S0-CRT-995

THE LANGUAGE OF THE CLASSROOM

THE LANGUAGE OF THE CLASSROOM

Arno A. Bellack
Herbert M. Kliebard
Ronald T. Hyman
Frank L. Smith, Jr.

TEACHERS COLLEGE PRESS
Teachers College, Columbia University
New York

Library of Congress Catalog Card Number: 66-22926
Manufactured in the United States of America

The research reported herein was supported through the Cooperative Research Program of the Office of Education, U.S. Department of Health, Education, and Welfare

PREFACE

In this book we present a study of a familiar human activity: classroom teaching. Our approach is analytical rather than clinical; "an analytical science is for understanding but not for action, at least not directly." * Our purpose is to gain understanding of the special world of the classroom, rather than to identify the "good" teacher or the "best" teaching methods. This is not to say that we are unconcerned with the improvement of teaching. Rather it is to contend that only as teachers have available knowledge about the teaching process gained through research will they be able to exercise effective control over the process. We have depended too long on unexamined "conventional wisdom" about teaching in pre-service and in-service training of teachers.

Our three-year study of teaching has impressed us with the complexity of the events that occur in the classroom. We make no claim that the present research reveals the whole story of these complex events. Of necessity, we have limited our attention to certain features of the activities of teachers and pupils in the classes under study, realizing full well that much additional research will be needed to round out the picture. The research reported in this book thus represents an initial stage in a continuing series of studies into the fascinating and little-understood life of the classroom. And because so little is known about teaching, we hope that this report of our initial investigations will encourage others to join in the search for more adequate knowledge about it. Given our current stage of knowledge (or, more accurately, our current stage of ignorance) about the teaching process, other researchers will undoubtedly describe and analyze the phenomena observed in the classroom in ways quite different from ours.

We are greatly indebted to the following people for assistance in conducting the research and in preparing the report for publication:

Teachers and students in the seven high schools, located in the

* Homans, G. *The Human Group.* New York, Harcourt, Brace & World, 1950, p. 15.

metropolitan New York City area, whose class sessions we recorded in this study of classroom discourse. We are indeed grateful to them for their cooperation in making this study possible. By agreement with the teachers, results of this research are reported anonymously and therefore the names of the teachers and their schools are not recorded here.

Members of the research staff, including Professor Joel Davitz, who collaborated with us in the first phase of the research; Dr. Lois Davitz, Mr. Raymond Gerson, and Miss Lillian Russo, each of whom was for a period of time a member of the staff; Mrs. Suzanne Hyman and Miss Frances Israelstam, who assisted in the coding; Dr. John Torosian and Mr. Woodrow Zaros, who served as technicians in recording the class sessions; Miss Penny Leka and Miss Lois Thompson, who transcribed the recordings and served as secretaries; Mrs. Helen Hardy, Mr. Robert Lundberg, and Mr. Kenneth Buell, who typed sections of the various drafts of the final report; and Mr. Paul Barbuto, who wrote the program for the IBM Computer.

Colleagues at Teachers College, Columbia University, including Professor Rosedith Sitgreaves, who served as statistics consultant and to whom we turned for advice in connection with many aspects of the research; and Professors Millie Almy and Charles Morris, who read an early draft of the report and made valuable suggestions.

The authors were associated with the Institute of Psychological Research, Teachers College, Columbia University, during the period in which the research was done.

The planning stage of our research was financed by a grant from the Bailey K. Howard Faculty Fund at Teachers College. Subsequently, the study was supported by two grants from the Cooperative Research Branch of the U.S. Office of Education. We acknowledge with thanks both these sources of financial support.

A.A.B.
H.M.K.
R.T.H.
F.L.S.

September, 1966

CONTENTS

LIST OF TABLES

CHAPTER ONE

DESIGN OF THE RESEARCH

Few classroom activities can be carried on without the use of language. Indeed, observation of what goes on in elementary and secondary schools reveals that classroom activities are carried on in large part by means of verbal interaction between students and teachers. The purpose of the research presented here is to study the teaching process through analysis of the linguistic behavior of teachers and students in the classroom. We focused on language as the main instrument of communication in teaching. Our major task was to describe the patterned processes of verbal interaction that characterize classrooms in action; a subsidiary aim, viewed primarily as an exploratory phase of the general line of research, was to study linguistic variables of classroom discourse in relation to subsequent pupil learning.

The research addressed itself specifically to description and analysis of the linguistic behavior of teachers and students in high school social studies classes. The subjects were 15 high school teachers and 345 students in classes studying a unit on international trade. The basic data were tape recordings and verbatim transcriptions of four class lessons for each of the 15 classes.

Theoretical Viewpoint

This section presents the theoretical view of classroom behavior developed during this study which served as the basis for the system of analysis used to describe linguistic events in the classroom. The approach to the study of classroom discourse was influenced by recently developed concepts in the study of language and meaning by contemporary philosophers and psychologists, including Wittgenstein (22),

Feigl (9), and Brown (4). The abstract, theoretical concepts from these sources were adapted, revised, and modified in the course of the work with the empirical data of classroom discussion. It was necessary to work out the empirical referents of existing concepts and to develop new concepts to describe significant characteristics of classroom discourse for which adequate concepts were not available.

Classroom Verbal Behavior

The verbal actions typical of classroom discussion are of such a nature that they invite, encourage, and sometimes demand attention or an active response on the part of persons addressed. Questions are asked to be answered; assignments are made to be carried out; explanations are made to be understood. Clearly, the verbal activities involved in teaching are reciprocal affairs involving both teachers and students. It follows, therefore, that the role played by the teacher can be adequately described only in relation to the role played by students. Studying the activities of teachers in the classroom without at the same time analyzing the actions of students would give a distorted and incomplete view of the teaching process.

The roles played by teachers and students are different, to be sure, and participants enter the classroom with roles more or less clearly defined. To identify the specialized functions of teachers and of students was one of the major tasks of this research. We were interested in finding out which participant—teacher or student—speaks about what; how much, when, under what conditions, and with what effect. The study of the division of labor in the classroom was in terms of actual behavior or performance, rather than role expectations expressed by the participants.

We assumed that the primary function of language is the communication of meaning and that describing linguistic events in the classroom in terms of the meanings expressed by teachers and students was a potentially fruitful direction for research. Our concept of the nature of meaning was derived in large measure from Wittgenstein's view that "the meaning of a word is its use in the language." (22:20) Equation of meaning and use suggested that the problem here was that of identifying the distinctive functions language actually serves in the verbal interplay between students and teachers and hence what meanings are conveyed through the words they use.

In searching for the meaning of what teachers and students communicate in the classroom, we found it helpful to identify (1) what the speaker was saying—whether, for example, he was structuring the class time, and (2) *what* he was saying. That is, in analyzing the utterance of a teacher or student at a given point in class discussion, we were first of all concerned with the pedagogical significance of what the speaker was saying—whether, for example, he was structuring the class discussion by launching or focusing attention on a topic or problem, eliciting a response from a member of the class, answering a question posed by a previous speaker, or reacting to a comment previously made. Secondly, we were interested in identifying the content of the communication—what topic was the focus of discussion, what facts the question called for, what explanation was being offered, or what assignment was being made.

An important methodological problem was that of devising the means whereby these dimensions of meaning could be defined operationally. As we dealt with this problem, we were again influenced by Wittgenstein's approach to language. In his view, "the *speaking* of language is part of an activity, or of a form of life." (22:11) Language is adaptable to many uses and functions in carrying on various types of activities that are essentially linguistic in nature. Wittgenstein refers to these activities as "language games," a metaphor used to point up the fact that linguistic activities assume different forms and structures according to the functions they come to serve in different contexts. A game has a definite structure, and there are certain moves that a player is bound to make insofar as he is playing the game at all. The following are some of the verbal activities that he identified as language games (22:11–12):

Giving orders and obeying them
Reporting an event
Forming and testing a hypothesis
Play acting
Making a joke and telling it
Making up a story and reading it

Carrying the game metaphor a step further, Wittgenstein observed that verbal activities in various contexts follow certain rules or conventions appropriate to the activities under way. Learning to participate appropriately in various kinds of language activities is very much like learning to play a game. Players have to learn the rules, the purpose of the rules, and how the various parts of the game are related. Only by learning these rules can one play the game successfully. Similarly, successful communication in various types of linguistic activities depends on understanding the language rules that govern the use of words in these activities.

Viewing classroom discourse as a kind of language game was a useful approach for purposes of this research, in that it suggested a framework of analysis within which we could identify verbal expressions that communicate various kinds of meaning. Teaching is similar to most games in at least two respects. It is a form of social activity in which the players (teachers and students) fill different but complementary roles. Furthermore, teaching is governed by certain ground rules that guide the actions or moves made by participants. We reasoned that if we could identify the various types of verbal moves teachers and students make in playing the game of teaching and the rules they implicitly follow in making these moves, we would be in a position to investigate the functions these verbal actions serve in classroom discourse and hence the meanings that are communicated.

Categories for Analysis

Examination of the transcripts of classroom discourse suggested that the verbal actions of students and teachers could be classified in four major categories. We labeled these basic verbal actions *pedagogical moves* and classified them in terms of the pedagogical functions they perform in classroom discourse:

Structuring. Structuring moves serve the pedagogical function of setting the context for subsequent behavior by either launching or halting-excluding interaction between students and teachers. For example, teachers frequently launch a class period with a structuring move in which they focus attention on the topic or problem to be discussed during that session.

Soliciting. Moves in this category are designed to elicit a verbal response, to encourage persons addressed to attend to something, or to elicit a physical response. All questions are solicitations, as are commands, imperatives, and requests.

Responding. These moves bear a reciprocal relationship to soliciting moves and occur only in relation to them. Their pedagogical function is to fulfill the expectation of soliciting moves; thus students' answers to teachers' questions are classified as responding moves.

Reacting. These moves are occasioned by a structuring, soliciting, responding, or prior reacting move, but are not directly elicited by them. Pedagogically, these moves serve to modify (by clarifying, synthesizing, or expanding) and/or to rate (positively or negatively) what has been said previously. Reacting moves differ from responding moves: while a responding move is always directly elicited by a solicitation, preceding moves serve only as the occasion for reactions. Rating by a teacher of a student's response, for example, is designated as a reacting move.

As we proceeded with the analysis of the data in terms of pedagogical moves it became evident that these moves occur in classroom discourse in certain cyclical patterns or combinations, which we designated *teaching cycles.* A teaching cycle begins either with a structuring or with a soliciting move, both of which are *initiating* maneuvers; they serve the function of getting a cycle under way. In contrast, responding and reacting moves are *reflexive* in nature; they are either solicited or occasioned by a preceding move and therefore cannot begin a cycle. A cycle frequently begins, for example, with a soliciting move by the teacher in the form of a question, continues with a responding move by the student addressed, and ends with an evaluative reaction by the teacher. A cycle might also get under way with a structuring move by the teacher in which he focuses attention on the topic to be discussed, continue with a question related to the topic, and end with responding moves by one or more students.

As we focused attention on the cyclical patterning of classroom discourse, the concept of teaching cycles made it possible to trace recurrent sequences in the verbal exchange among teachers and students and thus to describe the ebb and flow of the teaching process as it develops over time.

Using the concepts of pedagogical moves and teaching cycles, we were able to describe classroom discourse in terms of one of the dimensions of meaning with which this research was concerned—meaning from the viewpoint of the pedagogical significance of what teachers and students communicate. But we were also interested in the dimension of meaning represented by the content of the messages communicated. Analysis of classroom discourse in terms of what teachers and students communicate revealed four functionally different types of meanings: (a) substantive with associated (b) substantive-logical meanings, and (c) instructional with associated (d) instructional-logical meanings.

Substantive meanings refer to the subject matter of the class; that is, specific concepts such as multilateral trade and generalizations involving, for example, the relations between specialization and the factors of production. *Substantive-logical* meanings * refer to the cognitive processes involved in dealing with the subject matter, such as defining, interpreting, explaining, fact-stating, opining, and justifying. *Instructional* meanings involve such matters as assignments, materials, and routine classroom procedures that are part of the in-

* The system for the analysis of substantive-logical meanings draws on the research of Smith, Meux, *et al.* (17).

structional process. *Instructional-logical* meanings refer to distinctively didactic verbal processes such as those involved in positive and negative rating, explaining procedures, and giving directions.

Research Method

To accomplish the aims of the study, the research procedure included the following steps: (1) selection of high school classes; (2) selection and analysis of a unit of instruction; (3) development of measures of learning and attitude change; (4) collection of data, involving pre- and post-measures of knowledge and attitudes as well as recordings and transcriptions of classroom discussions; (5) development of a system of analysis dealing with the several kinds of meaning conveyed by the linguistic behaviors of teachers and pupils; (6) coding of the 60 protocols using the system of analysis; and (7) application of statistical methods for an analysis of the results.

Subject Matter for Instruction

In order to establish some reasonable limits within which the groups of students and teachers could conduct their classroom work and to provide a relatively stable basis both for testing changes in knowledge and for analyzing the substantive meanings of the classroom discussion, a specific unit of instruction was selected for all classes participating in the research. This unit was based on the first four chapters of the pamphlet *International Economic Problems* by James D. Calderwood (5).

Beginning with a general definition of trade and an explanation of the reasons for trade, the pamphlet discusses the differences between domestic and international trade, problems of foreign investments, imports and exports, various kinds of trade barriers, and reasons for such barriers, and then focuses on the reduction of trade barriers, arguments for and against international trade barriers, and some current methods for reduction of tariffs and other barriers. It provides a clear exposition of a delimited amount of substantive material at a level of difficulty appropriate to the senior high school classes involved in the study. The problems discussed were also of current public interest at the time this research was undertaken.

Before collecting the data to be considered in the final analysis, a member of the project staff taught the instructional unit to two high school classes similar to those that participated in the major part of the research. In general, the information obtained in this preliminary work supported the assumption that the unit was appropriate for the purposes of the research.

Measures of Learning and Attitude Change

Test of knowledge. To evaluate students' prior knowledge of the subject matter and to obtain an estimate of the amount of learning that occurred during the experimental period, the staff developed a test of knowledge related to the substantive material of the instructional unit. This test was based on a detailed analysis of the material covered in the pamphlet that served as the basis of the instructional unit. Moreover, the specific logical processes required by the test and the particular substantive items covered were selected to parallel the content analysis of logical and substantive meanings contained in the classroom discourse.

The test, designed in short essay form, includes three sections. Section One deals with connotative and denotative definitions of ten significant terms used in the pamphlet for the discussion of international trade; for example, one item concerns the term *specialization.* The student is required first to write a general definition of specialization as the term is used in discussions of international trade, giving the major ideas or characteristics to which the term refers; then, the student is asked to give a specific example to illustrate the concept of specialization.

Section Two of the test concerns a knowledge of general principles related to explanations of various economic phenomena or the justification of economic policies. The student, for example, is asked to answer briefly the following question: "Why is the largest amount of international trade between highly industrialized countries?" In each case, the student is instructed simply to write the main idea or major points in answering each question, without going into much detail.

Section Three parallels the general items contained in the second section but requires the students to apply their knowledge of economic principles by explaining concrete instances involved in international trade or justifying particular trade policies. Paralleling the item cited above to illustrate the previous section, the question asked in Section Three was: "Burmese farmers desperately need American farm equipment and other American goods. Yet, there is relatively little trade between Burma and the U.S. today. Why?"

The time required for administration of the test is 40 minutes: 10 minutes for Section One and 15 minutes each for Sections Two and Three. To eliminate the effect of order of items in each section, which might have played a significant role under the rather short time limits, two forms of the test were used. The two forms contained identical items, but within each section the order of the items was reversed from one to the other. For example, the first item in Section

One of Form A asked for a definition of the term *specialization,* while in Form B, this item was the last question in the section. Half the students in each class received each form, thus providing some control for differences in time that might be spent on a given item as a function of its place in the order of questions.

A comprehensive and detailed key was prepared for scoring. The key, based primarily on the information contained in the instructional pamphlet, contains explicit rules and examples for evaluating the answers to each question. Each section was alloted a total weight of 20 points, two points assigned to each of the ten items in a section. Reliability of scoring was estimated by comparing total scores of 43 tests scored independently by two judges. A product-moment correlation of .84 was obtained between the scores assigned by the two judges, indicating a degree of interjudge reliability sufficiently high for purposes of this research. A copy of the test is included in Appendix C.

The attitude scale. A subsidiary aim of this study was to explore the relationship between various aspects of classroom discourse and students' attitudes toward studying economics. A seven-point scale was developed to measure these attitudes, and the student was asked to check the statement which best described how he felt about studying economics. In an early form of the scale, statements ran from very positive to very negative attitudes, but in a preliminary study the data showed that very few students checked the negative points on the scale. For research purposes, therefore, the clearly negative statements had little functional value and, in fact, decreased the possible discriminative value of the scale. Thus the final form of the scale ran from a very positive to a relatively neutral attitude. The statement reflecting the most positive attitude was:

> Studying economics is of tremendous value, and I'd really enjoy it. It is one of the most important subjects I know, and everyone should be required to study it.

The statement reflecting the least positive attitude was:

> Studying economics won't to anybody any harm. I haven't any definite like or dislike for this subject. It might be worthwhile if it were taught right.

Between these two extremes were five statements reflecting varying degrees of positive attitude toward the study of economics. Although it cannot be assumed that the seven points on the scale represent equal intervals, the results of preliminary research in the development of the scale, involving an investigation of the relative strength of each statement, lend credence to the assumption that the scale validly reflects a rank order of positive to neutral attitudes about studying economics. A copy of the scale is contained in Appendix C.

Verbal intelligence. An estimate of verbal intelligence of the students was obtained by means of a 40-item vocabulary test developed by Thorndike (19). It is a relatively brief measure of verbal ability, but previous research indicates a rather high reliability and concurrent validity in terms of substantial correlations with other group measures of intelligence.

Subjects

The original plan for the research called for an analysis of discourse in 15 high school classes, selected on the basis of the willingness of the teachers to participate in the study. No effort was made to select teachers or students in terms of specific criteria. Anticipating some dropouts, data were collected in a total of 19 classes. Because of the illness of one teacher during the period of data collection and because of technical difficulties in recording 3 other classes, the final sample included 15 classes as original planned.

The sample consisted of 345 10th- and 12th-grade students and 15 teachers in problems of democracy classes in seven high schools in the metropolitan and suburban area of New York City. For purposes of the study, each class had a different teacher, and the instructional unit was included in the regular course schedule. Table 1 provides a summary of the data describing characteristics of each class.

The number of students for each class, as shown in Table 1, is based on the number of students who took both the pre-test and the post-test and therefore does not include absentees. Informal observations during the data collection, however, suggested relatively few absentees. As may be seen in Table 1, there was a considerable range in the size of the classes, with 15 pupils in Class 12, 34 in Class 2, and a mean of 23 pupils per class. The average vocabulary score in individual classes ranged from 22.30 in Class 11 to 30.00 in Class 9, with a mean of 25.11 for all pupils combined (perfect score, 40). There was considerable interclass variability in verbal intelligence, although the results indicate that the distribution of ability among the students was skewed somewhat positively toward the upper range in comparison with various national samples; for example, in terms of a voting sample obtained by Thorndike and Gallup (20), the average score in the present sample falls in approximately the 70th percentile.

Estimates of socio-economic class status, based on parent's occupation, were obtained by means of a seven-point scale of occupational ratings developed by the Horace Mann-Lincoln Institute of School Experimentation, Teachers College, Columbia University (11). In the present sample, social class ratings ranged from 1.77 for Class 10 to 3.84 for Class 1, with a mean of 2.93. Occupations in level 3, the ap-

TABLE 1

Number of Students, Average Vocabulary Score, and Social Class Rating for Each Class and for All Classes Combined

Class	*Number Students in Class*	*Average Vocabulary Score*	*Average Social Class Rating*
1	25	25.11	3.84
2	34	25.97	2.67
3	18	23.56	3.42
4	30	25.23	3.06
5	29	25.43	2.88
6	20	23.38	3.50
7	23	24.75	2.67
8	20	27.35	2.54
9	28	30.00	2.34
10	16	28.11	1.77
11	23	22.30	3.25
12	15	27.28	2.00
13	22	23.44	3.19
14	20	23.00	2.82
15	22	21.65	3.52
$\bar{X}$	23.1	25.11	2.93

proximate mean of the sample, include social workers, librarians, commercial artists, office managers, auto salesmen, detectives, and administrative secretaries. In contrast, occupations in level 2 include professional nurses, teachers and ministers with college degrees, and FBI agents; and occupations in level 4 include laboratory technicians, bookkeepers, stenographers, machinists, and policemen. These, of course, represent only examples of occupations classified at these levels.

Procedure

Several weeks before a class participated in the actual study, a member of the research staff met with members of the administration of each school and the cooperating teachers. The aims of the project were discussed in general terms, and the procedure was described. Teachers were told that the major purpose of the study was to develop a method of describing the language of the classroom. They were given copies of the pamphlet on international trade, as well as a teacher's guide paralleling the material in the pamphlet, and were asked to base their unit of instruction during the experimental period on the subject matter contained in the first four chapters of the pamphlet.

The procedure involved (1) pre-test; (2) the experimental class sessions; and (3) post-test. In most instances, the pre-test was administered on the Friday before the week in which the class participated in the experimental instruction. In a few instances, because of scheduling problems, the pre-test preceded the experimental sessions by a somewhat longer period, but this period was in no case longer than six days. During the pre-test session, both the test of knowledge and the attitude scale were administered.

The four experimental class sessions usually met Monday through Thursday of a given week, although a few classes deviated from this pattern because of conflict with other aspects of the school program. In all cases, however, the experimental sessions involved four successive meetings of the class. Teachers were instructed to use whatever methods they normally followed in class, emphasizing the goal of describing "normal" classroom discourse with minimal external interference. It was realized that the presence of a tape recorder and the teachers' and students' knowledge that they were participating in a research study would probably influence their behavior. Instructions were therefore designed to minimize this interference. The instructions to the teachers, for example, reassured them that the research did not involve an evaluation of their performance and that complete anonymity would be maintained. Observations during the data collection and subsequent analyses of the data indicated a remarkably high degree of cooperation both from teachers and from students. Although it cannot be assumed that the research procedures had no effect on the classroom behavior, it seems reasonable to conclude that this effect was minimal.

During the last few minutes of the fourth experimental class session, the pamphlets were collected from the students and the attitude post-test was administered. At the next meeting of the class, which typically was the following day, the post-test of knowledge of subject matter was administered.

Recording the classroom discourse involved the use of two microphones, one to record the teacher's speech and the other placed among the students to record their discussion. In the first few classes studied, the teacher's speech was recorded by means of a nondirectional microphone placed on the teacher's desk, but it was later found that a microphone worn by the teacher provided somewhat better fidelity. According to the teachers' reports this did not interfere with their work. Subsequent classes, therefore, were recorded by means of a microphone worn by the teacher and a microphone placed among the students, both of which were fed into a Switchcraft 301 TR mixer which was in turn connected to a T-1500 Wollensak tape recorder. The tape recorder, placed at the side of the classroom, was operated by a technician attached to the project staff.

Typescript protocols of the tape recordings were prepared. These typescripts were then revised by a second person who audited the tape recording and made whatever corrections and additions were necessary. At this point, over 95 per cent of the classroom discussion was transcribed, but as a further check on accuracy of the transcriptions, the recordings were audited once again when the protocols were analyzed. In the final analysis, probably no more than three or four per cent of the classroom discussion was missed, and this material primarily involved instances in which several students spoke simultaneously for very brief periods of time.

Analysis of the Protocols

The theoretical framework that served as the basis for the system of analysis used to describe linguistic events in the classroom has already been discussed (pp. 1–16). The content analysis system itself will be described in detail in Chapter Two, but it may be helpful at this point to report briefly the development of the categories of analysis and the general procedures for describing the various kinds of meaning contained in a protocol of classroom discourse.

The initial research plan called for an analysis of the content ot classroom discourse in terms of substantive and substantive-logical meanings.* At the outset, it was assumed that the basis for this analysis would be the material presented in the pamphlet on international trade; and for the most part, this assumption was supported by later analysis. As the data were collected, however, two major problems became apparent: first, before classifying the discourse in terms of substantive and substantive-logical meanings, a unit of discourse had to be defined; and secondly, discussion related to classroom activities but substantively different from the specific subject matter of international trade was obviously present in the discourse and could not reasonably be omitted from the analysis. Such discussion, for example, concerned assignments, teachers' reactions to student behavior, and other statements related to the process of instruction.

Solution of the first problem, the definition of a unit of analysis, turned out to be one of the most fruitful aspects of the entire analysis.

* The initial research plan also called for the analysis of emotional meanings to parallel the analysis of substantive and substantive-logical meanings. However, for a variety of reasons it was not possible to work out a reliable system for describing emotional meanings within the context of pedagogical moves and teaching cycles. See Bellack, *et al., The Language of the Classroom* (1963), pp. 63–71, 134–141.

As explained previously, classroom discourse is viewed as a language game, following the theoretical framework proposed by Wittgenstein (22), and the unit of discourse is defined as a pedagogical move. As already indicated, these moves are classified into four major categories (structuring, soliciting, responding, and reacting), and each move is defined in terms of its pedagogical function in the discourse. Each of these categories will be defined more fully in subsequent chapters but the important point to note here is that this relatively simple system of classification serves as a highly reliable basis for coding and describing classroom interaction in terms that have considerable apparent pedagogical use and functional meaning.

Solution of the second problem, involving material other than that specifically presented in the pamphlet upon which the teaching unit was based, required a major extension of the original plan of analysis. As indicated, the content of classroom discussions was originally to be analyzed primarily from two points of view, the logical and the substantive. Substantive meanings included definitions, facts, and principles of economics relevant to a discussion of international trade. In a sense, this would be the subject matter of instruction as viewed from the role of an economist. However, the teacher and the students not only played the role of an economist discussing trade but also played a variety of pedagogical roles. The teacher made assignments, specified classroom procedures to be followed, and evaluated the appropriateness of student behavior; the students, in turn, asked questions about procedures, reacted to each other's behavior, and commented about the value of the pamphlet and about other material. Inclusion of the discourse related primarily to instructional meanings and associated instructional-logical meanings in effect doubled the number of categories.

Development of the code for analysis was a long and detailed process requiring the participation of several researchers who constantly reviewed and revised successive approximations of the final code in the light of actual protocols. This provided an immediate empirical check on the more abstract concepts of analysis that gradually emerged in the course of the work. This daily encounter between relatively abstract, theoretical concepts of meaning and the empirical data of the classroom discussions provided a fruitful and realistic means of developing the system of analysis.

After revision, modification, and refinement of the coding system, the analysis of the material was begun. Even at this stage of the research, however, further revisions of the code were necessitated by problems encountered in particular protocols. On several occasions, all of the protocols analyzed on the basis of a previous draft of the code had to be reanalyzed to account for new revisions in the rules of analysis. Although this procedure appears to be somewhat inefficient in terms of the expenditure of time and effort, experience demonstrated that within the limitations of current knowledge about the teaching process this was the only way we could do justice to the extraordinarily complex interactions contained in the classroom discourse.

In view of the complexity inherent both in the material and in the system of analysis, it seemed unreasonable to expect that any one person, no matter how well trained, would be able to code large sections of the data reliably without the checks offered by consultation with another coder. Therefore, the following procedure was used in all of the final coding of the data: (1) each protocol of a single class session was first coded by one member of the coding team; (2) this initial coding was then reviewed by a second person, who noted his disagreements with the original analysis; (3) finally, these disagreements were arbitrated by two coders, who, whenever possible, were not involved in the initial coding of the protocol. Despite the intrinsic difficulties involved in the analysis, this procedure resulted in a consistently high level of reliability in coding.

After the protocols had been coded, the data were transferred to data processing cards, and a program was prepared for the IBM 7090 computer. The initial program consisted essentially of a series of tabulations and cross-tabulations computed by number and percentage of lines of transcript in each category and moves in each category for each class session, for the total of four class sessions of each teacher, and for the sum of these results for all classes. Later a more complex program using Markov chains (14) was used for the analysis of teaching cycles. The analysis of data in various categories was made on the basis of number of lines and number of moves, but because classes differed somewhat in total time devoted to the four experimental sessions, for the report the results were converted to percentage of total lines and moves in each category of the analysis.

The analysis of the data using the basic coding system reported in Chapter Three suggested several possible additional directions for research. While the initial analysis provided a general picture of the distribution of pedagogical moves and something of their recurring patterning, further analysis helped clarify the rules of the game followed by teachers and pupils in the classroom. This refinement and extension of the original analysis in terms of pedagogical moves is presented in Chapters Four, Five, and Six. Analysis of the patterning and sequence of linguistic events in terms of teaching cycles is presented in Chapter Seven.

CHAPTER TWO

BASIC SYSTEM FOR ANALYSIS

OUR ANALYSIS of classroom discourse is based on a system of categories devised to describe the verbal performance of teachers and students. Protocols of classroom discourse were analyzed in terms of these categories. Excerpts from coded protocols are included in this discussion of the system for analysis to illustrate the coding process, and results of the reliability test of the system are reported.

Content Analysis System

Overview of the Analysis System

The basic categories of analysis include types of pedagogical moves, teaching cycles, and various categories of meaning. This section presents a general overview of these basic categories.

Pedagogical moves. Following Wittgenstein's view of language (22), classroom discourse is viewed as a kind of "language game." The basic unit of discourse is defined as a pedagogical move. These moves are classified in four major categories according to the pedagogical functions they serve in classroom discussion: structuring, soliciting, responding, and reacting. These four types of move describe the verbal maneuvers of both teachers and students in classroom discourse and set the framework for the analysis of meanings communicated in the classroom.

Teaching cycles. Pedagogical moves occur in classroom discourse in certain cyclical patterns and combinations that are designated teaching cycles.

Categories of meanings. Four functionally different types of meaning are communicated by teachers and pupils in the classroom: (1)

substantive with associated (2) substantive-logical meanings; and (3) instructional with associated (4) instructional-logical meanings. Within each pedagogical move these four types of meaning are identified when they appear in the discourse and are coded according to the rules of analysis described in Appendix A.

Coding format. The four types of pedagogical move are the basic units for analyzing the discourse both of teachers and of pupils. One or more pedagogical moves may occur within an utterance, which is defined as a complete statement by a teacher or pupil at any one time in the discourse. Coding is done from the viewpoint of the observer, with pedagogical meaning inferred from the speaker's verbal behavior. Coders listened to tape recordings of class sessions and also followed the transcribed protocols. Sample pages of coded protocols are given in Appendix B.

Each pedagogical move is coded as follows:

(1) Speaker (Teacher, Pupil, or Audio-Visual Device)
(2) Type of Pedagogical Move
(3) Substantive Meanings
(4) Substantive-Logical Meanings
(5) Number of Lines in (3) and (4)
(6) Instructional Meanings
(7) Instructional-Logical Meanings
(8) Number of lines in (6) and (7)

An example of a coded pedagogical move is:

T / STR / IMX / XPL / 4 / PRC / FAC / 2
(1) / (2) / (3) / (4) / (5) / (6) / (7) / (8)

This is interpreted as follows: a *teacher* makes a *structuring* move in which he *explains* something about *imports and exports* for *four* lines of transcript and also states *facts* about class *procedures* for *two* lines of transcript.

Pedagogical Moves and Teaching Cycles

1. *Pedagogical moves.* Pedagogical moves, the basic units of classroom discourse, describe the verbal activities of teachers and pupils in the classroom. There are four basic types of move which characterize the verbal interplay of teachers and pupils: structuring and soliciting, which are initiatory moves; and responding and reacting, which are reflexive moves.

1.1. *Structuring* (STR). Structuring moves serve the function of setting the context for subsequent behavior by (1) launching or halting-excluding interactions between teacher and pupils, and (2) indicating the nature of the interaction in terms of the dimensions of time, agent, activity, topic and cognitive process, regulations, reasons, and instructional aids. A structuring move may set the context for the entire classroom game or a part of the game.

Since structuring moves set the context for subsequent behavior or performance, they are pivotal points in classroom discourse. They convey an implicit directive by launching classroom discussion in specified directions and by focusing on topics, subjects or problems to be discussed, or procedures to be followed.

Structuring moves do not elicit a response, are not in themselves direct responses, and are not called out by anything in the immediate classroom situation except the speaker's concept of what should be said or taught.

Examples

T/STR: Last night I was sitting out on the porch trying to cool off and also trying to ask myself how to best begin this unit on international economics, international trade, world trade, or whatever else one wants to call it. And after thinking over a number of approaches, I wrote down on paper a number of items that are connected with our story. Some of them are within your experience. Some of them are found in your pamphlet.

T/STR: Well, tomorrow, we'll continue to talk about the problem of investments. I'd like to show you tomorrow another slide through the projector so that you can perhaps understand this more fully. Also tomorrow we'll move into the realm of some of the problems that people face when trying to engage in trade abroad.

T/STR: All right, getting down to it now, I think international trade, then, or international economic relations, whatever you want to call it, is a field of study within economics which in many cases has been unfortunately divorced from or too far divorced from domestic trade because there are great similarities, and also there are some rather distinct differences.

The postscript -A is added to structuring (STR-A) when it occurs as a result of an assignment, such as student reports or debates. The postscript serves to distinguish these moves from those structuring moves that have not been previously assigned.

Example

P/STR-A: Well, I was asking my father on, well, he imports watches—that's his business. I wasn't able to interview him, but there was one thing I found out from—you know—when he just started importing. When you import watches from Switzerland, you have to have a code of letters you get from the Swiss government so that you can be shown that these watches aren't smuggled, and I thought this was a very interesting thing, and that way the American buyer can check also as they're brought over, these are not smuggled watches, or that, that they're not fake watches.

1.2. *Soliciting* (SOL). Moves in this category are intended to elicit (a) an active verbal response on the part of the persons addressed; (b) a cognitive response, e.g., encouraging persons addressed to attend to something; or (c) a physical response.

Soliciting moves are clearly directive in intent and function and are crucial in any active classroom interchange between teachers and pupils. Although these moves may take all grammatical forms—declarative, interrogative, and imperative—the interrogative occurs most frequently. In coding soliciting moves, the various categories of analysis are coded in terms of the response expected rather than the solicitation itself.*

Examples

T/SOL: What are the factors of production?

P/SOL: May we keep our books open?

T/SOL: Turn the lights out, Bobby!

T/SOL: Pay attention to this!

1.3. *Responding* (RES). Responding moves bear a reciprocal relationship to soliciting moves and occur only in relation to them. Their pedagogical function is to fulfill the expectation of soliciting moves and is, therefore, reflexive in nature. Since solicitations and responses are defined in relationship to each other, there can be no solicitation that is not intended to elicit a response, and no response that has not been directly elicited by a solicitation.

Examples

T/SOL: What are the factors of production?
P/RES: Land, labor, and capital.

T/SOL: Why didn't you do the assignment?
P/RES: I was absent yesterday.

T/SOL: What is exchange control?
P/RES: I don't know.

1.4. *Reacting* (REA). These moves are *occasioned* by a structuring, soliciting, responding, or a prior reacting move, but are not

* This procedure is adapted from Smith, Meux, *et al.* (17).

directly elicited by them. Pedagogically, these moves serve to modify (by clarifying, synthesizing, or expanding) and/or to rate (positively or negatively) what was said in the move(s) that occasioned them. Reacting moves differ from responding moves: while a responding move is always directly elicited by a solicitation, *preceding moves serve only as the occasion for reactions.* For example, the rating by a teacher of a student's response is designated a reacting move; that is, the student's response is the occasion for the teacher's rating reaction but does not actively elicit it.

Examples

T/REA: All right.

T/REA: That's partly it.

P/REA: But he left out the most important part.

T/REA: Good. It limits specifically the number of items of one type or another which can come into this country. For example, we might decide that no more than one thousand of German automobiles will be imported in any one calendar year. This is a specific quota which the government checks.

When the coding symbol for a reacting move is italicized (*REA*), it indicates that the reaction is occasioned by more than a single move.

Examples

T/*REA*: Now Kathy has mentioned natural resources and you raise the problem of human skills. Both are factors of production.

T/*REA*: All of the instances of foreign investment that we have discussed here can be classified as either direct or portfolio types of investment.

2. *Teaching cycles.* Pedagogical moves occur in classroom discourse in certain cyclical patterns and combinations, which are designated teaching cycles. A teaching cycle begins either with a structuring move or with a solicitation that is not preceded by a structuring move. A cycle ends with the move that precedes a new cycle. Teaching cycles are coded only after all pedagogical moves within a protocol have been coded individually. By defining structuring and soliciting moves as *initiatory,* and responding and reacting moves as *reflexive moves,* 21 types of teaching cycles are possible. The first 12 are structure-initiated; the next 9 are initiated by soliciting moves.

Each of the 21 cycles represents a different pattern of pedagogical moves. Cycle 9, for example, represents a pattern of discourse that is initiated by a structuring move and is followed by a solicitation; this solicitation elicits a response that is the occasion for a reaction. Cycle

21 is initiated by a solicitation that elicits multiple responses which are in turn the occasion for multiple reactions.

Teaching cycles provide a way of describing pedagogical moves in relationship to each other. Using teaching cycles it is possible, for example, to determine the extent to which solicitations elicit single or multiple responses or the regularity with which reactions follow responses. If a single pedagogical move may be compared to a move in chess or a single play in football, then the teaching cycle may be seen as an interrelated series of moves or plays. The focus in teaching cycles is on combinations of pedagogical moves and sequences of linguistic events in the classroom.

1.	STR					
2.	STR	SOL				
3.	STR	REA				
4.	STR	REA	REA . . .			
5.	STR	SOL	RES			
6.	STR	SOL	RES	RES . . .		
7.	STR	SOL	REA			
8.	STR	SOL	REA	REA . . .		
9.	STR	SOL	RES	REA		
10.	STR	SOL	RES	REA	REA . . .	
11.	STR	SOL	RES	REA	RES . . .	
12.	STR	SOL	RES	REA	RES . . .	REA . . .
13.	SOL					
14.	SOL	RES				
15.	SOL	RES	RES . . .			
16.	SOL	REA				
17.	SOL	REA	REA . . .			
18.	SOL	RES	REA			
19.	SOL	RES	REA	REA . . .		
20.	SOL	RES	REA	RES . . .		
21.	SOL	RES	REA	RES . . .	REA . . .	

Legend

STR—Structuring RES—Responding
SOL—Soliciting REA—Reacting
. . .—One or more additional moves of the kind designated. For example, RES . . . means one or more additional responses to the same solicitation.

Categories of Meaning

Four functionally different types of meaning are communicated by teachers and students in the classroom: *substantive* with associated *substantive-logical* meanings; and *instructional* with associated *instructional-logical* meanings. Within each pedagogical move these four types of meaning are identified when they appear in the discourse and are coded according to the rules for analysis described in Appendix A.

1. *Substantive meanings.* Substantive meanings refer to the subject matter under study by the class. In the present research, the categories of substantive meaning relate to the topic of international trade. The categories listed below were developed by means of a content analysis of the pamphlet on which this teaching unit was based: *International Economic Problems* by James D. Calderwood (5).

1.1. *Trade* (TRA). General discussion of trade; nature of trade in broad terms; definition of trade; why trade takes place.

1.11 *Trade—Domestic and International* (TDI). Domestic trade compared and contrasted with international trade; discussion of consequences or differences between international and domestic trade when these differences are the focus of discussion.

1.12 *Trade—Money and Banking* (TMB). Money and banking related to trade (not primarily aid); rate of exchange; balance of payments.

1.13 *Trade—Who Trades With Whom* (TWH). Who (countries or individual corporations) trades with whom; discussion of multilateral trade.

1.2. *Factors of Production and/or Specialization* (FSP). General discussion of factors of production; what the factors are; specialization; absolute and comparative advantage.

1.21 *Factor of Production—Natural Resources* (FNR). Specific discussion of natural resources as a factor of production.

1.22 *Factor of Production—Human Skills* (FHS). Specific discussion of labor as a factor of production.

1.23 *Factor of Production—Capital Equipment* (FCE). Specific discussion of capital equipment as a factor of production.

1.24 *Factors Other Than Natural Resources, Human Skills, and Capital Equipment Occurring in Discussion of Reasons for Trade* (FRE). Any discussion of reasons for trade or factors in addition to those specifically identified above (e.g., political reasons for trade).

1.3. *Imports and/or Exports* (IMX). What is imported and/or exported from any country; dependence on imports and/or exports; effects of imports and/or exports on economy; balance of trade.

1.4. *Foreign Investment—General* (FOR). General discussion of foreign investment.

1.41 *Foreign Investment—Direct* (FOD). Specific discussion of direct foreign investment.

1.42 *Foreign Investment—Portfolio* (FOP). Specific discussion of portfolio investment.

1.5. *Barriers to Trade* (BAR). General discussion of barriers, including policies directed toward maintaining or increasing barriers; how barriers work; effects of barriers.

1.51 *Barrier—Tariffs* (BAT). Specific discussion of tariffs.

1.52 *Barrier—Quotas* (BAQ). Specific discussion of quotas.

1.53 *Barrier—Exchange Control* (BAE). Specific discussion of exchange control.

1.54 *Barrier—Export Control* (BAX). Specific discussion of export control.

1.55 *Barrier—Administrative Protectionism* (BAA). Specific discussion of administrative protectionism or red tape as a barrier to trade.

1.6. *Promoting Free Trade* (PFT). Means of promoting free trade or reducing trade barriers; policies related to free trade; Common Market; Reciprocal Trade Agreements.

1.7. *Relevant to Trade* (REL). A topic relevant to trade or economics but not considered in the Calderwood text (e.g., foreign aid).

1.8. *Not Trade* (NTR). Discussion not about trade or economics and not related to either.

2. *Substantive-logical meanings.* Substantive-logical meanings refer to the cognitive processes involved in dealing with the subject matter under study. Substantive-logical meanings are categorized under three general headings: (a) analytic process; (b) empirical process; and (c) evaluative process.

2.1. *Analytic process.* Analytic statements are statements about the proposed use of language. Analytic statements are true by virtue of the meaning of the words of which they are composed. They depend for their truth on an agreed-upon set of rules and follow logically from accepted definitions. The statement "Mother is a female parent," for example, is necessarily true because "mother" means the same as "female parent." To define a term is to indicate what the term means, to state how it is used, or to give a verbal equivalent. A definition can be expressed in two ways: (1) by talking about the characteristics designated by a term; or (2) by talking about specific instances of the class designated by a term. Interpreting bears the same relationship to *statements* that defining does to *terms.*

2.11 *Defining—General* (DEF). To define in a general manner is to give the defining characteristics of a class *and* to give a specific example of an item within the class. DEF is also coded when the type of definition asked for or given is not clear.

Example	*Code* *
T: What is a barrier?	T/SOL/BAR/*DEF*/1/-/-/-
P: It's something that hinders trade, like a tariff.	P/RES/BAR/*DEF*/2/-/-/-

2.111 *Defining—Denotative* (DED). To define denotatively is to refer to the objects (abstract or concrete) to which the term is applicable. A denotative definition cites the objects to which the term may correctly be applied, and these objects constitute the denotation of the term. Thus, to give actual instances or examples of international trade (U.S. trading with Britain, Germany trading with France) is to give a denotative definition of the term *international trade.*

Examples	*Code*
T: What are public utilities?	T/SOL/NTR/DEF/1/-/-/-
P: Light, power, gas, water.	P/RES/NTR/*DED*/1/-/-/-
T: Can you give an example of a machine tool, Alex?	T/SOL/FSP/*DED*/2/-/-/-
P: A press.	P/RES/FSP/*DED*/1/-/-/-

2.112 *Defining—Connotative* (DEC). To define connotatively is to give the set of properties or characteristics that an object (abstract or concrete) must have for the term to be applicable. DEC thus refers to the defining characteristics of a given term.

Examples	*Code*
T: Now what do we mean by quotas?	T/SOL/BAQ/DEF/1/-/-/-
P: The government sets a special amount of things that can come into the country in one year, and no more can come in.	P/RES/BAQ/*DEC*/4/-/-/-
T: What are machine tools?	T/SOL/FSP/DEF/1/-/-/-
P: Tools that make tools.	P/RES/FSP/*DEC*/1/-/-/-

2.12 *Interpreting* (INT). To interpret a statement is to give its verbal equivalent, usually for the purpose of rendering its meaning clear.

Examples	*Code*
T: What does President Kennedy mean when he says, "We must trade or fade?"	T/SOL/TRA/*INT*/2/-/-/-

* Italicized symbols indicate specific part of code being illustrated. Line counts refer to lines of typescript in printed example, not to lines in actual protocols.

T: What does the slogan mean, "Buy American—the job you save may be your own?"	T/SOL/BAR/*INT*/3/–/–/–

2.2. *Empirical process.* Empirical statements give information about the world, based on one's experience of it. The distinguishing mark of empirical statements is that they are verified by tests conducted in terms of one's experience. In other words, one makes observations and decides whether the statement is true or false.

2.21 *Fact-Stating* (FAC). Fact-stating is giving an account, description, or report of an event or state of affairs. To state a fact is to state what is, what was in the past, or what will be in the future. For example, a statement of a past event is, "Yesterday we reviewed some of the terms used by economists in talking about international trade." A statement of a present state of affairs is, "We are studying the problems relating to international trade." A statement referring to future events is, "We will discuss international monetary policies tomorrow."

The facts stated or reported need not be singular to be coded as FAC. Generalizations or universal statements are also coded FAC. For example, such general statements as "No country is self-supporting" and "All people need food" are coded FAC.

Examples	*Code*
T: Now in 1934 . . . in 1934 . . . who was President?	T/SOL/PFT/*FAC*/2/–/–/–
P: Roosevelt.	P/RES/PFT/*FAC*/1/–/–/–
T: The United States will say that the French franc is exchanged at how many per dollar?	T/SOL/TMB/*FAC*/3/–/–/–
P: Five.	P/RES/TMB/*FAC*/1/–/–/–

2.22 *Explaining* (XPL). To explain is to relate an object, event, action, or state of affairs to some other object, event, action, or state of affairs; or to show the relation between an event or state of affairs and a principle or generalization; or to state the relationships between principles or generalizations.

Following Copi (7:420), explaining and inferring are regarded as the same process:

> An explanation is a group of statements or a story from which the thing to be explained can logically be inferred and whose assumption removes or diminishes its problematic or puzzling character. . . . It thus appears that explanation and inference are very closely related. They are, in

fact, the same process regarded from opposite points of view. Given certain premisses, any conclusion which can logically be inferred from them is regarded as being explained by them. And given a fact to be explained, we say that we have found an explanation for it when we have found a set of premisses from which it can be logically inferred.

A statement is coded XPL when it concerns the *effect* of some event or state of affairs on some other event or state of affairs; or when the statement gives the *reasons* for an event or state of affairs (i.e., relates an event to some general principle). The relationship between two events, facts, or states of affairs is often expressed in terms of "If . . . , then . . . ." One way of showing relationships is by comparing and contrasting. Therefore, all *explicit* instances of comparing and contrasting are coded XPL.

Explanations frequently are given in response to questions asking why or how some events occur. The "why" or "how" may be explicit (i.e., in a preceding question) or implicit in the context of the statement. Also, the word "because" is frequently a verbal cue indicating the explanatory nature of the statement.

Examples	*Code*
T: Why do industrialized countries trade the most?	T/SOL/TWH/*XPL*/1/–/–/–
P: Because they have more . . . more to offer each other.	P/RES/TWH/*XPL*/2/–/–/–
T: What would happen if we raised the tariff on transistor radios?	T/SOL/BAT/*XPL*/2/–/–/–
P: Prices would go up.	P/RES/BAT/*XPL*/1/–/–/–
P: Japan would raise its tariffs on American stuff.	P/RES-M2/BAT/*XPL*/2/–/–/–

2.3. *Evaluative process.* Evaluative statements are statements that grade, praise, blame, commend, or criticize something. Evaluative statements are verified by reference to a set of criteria or principles of judgment. A common set of criteria is essential if individuals are to reach agreement regarding the value of a given act, object, or state of affairs.

2.31 *Opining* (OPN). To opine is to make statements in which the speaker gives his own valuation regarding (a) what should or ought to be done, or (b) fairness, worth, importance, or quality of an action, event, person, idea, plan, or policy.

Examples	*Code*
P: I think the farmer is being exploited.	P/REA/BAT/*OPN*/1/–/–/–

T: Do you feel that a company who has gone into another country, has invested time, has invested money, has invested its knowledge, its skill and so on, has a right to make a profit?	T/SOL/FOD/*OPN*/6/–/–/–
P: Yes.	P/RES/FOD/*OPN*/1/–/–/–

2.32 *Justifying* (JUS). To justify is to give *reasons* for holding an opinion regarding (a) what should or ought to be done, or (b) fairness, worth, importance, or quality of an action, event, policy, idea, plan, or thing.

Justifying statements are intended as support or criticism of opinions that either have been explicit in a previous statement or are implied within the context of the interaction. Justifying statements are frequently preceded by an opining statement, although this is not a necessary condition for coding JUS.

Examples	*Code*
P: I feel that the reason why the United States should not and probably will not in a number of years join the Common Markets is that because the Latin countries with which we are associated would feel that we are no longer interested in their opinion.	P/STR-A/PFT/*JUS*/8/–/–/–
T: Is it the government's responsibility then to train you for some other job, assuming that you couldn't get a job on your own?	T/SOL/PFT/OPN/4/–/–/–
P: I believe that they should train them over again and give them government jobs or something because, I mean, after all if it weren't for the tariff and barriers, they'd still be in work.	P/RES/PFT/*JUS*/6/–/–/–

2.4. *Not Clear* (NCL). When the wording or sense of a statement is ambiguous and the substantive-logical meaning cannot be determined, the logical process is coded NCL.

3. *Instructional meanings.* In addition to talking about a particular area of study, teachers and pupils also discuss matters per-

taining to classroom management, assignments, and procedures that are part of the instructional process. The items listed under instructional meanings categorize the content of this aspect of classroom discourse.

3.1. *Assignment* (ASG). Discussion of reports, homework, debates, tests, readings, and the like.

Examples	*Code*
P: What should we do for tomorrow?	P/SOL/TRA/–/–/*ASG*/FAC/1
T: For tomorrow, I'd like you to read Chapters One and Two in this booklet.	T/RES/TRA/–/–/*ASG*/FAC/2

3.2. *Material* (MAT). Discussion of textbooks, maps, chalkboard, teaching aids, films, newspapers, television programs, radio, and the like.

Examples	*Code*
T: Now, look at this graph.	T/SOL/IMX/–/–/*MAT*/PRF/1
P: I think this book is too easy.	P/REA/TRA/–/–/*MAT*/OPN/1

3.3. *Person* (PER). Discussion of teacher's or pupil's person, physiognomy, dress, expression, or appearance. Used also when a personal experience is the topic under discussion.

Examples	*Code*
T: That's a pretty dress.	T/REA/NTR/–/–/*PER*/OPN/1
T: Have you ever been to Canada?	T/SOL/TMB/–/–/*PER*/FAC/1

3.4. *Procedure* (PRC). Discussion of any course of action or set of activities, continuing activity, or future activity. Includes references to how class is to be conducted and what regulations are to be observed. Refers also to specific instances of class regulations or practice.

Examples	*Code*
T: Tomorrow we are going to discuss foreign investments.	T/STR/FOR/–/–/*PRC*/FAC/2
T: There will be no talking when I'm talking.	T/SOL/IMX/–/–/*PRC*/PRF/2
T: I think I've asked you to keep quiet.	T/SOL/TDI/–/–/*PRC*/PRF/1

3.5. *Statement* (STA). Reference to any verbal utterance, particularly the meaning, validity, truth, or propriety of that utterance. May refer to a single word, sentence, paragraph or longer statement.

Examples	*Code*
T: That's correct.	T/REA/IMX/–/–/*STA*/POS/1
P: I think you're wrong.	P/REA/PFT/–/–/*STA*/NEG/1

3.6. *Logical Process* (LOG). Discussion of the way language is used or of a logical process. Includes references to definitions, explanations, reasoning, arguments, and the like.

Examples	*Code*
T: What is a definition?	T/SOL/TRA/–/–/*LOG*/DEF/1
T: That's a negative argument.	T/REA/TRA/–/–/*LOG*/FAC/1

3.7. *Action—General* (ACT). Reference to performance, action, or event where the nature of the performance (whether vocal, non-vocal, cognitive, or emotional) cannot be determined or when more than one of the subcategories 3.71 through 3.74 are involved.

Examples	*Code*
T: Stop that!	T/SOL/FOR/–/–/*ACT*/PRF/1
T: Think about that for a few minutes and then write your answers.	T/SOL/TRA/–/–/*ACT*/PRF/2

3.71 *Action—Vocal* (ACV). Reference to action involving the emission of speech or sound. Used for the physical qualities of the action or the act of saying something. This includes references to the act of reading aloud, or to the pace, volume, pitch, and diction of vocal action.

Examples	*Code*
T: Bobby, you said that before.	T/REA/TWH/–/–/*ACV*/FAC/1
T: Repeat that, please.	T/SOL/IMX/–/–/*ACV*/RPT/1

3.72 *Action—Physical* (ACP). Reference to action where physical movements are primary. Includes writing, passing papers, walking, hearing, and seeing.

Examples	*Code*
T: Turn out the lights, please.	T/SOL/PFT/–/–/*ACP*/PRF/1
P: May I leave the room?	P/SOL/BAT/–/–/*ACP*/AON/1

3.73 *Action—Cognitive* (ACC). Reference to action where a cognitive process is principally involved. This includes thinking, imagining, knowing, supposing, understanding or not understanding, listening, believing, and reading (silent).

Examples	*Code*
P: I don't know.	P/RES/FCE/–/–/*ACC*/FAC/1
T: Now keep this in mind.	T/SOL/BAQ/–/–/*ACC*/PRF/1

3.74 *Action—Emotional* (ACE). Reference to action where feelings or emotions are principally involved. Includes feeling bad, good, sorry, thankful, grateful, relieved, or upset.

Examples	*Code*
P: Thanks a lot.	P/REA/FHS/–/–/*ACE*/FAC/1
T: Keep your feelings out of this.	T/SOL/BAR/–/–/*ACE*/PRF/1

3.8 *Language Mechanics* (LAM). Discussion of language usage or grammar.

Examples	*Code*
T: "I seen" or "I saw"?	T/SOL/TMB/–/–/*LAM*/FAC/1
P: How do you spell "reciprocal?"	P/SOL/PFT/–/–/*LAM*/FAC/1
T: R-E-C-I-P-R-O-C-A-L.	T/RES/PFT/–/–/*LAM*/FAC/1

4. *Instructional-Logical Meanings.* While instructional-logical meanings include those processes listed under substantive-logical meanings, they also refer to distinctly didactic verbal moves such as those involved in positive and negative rating and giving instructions. For this reason, additional subcategories under the logical processes are necessary.

4.1. *Analytic process* (same as in substantive-logical meanings)

4.11 *Defining—General* (DEF)

4.111 *Defining—Denotative* (DED)

4.112 *Defining—Connotative* (DEC)

4.12 *Interpreting* (INT)

4.2. *Empirical process* (same as in substantive-logical meanings)

4.21 *Fact-Stating* (FAC)

4.22 *Explaining* (XPL)

4.3. *Evaluative process*

4.31 *Opining* (OPN) (same as in substantive-logical meanings)

4.32 *Justifying* (JUS) (same as in substantive-logical meanings)

4.33 *Rating.* The categories under rating include judgments about the truth or falsity, or appropriateness or inappropriateness, of preceding statements.

4.331 *Positive* (POS). Distinctly affirmative rating, usually in a reaction to a statement.

Examples	*Code*
T: Right.	T/REA/TDI/–/–/STA/*POS*/1
T: Yeah.	T/REA/FSP/–/–/STA/*POS*/1
T: Good.	T/REA/FOD/–/–/STA/*POS*/1

4.332 *Admitting* (ADM). Hesitation on part of rater; mildly accepting or equivocally positive rating, usually in a reaction to a statement.

Examples	*Code*
T: Mm-hmm.	T/REA/PFT/–/–/STA/*ADM*/1
T: Oh, all right.	T/REA/FOR/–/–/STA/*ADM*/1
T: O.K.	T/REA/BAR/–/–/STA/*ADM*/1

4.333 *Repeating* (RPT). Implicit rating in reaction in which there is only a repetition, rephrasing, or restatement of a preceding move with no explicit evaluative comment. Also coded for solicitations and responses that ask for or give a repetition of a previous statement.

Examples	*Code*
T: What countries belong to the Common Market?	T/SOL/PFT/FAC/2/–/–/–
P: France.	P/RES/PFT/FAC/1/–/–/–
T: France.	T/REA/PFT/–/–/STA/*RPT*/1
T: What?	T/SOL/IMX/–/–/ACV/*RPT*/1
P: Tin (a repetition).	P/RES/IMX/–/–/ACV/*RPT*/1

4.334 *Qualifying* (QAL). Any indication of reservation, however mild or oblique, usually in reactions to statements.

Examples	*Code*
T: That's partly it.	T/REA/FSP/–/–/STA/*QAL*/1
T: That's one way of looking at it.	T/REA/BAR/–/–/STA/*QAL*/1
P: Yes, but . . .	P/REA/PFT/–/–/STA/*QAL*/1

4.335 *Not Admitting* (NAD). Ratings that reject by stating the contrary rather than by making an explicitly negative comment.

Examples	*Code*
T: Imports and exports are *not* the factors of production.	T/REA/FSP/–/–/STA/*NAD*/2
T: We *do* trade with Yugoslavia.	T/REA/TWH/–/–/STA/*NAD*/1

4.336 *Negative* (NEG). Distinctly negative rating, usually in reaction to a statement.

Examples	*Code*
T: No.	T/REA/FOP/–/–/STA/*NEG*/1
T: You're wrong.	T/REA/BAE/–/–/STA/*NEG*/1

4.337 *Positive or Negative* (PON). Solicitations in which a request is made for either a positive or a negative rating.

Examples	*Code*
T: Right?	T/SOL/IMX/–/–/STA/*PON*/1
P: Am I wrong?	P/SOL/BAT/–/–/STA/*PON*/1

4.338 *Admitting or Not Admitting* (AON). Solicitations in which a request is made to give an evaluation or to permit a given procedure or action.

Examples	*Code*
P: Is my homework O.K.?	P/SOL/TRA/–/–/ASG/*AON*/1
P: Is this all right?	P/SOL/PFT/–/–/PRC/*AON*/1

4.4. *Extra-logical Process.* The two categories listed under extra-logical process involve solicitations that call for the performance of a physical or cognitive act or solicitations which invite responses that are nonpropositional verbal utterances (e.g., commands, questions, or directives).

4.41 *Performing* (PRF). Solicitations that ask or demand of someone to do something. These include directives and imperatives.

Examples	*Code*
T: Read chapters one and two.	T/SOL/TRA/–/–/ASG/*PRF*/1
T: John?	T/SOL/REL/–/–/ACV/*PRF*/1
T: Pay attention now!	T/SOL/TDI/–/–/ACC/*PRF*/1

4.42 *Directing* (DIR). Solicitations that ask for a directive (a further solicitation). The solicitation must be general or involve more than one alternative rather than ask for approval or prohibition (AON) of a single given procedure or action.

Examples	*Code*
T: How shall we handle this problem?	T/SOL/TRA/–/–/PRC/*DIR*/1
T: What ought we to do today?	T/SOL/TRA/–/–/PRC/*DIR*/1

Scales for Rating Reactions

Positively Toned

POSITIVE (POS)	ADMITTING (ADM)	REPEATING (RPT)
An explicitly positive statement	A mild or equivocally positive statement.	An implicit admitting by a simple repetition, rephrasing, or restatement.
Yes. Right. Correct. A Good answer. Exactly. Precisely.	All right. O.K. Uh-huh.	Land, labor, and capital.

Negatively Toned

QUALIFYING (QAL)	NOT ADMITTING (NAD)	NEGATIVE (NEG)
Any indication of reservation, however mild or oblique.	Making no explicitly negative statement, but refusing to admit by stating the direct contrary. Indicated by restating a positive utterance in negative terms or a negative utterance in positive terms.	An explicitly negative statement.
Yes, but . . . . However . . . . Nevertheless . . . . That's one way of saying it.	England is *not* in the Common Market. We *do* have bauxite resources.	No. Wrong. That's a terrible answer. Nope. Uh-uh.

Example	*Code*
T: Give an example of a natural resource.	T/SOL/FNR/DED/1/–/–/–
P: Automobiles.	P/RES/FNR/DED/1/–/–/–

To this response, there may be the following kinds of evaluative reaction:

Basically positive		*Basically negative*	
STA/POS	T: Right.	STA/QAL	T: Well, that's one way of looking at it.
STA/ADM	T: All right.	STA/NAD	T: An automobile is not a natural resource.
STA/RPT	T: Automobiles.	STA/NEG	T: Wrong

Coding the Protocols

In this section several excerpts from the coded protocols are given to illustrate coding procedures and interpretations of the coded information.

Example No. 1

Excerpt from protocol

Teacher (Move #1): Now, in order to pacify, or help satisfy, certain groups in American industry and American politics who want high protective tariffs, or who are clamoring for protection, we have inserted into our reciprocal agreements two—what you might call—safeguards which are coming up now as President Kennedy looks for greater authority in the tariff business. (Move #2): What have we inserted in here to give an element of protection or to stifle the outcries of American businessmen who want protection? Two clauses which we call. . . ? Yes?

Pupil (Move #3): The peril point and the escape clause.
Teacher (Move #4): Right. The peril point and the escape clause.

Code

Move #1 T/STR/BAT/XPL/5/–/–/–
Move #2 T/SOL/BAT/FAC/2/–/–/–
Move #3 P/RES/BAT/FAC/1/–/–/–
Move #4 T/REA/BAT/–/–/STA/POS/1

Interpretation

The teacher focuses on a substantive area by explaining something having to do with tariffs to the extent of five lines (Move #1). He then solicits for two lines with the expectation that a factual response on tariffs will be given (Move #2). A pupil gives a one-line response by stating a fact about tariffs (Move #3). The teacher positively evaluates the statement by the pupil (Move #4).

The entire segment of discourse is an example of a teacher-initiated cycle 9 (STR SOL RES REA).

Example No. 2

Excerpt from protocol

Teacher (Move #1): We specialize in what—manufacturing or agriculture?

Pupil (Move #2): Manufacturing.

Teacher (Move #3): All right. We're able to support our people on a very small number of agricultural workers because we can specialize and make the trade with many places.

Code

Move #1 T/SOL/FSP/FAC/1/–/–/–
Move #2 P/RES/FSP/FAC/1/–/–/–
Move #3 T/REA/FSP/XPL/2/STA/ADM/1

Interpretation

The teacher asks for factual information relating to factors of production or specialization to the extent of one line (Move #1). A pupil gives a one-line factual response (Move #2). The teacher reacts by admitting the previous statement and adding two lines of explanation on the same subject (Move #3).

The entire segment of discourse is an example of a teacher-initiated cycle 18 (SOL RES REA).

Example No. 3

Excerpt from protocol

Teacher (Move #1): For instance, what were your 1934 Reciprocal Trade Agreements? How did they work? What were they designed to do? Ellen?

Pupil (Move #2): I don't know.

Teacher (Move #3): We studied that just last week when we were studying the New Deal. (Move #4): All right, Ron?

Pupil (Move #5): Well, we agreed, I think we agreed to lower the tariffs for import duty in our country. Then the other country would reciprocate by agreeing to lower theirs.

Teacher (Move #6): Very good.

Code

Move #1 T/SOL/PFT/XPL/2/–/–/–
Move #2 P/RES/PFT/–/–/ACC/FAC/1
Move #3 T/REA/PFT/–/–/PRC/FAC/1
Move #4 T/SOL/PFT/–/–/ACV/PRF/1
Move #5 P/RES-M4/PFT/XPL/3/–/–/–
Move #6 T/REA/PFT/–/–/STA/POS/1

Interpretation

The teacher asks for an explanation concerning the promotion of free trade to the extent of two lines (Move #1). A pupil responds by making a one-line statement about her cognition (Move #2). The teacher reacts to the statement by stating factual information about a class procedure to the extent of one line (Move #3). He then calls upon a student to perform a vocal action (Move #4). A pupil responds to a solicitation that occurred four moves earlier by giving a two-line explanation relating to promoting free trade (Move #5). The teacher reacts by making a positive evaluation of the previous move (Move #6).

The entire segment of discourse is an example of a teacher-initiated cycle 21 (SOL RES REA RES . . . REA . . .).

Reliability Test

Although preliminary studies conducted during the course of developing the content analysis system had indicated high agreement between coders, it was necessary to test the reliability of the final system of analysis under rigorously controlled conditions and to obtain a quantitative estimate of the degree of reliability for each of the major kinds of meaning considered in the research.

Four members of the research staff participated in the reliability test. Twelve five-page samples were selected at random from protocols of six different teachers. The segments of the protocols were verbatim transcriptions of the recorded class sessions. No attempt was made to prestructure the coding by delineating where moves began or ended. The four coders were divided into two teams. Assignment of coders to the two coding teams was rotated so that all possible permutations of team membership were compared. Following our general procedures for analysis, one member of each team coded a given sample, the other member reviewed the coding, and both members of each team then arbitrated any disagreements between the initial coder and the reviewer.

After each of the 12 samples had been coded independently by the two teams, the codings of the teams were compared, and the percentage of agreement was computed in terms of both number of lines and number of moves. The results as presented in Table 2 indicate a consistently high degree of reliability for all major categories of analysis: agreement ranged from 84 to 96 per cent. Thus, the data

TABLE 2

Percentage of Agreement among Coding Teams for Each Major Category in the Content Analysis

Major Categories	*Per Cent Agreement Moves*	*Per Cent Agreement Lines*
Pedagogical Moves	94	93
Substantive Meanings	95	96
Substantive-Logical Meanings	88	91
Instructional Meanings	88	91
Instructional-Logical Meanings	87	84

strongly support the conclusion that the system devised in this research for a content analysis of classroom discourse is highly reliable.

Problems in Coding

In the course of developing the content analysis system, numerous problems were encountered in defining categories and establishing rules of coding with sufficient rigor and clarity to insure reliable coding. As the results of the reliability test demonstrate, a majority of these problems were satisfactorily resolved. A brief description of some major issues faced during the development of the code may provide useful information for researchers who will either use this system in future work or devise similar techniques of analysis.

One of the earliest problems in coding involved the differentiation between the structuring and the reacting pedagogical moves. Solicitations and responses seemed to be distinctive enough to offer little difficulty, since they occur most frequently in conjunction with each other in the form of questions and answers. However, the unique characteristics of the pedagogical moves that framed the question-and-answer sequence were less obvious. A structuring move, which launches and frames the subsequent discourse, might also contain a passing reference to preceding discussion; and a reacting move, whose primary focus is some aspect of the previous discussion, might imply an introduction to a new topic of discourse. This problem was resolved by coding the material primarily on the basis of its manifest content, establishing comprehensive definitions of structuring and reacting, and providing numerous examples of each type of move. If doubt persisted with regard to differentiating structuring and reacting moves, the general rule was to code that pedagogical category which moved the discourse forward, thus coding structuring rather than reacting.

In the substantive-logical category, two frequent problems were encountered. The first involved discriminating between denotative defining and fact-stating. This was resolved by coding defining when the referent of the statement was words *per se,* and coding fact-stating when the referent was empirical. A second problem in the substantive-logical category concerned explaining and justifying. Both kinds of statement involved relationships of one sort or another, but explaining concerned facts which could conceivably be verified empirically, while justifying concerned personal opinions held by the speaker.

Perhaps the major difficulty in coding substantive meanings occurred when two or more of the major substantive topics, such as specialization and foreign investments, were contained in a single move. Because preliminary work in analyzing substantive meanings indicated that coding two or more substantive categories for one move would be likely to reduce, rather than raise, agreement among coders, double coding of substantive categories was prohibited. The general policy followed in the analysis was to code each statement within the context of the ongoing discourse unless there was a clear shift from one major topic to another. Thus a single statement about imports within the context of an ongoing discussion of foreign investment was coded in the "foreign investment" category.

In a sense, this compromise represents a possible weakness in the coding system, for while it led to high reliability of coding, discussions that concerned the relationship between one major topic and another, such as trade barriers and foreign investment, were somewhat obscured by the coding procedures. For the purposes of the present research, this was not a crucial issue; but it does suggest a possible line of development for further modifications of the content analysis system.

Coding of instructional meanings was aided by a specified order of precedence among the various subcategories that eliminated many of the possibly difficult decisions in this area; for example, a teacher might direct the pupils to engage in some classroom procedure (PRC) which required the use of materials (MAT). By order of precedence, "materials" would be coded rather than "procedure." This solution was especially useful in coding instructional meanings, but it also suggests that the technique of setting a rationally based order of precedence in other categories of analysis might be a useful procedure to follow in future work.

At the outset of the content analysis, a major difficulty in the instructional-logical category was specifying the particular kind of rating reaction contained in a given move. This problem was largely resolved by establishing scales for the positively oriented ratings and the negatively oriented ratings (p. 32).

These problems represent a sample of the issues dealt with in the development of the code. In many instances, solution of a problem depended upon a compromise between representing precisely the unique qualities of particular statements and establishing more abstract categories that lost some of the information conveyed by specific statements but also provided a reliable basis for classifying the meaning expressed. This is a problem encountered in almost all content analysis procedures, and these efforts represent a series of compromises which seemed to capture best the meanings expressed in classroom interactions. The relatively high degree of agreement obtained among coders lends credence to the final results obtained, but it should also be noted that the four coders who provided the data for the reliability test also participated in development of the code. Although the material used for estimating reliability was not used in developing the code, and thus represented an independent sample of discourse, the researchers who worked on various stages of the content analysis continuously interacted, discussed problems of coding, and probably developed, over time, a shared perspective that in part accounted for the high agreement in the final coding. A rigorous attempt has been made to make this perspective explicit in the definitions of categories and rules of coding, but it would be unreasonable to assume that the present system has completely objectified all aspects of the coding procedures. Nevertheless, it seems likely that researchers appropriately trained and thoroughly familiar with the code can use the present system of analysis reliably.

Summary of the Coding System *

(1) SPEAKER: indicates source of utterance
Teacher (T); *Pupil* (P); *Audio-Visual Device* (A)

(2) TYPE OF PEDAGOGICAL MOVE: reference to function of move
Initiatory Moves
Structuring (STR): sets context for subsequent behavior by launching or halting-excluding interaction
Soliciting (SOL): directly elicits verbal, physical, or mental response; coded in terms of response expected
Reflexive Moves
Responding (RES): fulfills expectation of solicitation; bears reciprocal relation only to solicitation
Reacting (REA): modifies (by clarifying, synthesizing, expanding) and/or rates (positively or negatively); occasioned by previous move, but not directly elicited; reactions to more than one previous move coded *REA*
Not Codable (NOC): function uncertain because tape is inaudible

(3) SUBSTANTIVE MEANING: reference to subject matter topic (see pp. 21–22).

(4) SUBSTANTIVE-LOGICAL MEANING: reference to cognitive process involved in dealing with the subject matter under study
Analytic Process: use of language or established rules of logic
Defining—General (DEF): defining characteristics of class or term with example of items within class explicitly given

* Italics indicate actual coding terminology.

Defining—Denotative (DED): object referent of term

Defining—Connotative (DEC): defining characteristics of class or term

Interpreting (INT): verbal equivalent of a statement, slogan, aphorism, or proverb

Empirical Process: sense experience as criterion of truth

Fact-Stating (FAC): what is, was, or will be without explanation or evaluation; account, report, description, statement of event or state of affairs.

Explaining (XPL): relation between objects, events, principles; conditional inference; cause-effect; explicit comparison-contrast; statement of principles, theories, or laws

Evaluative Process: set of criteria or value system as basis for verification

Opining (OPN): personal values for statement of policy, judgment or evaluation of event, idea, state of affairs; direct and indirect evaluation included

Justifying (JUS): reasons or argument for or against opinion or judgment

Logical Process Not Clear (NCL): cognitive process involved not clear

(5) NUMBER OF LINES IN 3 AND 4 ABOVE: see Appendix A for definition and procedures

(6) INSTRUCTIONAL MEANINGS: reference to factors related to classroom management

Assignment (ASG): suggested or required student activity; reports, tests, readings, debates, homework

Material (MAT): teaching aids and instructional devices

Person (PER): person as physical object or personal experiences

Procedure (PRC): a plan of activities or a course of action

Statement (STA): verbal utterance, particularly the meaning validity, truth, or propriety of an utterance

Logical Process (LOG): function of language or rule of logic; reference to definitions or arguments, but not presentation of such

Action—General (ACT): performance (vocal, non-vocal, cognitive, or emotional) the specific nature of which is uncertain or complex

Action—Vocal (ACV): physical qualities of vocal action

Action—Physical (ACP): physical movement or process

Action—Cognitive (ACC): cognitive process, but not the language or logic of a specific utterance; thinking, knowing, understanding, listening

Action—Emotional (ACE): emotion or feeling, but not expression of attitude or value

Language Mechanics (LAM): the rules of grammar and/or usage

(7) INSTRUCTIONAL-LOGIC MEANING: reference to cognitive processes related to the distinctly didactic verbal moves in the instructional situation

Analytic Process: see (4) above

Defining—General (DEF)

Defining—Denotative (DED)

Defining—Connotative (DEC)

Interpreting (INT)

Empirical Process: see (4) above

Fact-Stating (FAC)

Explaining (XPL)

Evaluative Process

Opining (OPN): see (4) above

Justifying (JUS): see (4) above

Rating: reference to metacommunication; usually an evaluative reaction (REA)

Positive (POS): distinctly affirmative rating

Admitting (ADM): mild or equivocally positive rating

Repeating (RPT): implicit positive rating when statement (STA) is repeated by another speaker; also for SOL to repeat vocal action (ACV)

Qualifying (QAL): explicit reservation stated in rating; exception

Not Admitting (NAD): rating that rejects by stating the contrary; direct refutation or correction excluded

Negative (NEG): distinctly negative rating

Positive/Negative (PON): SOL requesting positive or negative rating

Admitting/Not Admitting (AON): SOL asking to permit or not permit procedure or action

Extra-logical Process: SOL expecting physical action or when logical nature of verbal response cannot be determined

Performing (PRF): asking, demanding; explicit directive or imperative

Directing (DIR): SOL with or without stated alternatives; asking for directive, not permission for specific action

Extral-logical Process Not Clear (NCL): extra-logical process involved not clear

(8) NUMBER OF LINES IN 6 AND 7 ABOVE: see Appendix A for definition and procedures

CHAPTER THREE

OVERVIEW OF CLASSROOM DISCOURSE

To PROVIDE a setting for the detailed analysis of pedagogical moves and teaching cycles in subsequent chapters, we present here an overview of the general trends and similarities as well as the range of individual differences found in the discourse of the 15 classes studied.

Teacher-Pupil Activity

Activity in this context is defined as the percentage of total number of lines of transcript and moves spoken either by a teacher or by the pupils in a particular class.

Total Activity over All Sessions

Data relating to total activity over all sessions for teachers and pupils are summarized in Table 3. The 15 teachers did more talking than did the 345 pupils, although there were of course differences in the degree to which individual teachers dominated the classroom discourse.

Percentage of lines. In terms of lines spoken, the median percentage of lines for the 15 teachers is 72.6. The distribution is fairly peaked; 7 of the 15 teachers spoke between 70 and 75 per cent of the total lines of discourse for all sessions. In this sample of classes, therefore, the teacher-pupil ratio of amount spoken was approximately the same for all classes. There was a range of teacher activity, however, from 60.3 per cent to 92.8 per cent. In fact, there was a cluster of four teachers (Teachers 2, 4, 5, and 15) at the 60 per cent range. Only three of the 15 teachers spoke more than 80 per cent of the lines; these were Teacher 6 (82.2), Teacher 10 (81.2), and Teacher 9 (92.8). Not-

TABLE 3

Percentage of Lines and Moves for Teachers, Pupils, and Audio-Visual Devices in Each of the Fifteen Classes and for All Classes Combined

Class		*Teacher*	*Pupil*	*Audio-Visual Device*
1	Moves	60.6	39.4	—
	Lines	76.3	23.7	—
2	Moves	59.0	41.0	—
	Lines	61.5	38.5	—
3	Moves	65.8	34.2	—
	Lines	70.2	29.8	—
4	Moves	61.4	38.6	—
	Lines	60.3	39.7	—
5	Moves	58.3	41.7	—
	Lines	61.3	38.7	—
6	Moves	64.5	35.5	—
	Lines	82.2	17.8	—
7	Moves	63.7	36.3	—
	Lines	72.0	28.0	—
8	Moves	61.7	38.3	—
	Lines	73.5	26.5	—
9	Moves	72.1	27.9	—
	Lines	92.8	7.2	—
10	Moves	62.3	37.7	—
	Lines	81.2	18.8	—
11	Moves	66.9	33.1	—
	Lines	73.7	26.3	—
12	Moves	58.3	41.7	—
	Lines	73.4	26.6	—
13	Moves	60.1	39.9	—
	Lines	70.9	29.1	—
14	Moves	66.4	33.5	0.1
	Lines	72.6	20.3	7.1
15	Moves	57.8	41.3	0.9
	Lines	60.8	36.2	3.0
$\overline{X}$	Moves	61.7	38.2	0.1
	Lines	72.1	27.2	0.7

withstanding the clusters at the extremes of the distribution, the most remarkable characteristic of these data is the number of teachers clustering at the center of the distribution. Thus the teacher-pupil ratio of speech is about 3 to 1 in most of the classrooms sampled.

Percentage of moves. The analysis in terms of percentage of moves presents approximately the same picture, for the teachers not only speak the majority of lines but also make the majority of pedagogical moves. The teacher-pupil ratio in terms of percentage of moves, however, is somewhat lower than that for percentage of lines. The median percentage of moves for all teachers is 61.7, with a range from 57.8 per cent to 72 per cent. As in the analysis of percentage of lines, the distribution of moves is fairly peaked; the data for 10 of the 15 classrooms show that teachers made between 57.8 and 64.5 per cent of the total moves. For these classrooms, therefore, the teacher-pupil ratio of moves was approximately 3 to 2. In only three classes was the ratio 2 to 1: Teacher 11 made 66.9 per cent of the moves; Teacher 14 made 66.4 per cent of the moves; and Teacher 3 made 65.8 per cent of the moves. One class was distinctly different from all other classes in that the teacher made the great majority of pedagogical moves; Teacher 9 made 72.1 per cent of the total moves, with a teacher-pupil move ratio of 2.6 to 1.

The data summarized in Table 3 reveal a marked similarity in total number of lines and moves spoken by the various teachers. This is particularly noteworthy in view of the fact that the teachers were told they could conduct their classes in any way they wished. Undoubtedly they did not feel completely free, in part as a consequence of being recorded while teaching. It is nevertheless remarkable that so many of the teachers in different schools, given the freedom to conduct their classes as they chose, all spoke about the same proportion of the total number of lines and moves.

Activity in Each Session

Table 4 summarizes teacher and pupil activity for each of the four sessions for each of the 15 teachers. These data demonstrate a degree of consistency over sessions for each teacher. This is particularly true if one considers the first three class sessions. In terms of percentage of lines, for example, Teacher 1 in the first session spoke 78 per cent of the lines, in the second session 72.6 per cent, and in the third session 73.7 per cent. Teacher 9 spoke 92.2 per cent in session 1, 92.3 per cent in session 2, and 94.8 per cent in session 3. For some of the classes, the amount of teacher activity in the fourth session was

TABLE 4

Teacher-Pupil Activity in Terms of Percentage of Lines and Moves by Session for Each of the Fifteen Classes and for All Classes Combined

Class	Teacher Session I	II	III	IV	Unit of Four Sessions	Pupil Session I	II	III	IV	Unit of Four Sessions
1 Moves	61.1	58.6	60.6	64.8	60.6	38.9	41.4	39.4	35.2	39.3
Lines	78.0	72.6	73.7	82.6	76.3	22.0	27.4	26.3	17.4	23.7
2 Moves	52.9	58.0	63.2	62.5	59.0	47.1	42.0	36.8	37.5	41.0
Lines	45.1	53.2	67.8	76.6	61.5	54.9	46.8	32.2	23.4	38.5
3 Moves	69.1	66.9	62.4	63.5	65.8	30.9	33.1	37.6	36.6	34.2
Lines	80.7	74.4	71.7	50.9	70.2	19.3	25.6	28.3	49.1	29.8
4 Moves	63.5	57.6	63.6	60.9	61.4	36.5	42.4	36.5	39.1	38.6
Lines	58.0	55.4	58.4	70.3	60.3	42.0	44.6	41.6	29.7	39.7
5 Moves	64.6	60.3	62.8	43.7	58.3	35.4	39.7	37.3	56.3	41.7
Lines	76.1	72.6	66.9	28.2	61.3	23.9	27.4	33.1	71.8	38.7
6 Moves	63.9	66.5	63.4	64.1	64.5	36.2	33.5	36.7	35.9	35.5
Lines	87.4	82.9	76.3	82.1	82.2	12.6	17.1	23.7	17.9	17.8
7 Moves	63.6	62.5	63.7	65.8	63.7	36.4	37.5	36.3	34.3	36.3
Lines	68.2	76.6	75.7	67.4	72.0	31.8	23.4	24.3	32.6	28.0
8 Moves	61.2	61.9	61.9	62.0	61.7	38.8	38.2	38.1	38.0	38.4
Lines	67.8	74.1	78.7	77.3	73.5	32.2	25.9	21.3	22.8	26.5
9 Moves	71.3	68.8	76.9	72.9	72.1	28.7	31.2	23.1	27.1	27.9
Lines	92.2	92.3	94.8	92.3	92.8	7.8	7.7	5.2	7.8	7.2

Class	Teacher Session I	II	III	IV	Unit of Four Sessions	Pupil Session I	II	III	IV	Unit of Four Sessions
10 Moves	59.9	63.8	61.7	64.3	62.3	40.1	36.2	38.3	35.7	37.7
Lines	68.1	84.2	85.1	87.3	81.2	31.9	15.8	14.9	12.7	18.8
11 Moves	71.1	72.7	63.7	55.5	66.9	28.9	27.3	36.3	44.6	33.1
Lines	88.2	88.6	74.6	37.9	73.7	11.8	11.4	25.5	62.2	26.3
12 Moves	62.6	58.9	53.8	59.8	58.3	37.4	41.1	46.2	40.2	41.7
Lines	78.1	72.9	64.6	80.7	73.4	21.9	27.1	35.5	19.3	26.6
13 Moves	61.0	60.9	58.5	59.6	60.1	39.0	39.1	41.5	40.4	39.9
Lines	72.7	68.8	72.7	69.0	70.9	27.3	31.2	27.3	31.0	29.1
14 Moves	66.2	68.7	64.9	65.9	66.4	33.8	31.3	35.1	33.3	33.5
Lines	80.5	80.6	76.5	54.4	72.6	19.5	19.4	23.5	18.9	20.3
15 Moves	56.4	60.4	60.7	48.6	57.8	43.7	39.6	39.4	44.5	41.3
Lines	69.5	70.2	68.3	30.3	60.8	30.5	29.8	31.7	56.1	36.3
$\bar{X}$ Moves	62.4	62.2	61.7	60.5	61.7	37.6	37.8	38.3	39.5	38.2
Lines	73.6	74.6	73.5	68.3	72.1	26.4	25.4	26.5	31.7	27.2

somewhat different from the amount displayed in the first three sessions, probably reflecting the fact that some of the teachers assigned debates or student reports for the fourth class session. Thus Teacher 5 in the fourth session spoke only 28.2 per cent of the lines, while in the first three sessions he had spoken approximately 70 per cent of the lines. Similarly, Teacher 11 spoke only 37.9 per cent of the lines in the fourth session, while in the other three sessions he had spoken between 75 and 90 per cent of the total lines.

Despite these differences for the fourth session, however, the amount of teacher activity seems to be fairly stable over time. In all classrooms, the teachers spoke a majority of the lines. The teacher who spoke approximately 80 to 90 per cent of the lines in one session also tended to be in that range of activity for other sessions, unless some special classroom event such as a student debate was scheduled. Similarly, a teacher who was at the lower end of the distribution of activity for the first sessions, such as one who spoke only 60 per cent of the lines, tended to remain at that level of verbal activity over all class sessions. This means that there are some teachers who are more active than others, and this degree of teacher activity is a stable characteristic of the discourse in a given classroom.

Pedagogical Roles of the Teacher and the Pupil

Aside from the sheer volume of activity, teachers and pupils differ markedly in the types of activity that characterize their classroom performances. Pedagogically speaking, the teacher and the pupil play different but complementary roles in the classroom game. The roles of the teacher and the pupil may be defined in terms of frequency of behavior in each category of pedagogical moves, as indicated by the following data summarized for all 15 classes:

Pedagogical Move		*f*	*Total*	*Percentage of Moves by Teachers*	*Percentage of Moves by Pupils*	*Percentage of Moves by Audio-Visual Devices*
Soliciting	SOL	5,135	100.	86.0	14.0	—
Responding	RES	4,385	100.	12.0	88.0	—
Structuring	STR	854	100.	86.0	12.0	2.0
Reacting	REA	4,649	100.	81.0	19.0	—

The teacher dominates the structuring, soliciting, and reacting moves, speaking 86 per cent, 86 per cent, and 81 per cent of these moves respectively. In contrast, the teacher is responsible for only 12 per cent of the responding moves. Control by the teacher of three of the pedagogical moves leaves the pupil with a very limited role to play in classroom discussions. The pupil dominates the responding move, as demonstrated by the fact that he speaks 88 per cent of all moves of this type. The pupil reacts infrequently; his reactions account for only 19 per cent of all reacting moves. Even less frequently does the pupil solicit or structure; he is responsible for only 14 per cent and 12 per cent of these moves respectively.

Differences in the role patterns of the teacher and the pupil are also apparent when the percentage of the teacher's and the pupil's discourse devoted to each of the moves is considered. Data relating to the percentage distribution of moves and lines in the teacher's discourse (that is, moves and lines spoken by the 15 teachers in all sessions) are summarized below:

Pedagogical Move		*Percentage of Teachers' Moves*	*Percentage of Teachers' Lines*
Soliciting	SOL	46.6	28.0
Responding	RES	5.5	6.8
Structuring	STR	7.7	20.1
Reacting	REA	39.2	44.7
Not Codable	NOC	1.0	0.4
f (Moves) =	9,565		
f (Lines) =	30,897		

The teacher's principal responsibilities are to solicit and to react. Soliciting accounts for 46.6 per cent and reacting for 39.2 per cent of the teacher's moves. In contrast, very much smaller percentages of the teacher's discourse are responding and structuring moves; structuring accounts for 7.7 per cent and responding for only 5.5 per cent of the teacher's moves.

When the teacher's discourse is considered in terms of percentage of lines, the results for soliciting and reacting are slightly changed. While the analysis based on percentage of moves shows that the teacher solicited more than he reacted, there was in fact a larger proportion of lines devoted to reacting—44.7 per cent, with 28 per cent accounted for by soliciting. This indicates that although a larger number of moves was devoted to soliciting, the length of reacting moves in terms of number of lines was generally greater. These differences, however, do not change the general picture of the teaching pattern: whether one considers percentage of lines or percentage of moves, the teacher's role is characterized by a high proportion of soliciting and reacting. Structuring moves, with 20.1 per cent of lines spoken, also assume a more significant role in the teacher's discourse than they do in terms of moves (7.7 per cent). In contrast with other moves, responding accounts for a very small percentage of the teacher's discourse—only 6.8 per cent of the lines spoken.

The pupil's discourse (that is, moves and lines spoken by all pupils in 15 classes) is distinguished from the teacher's discourse by significantly different percentages of moves and lines devoted to the four pedagogical moves.

Pedagogical Move		*Percentage of Pupils' Moves*	*Percentage of Pupils' Lines*
Soliciting	SOL	11.3	8.7
Responding	RES	65.4	57.5
Structuring	STR	1.8	11.1
Reacting	REA	15.1	19.1
Not Codable	NOC	6.4	3.6

f (Moves) = 5,910
f (Lines) = 11,659

The pupil's primary job is to respond, as shown by the fact that the largest percentage of his moves (65.4 per cent) is devoted to responding. In marked contrast, smaller percentages of the pupil's discourse are given over to reacting (15.1 per cent) and soliciting (11.3 per cent). The pupil rarely structures; only 1.8 per cent of his moves is accounted for by structuring.

In terms of lines spoken by the pupil, the picture is little changed. Again the greatest percentage (57.5 per cent) is given over to responding, considerably smaller percentages to reacting (19.1 per cent) and to soliciting (8.7 per cent). Structuring moves again account for a higher percentage of the discourse in terms of lines (11.1 per cent) than in terms of moves (1.8 per cent).

The data therefore reveal that the roles of the teacher and of the pupil are characterized by the different percentages of their discourse devoted to the four pedagogical moves. Whereas 46.6 per cent of the teacher's moves are solicitations, only 11.3 per cent of the pupil's moves are included in this category. The reverse is the case when it comes to responding: 65.4 per cent of the pupil's moves are responding moves, while only 5.5 per cent of the teacher's moves are in this category. In contrast, 39.2 per cent of the teacher's moves are accounted for by reactions, but only 15.1 per cent of pupil moves are reactions. Structuring moves account for 7.7 per cent of the teacher's moves, but only 1.8 per cent of the pupil's moves are in this category.

Pedagogical Moves in Individual Classes: Teacher's Role

Individual teachers deviate little from the pedagogical role patterns that characterize the group as a whole, as indicated by the data summarized in Table 5. Reviewing the data in terms of percentage of total lines of transcript for each class and percentage of various types of pedagogical move for each class provides a reasonable basis for comparing and contrasting the discourse in the various classes, despite the small differences in total time among the 15 classes. In most parts of the analysis, the results obtained in terms of percentage of lines are essentially the same as those obtained for percentage of moves. For economy of presentation, therefore, the results are discussed in terms of percentage of lines unless the patterns of discourse are different when stated in terms of percentage of moves—in which case both lines and moves are discussed.

Structuring. The median amount of structuring (STR) for teachers is 11.2 per cent, with a low of 1.7 per cent and a high of 46.6 per cent. The high of 46.6, which means nearly half of the classroom discourse was devoted to teacher structuring, is represented by Teacher 9. He is clearly different from the majority of other teachers, for the next highest percentage of structuring is 24. The effective range for structuring, aside from Teacher 9, is thus between 1.7 per cent for Teacher 13 and 24 per cent for Teacher 7. Seven of the teachers range between 6 and 11 per cent, so that nearly half of the teachers are clustered in this relatively small range.

Soliciting. The median percentage of soliciting (SOL) is 20.2, represented by Teacher 6. The range is from 12 per cent for Teacher 10 to 30.1 per cent for Teacher 3. Eight of the 15 teachers are clustered between 15 and 20 per cent. Thus for most teachers five to ten per cent more lines are given over to soliciting than to structuring, despite the fact that a solicitation is typically much shorter than a structuring move.

Reacting. For most teachers the largest proportion of lines is devoted to reacting (REA). The median percentage of lines involving reacting is 25.5, with a range from 17.3 per cent to 36.9 per cent. The high of 36.9 per cent is represented by Teacher 1, whose pattern of teaching was consistently a question by the teacher followed by a student response which in turn was almost always followed by a teacher reaction. The effective range for reacting is even more restricted than that for either structuring or soliciting. Eleven of the 15 teachers are clustered between 22 and 30 per cent of the lines devoted to reacting. Outside of this range are only four teachers: two at the lower end of

TABLE 5

Percentage of Lines and Moves in Each Pedagogical Category for Teachers and Pupils in Each of the Fifteen Classes and for All Classes Combined

	TEACHER						*PUPIL*						
Class	SOL	RES	STR	REA	*REA*	REA *Total*	SOL	RES	STR	STR-A	REA	*REA*	REA *Total*
1 Moves	29.9	1.4	2.5	25.3	0.9	26.2	1.7	30.0	0.4	—	3.4	—	3.4
Lines	27.5	1.4	7.2	36.9	3.1	40.0	1.2	18.0	0.4	—	2.3	—	2.3
2 Moves	29.9	1.2	4.8	20.8	1.6	22.4	2.6	26.6	0.7	—	7.5	0.2	7.7
Lines	20.1	1.0	11.2	25.5	3.4	28.9	1.6	23.9	0.8	—	10.2	0.4	10.6
3 Moves	36.6	2.1	7.0	18.8	1.2	20.0	3.1	24.4	0.03	1.2	3.7	—	3.7
Lines	30.1	3.7	10.1	22.9	3.3	26.2	2.1	18.2	0.02	6.3	2.5	—	2.5
4 Moves	29.6	2.8	4.1	23.5	1.3	24.8	3.1	24.6	0.04	0.1	8.6	—	8.6
Lines	20.7	3.7	5.9	26.7	3.3	30.0	1.8	24.8	0.6	4.8	7.0	—	7.0
5 Moves	24.5	5.8	5.2	20.4	1.6	22.0	9.4	17.9	0.4	1.2	9.0	0.1	9.1
Lines	15.5	9.4	15.5	17.3	3.4	20.7	5.4	14.4	0.5	6.1	10.7	0.2	10.9
6 Moves	33.7	3.3	3.7	20.7	2.8	23.5	2.7	27.5	0.2	—	2.5	—	2.5
Lines	20.2	5.9	16.2	25.5	14.4	39.9	1.1	14.3	0.04	—	1.6	—	1.6
7 Moves	25.7	5.8	7.8	22.5	1.1	23.6	6.6	21.4	1.7	0.2	4.9	—	4.9
Lines	15.5	7.5	24.0	22.2	2.4	24.6	4.2	13.5	2.4	3.3	4.1	—	4.1
8 Moves	27.6	4.4	3.7	23.5	1.7	25.2	4.7	22.9	0.4	—	8.0	—	8.0
Lines	20.4	8.8	8.8	30.5	4.5	35.0	2.9	15.0	0.3	—	7.3	—	7.3
9 Moves	29.0	1.7	13.2	25.8	2.2	28.0	1.5	22.5	—	—	2.8	—	2.8
Lines	12.8	0.9	46.6	29.5	2.8	32.3	0.3	5.8	—	—	0.9	—	0.9

Class	TEACHER						PUPIL						
	SOL	RES	STR	REA	*REA*	REA *Total*	SOL	RES	STR	STR-A	REA	*REA*	REA *Total*
10 Moves	28.3	2.4	5.5	23.4	2.1	25.5	3.1	25.3	0.1	—	5.5	—	5.5
Lines	12.0	5.3	19.7	34.7	9.4	44.1	1.2	10.6	0.03	—	5.9	—	5.9
11 Moves	32.9	2.1	8.6	20.7	2.2	22.9	2.6	26.7	0.4	0.7	1.3	—	1.3
Lines	23.2	2.8	22.4	18.2	6.8	25.0	0.9	13.4	0.5	9.8	1.2	—	1.2
12 Moves	21.5	5.8	7.3	21.3	1.1	22.4	8.0	18.6	0.1	0.1	11.2	—	11.2
Lines	16.0	6.2	22.0	25.3	3.3	28.6	4.1	10.0	0.1	3.1	7.9	—	7.9
13 Moves	30.1	3.7	1.2	22.0	2.3	24.2	4.2	30.1	0.4	—	3.9	—	3.9
Lines	28.9	6.1	1.7	27.5	6.6	34.1	3.0	21.4	0.7	—	3.3	—	3.3
14 Moves	29.8	2.7	4.5	25.9	2.5	28.4	2.7	25.2	—	0.6	1.5	—	1.5
Lines	23.8	3.5	8.0	28.3	8.5	36.8	1.3	13.0	—	4.3	0.6	—	0.6
15 Moves	24.6	5.3	3.6	23.0	1.2	24.2	7.3	22.9	0.4	0.2	9.2	—	9.2
Lines	14.7	9.1	8.7	24.2	4.0	28.2	5.5	15.6	0.2	3.6	10.8	—	10.8
$\overline{X}$ Moves	28.8	3.5	4.8	22.6	1.7	24.2	4.4	25.0	0.4	0.3	5.7	0.02	5.7
Lines	20.3	5.0	14.5	26.7	5.3	32.0	2.5	15.6	0.4	2.6	5.1	0.03	5.1

the distribution, with 17 and 18 per cent respectively; and two at the upper end, with 35 and 37 per cent.

If these data are considered in terms of percentage of moves, rather than lines, the results for soliciting and reacting are slightly changed. While the analysis based on percentage of lines shows that teachers reacted more than they solicited, there was in fact a larger proportion of discrete moves devoted to soliciting. The median percentage of moves concerned with soliciting was 29.6, while the median percentage of reacting moves was 22.5. This suggests that although a larger number of moves was devoted to soliciting, the length of the reacting moves was generally greater. These small differences, however, do not change the general picture of the teaching pattern, for regardless of whether one considers percentage of lines or of moves, the teacher's role is characterized by a relatively high proportion of soliciting and reacting.

In contrast to the usual reacting statements, coded REA, the reactive statements that summarize, coded *REA* (italicized), represent much less of the teachers' activity. In this category, the range of percentage of lines is from 2.4 per cent to 14.4 per cent, with a median of 3.4 per cent. The high of 14.4 per cent for Teacher 6, who is also a highly structuring teacher, is clearly different from most of the other teachers. The next highest percentage of *REA* is 9.4 for Teacher 10. Of the total sample of 15 teachers, ten cluster within a range from 2 to 4 per cent of lines devoted to *REA;* in other words, nearly 80 per cent of the entire sample falls within a range of two percentage points. This underscores the fact that in certain respects the 15 teachers were remarkably similar to each other in their classroom behavior.

Responding. In comparison with their use of other types of moves, teachers respond (RES) very infrequently. The median percentage of responding for teachers is 5.3. The range is from 0.9 per cent for Teacher 9 to 9.4 per cent for Teacher 5. This low proportion of teacher responding is obviously related to a comparably low incidence of pupil soliciting.

Pedagogical Patterns in Individual Classes: Pupils' Role

Table 5 also presents the percentage distributions for the pupils' pedagogical moves in each of the 15 classes. As in the case of the teachers, pupils in each of the classes deviate little from the role patterns that characterize the students as a group.

Responding. The pupils' primary job is to respond, as illustrated by the fact that for pupils the largest proportion of lines is devoted to responding (RES), with a range from 5.8 per cent to 24.8 per cent and a median of 14.4 per cent. The majority of classes fall within a range of a few percentage points. Nine of the classes cluster between 13 and 18 per cent, so that a range of only five percentage points accounts for 60 per cent of the sample in terms of the amount of discourse concerned with pupil responding.

As one might infer from the data on teacher-pupil activity, the low of 5.8 per cent for pupil responding is represented by the classroom in which the teacher showed the highest amount of activity. This was Class 9, in which pupils were responsible principally for listening rather than responding. In contrast, the high of 24.8 per cent is represented by the pupils in Class 4, whose main job was responding to the teacher's repeated questions. In this class, the teacher asked many relatively brief questions, requiring the pupils to respond with relatively long answers. Despite these differences among the classrooms, however, the data clearly demonstrate that in all classrooms sampled the pupil's task was to respond to the teacher's solicitations.

Soliciting. The amount of pupil soliciting (SOL) is in marked contrast to the percentage of lines devoted to pupil responding. Pupils infrequently ask questions. The range for pupil soliciting in terms of percentage of lines is from 0.3 to 5.5 with a median of 2.1. In terms of median percentage of lines, pupils thus respond approximately seven times more frequently than they solicit. The lowest soliciting rate is in Teacher 9's class, where pupils solicit only 0.3 per cent of the time. The similarity of the classrooms is emphasized by the fact that all of the classrooms are accounted for by a range of only five percentage points in terms of the amount of pupil soliciting. It is clear that the teacher's job is to solicit, and the pupils rarely assume this aspect of the teacher's role.

Reacting. Although responding comprises by far the largest proportion of pupil activity, reacting (REA) accounts for an appreciable, though small, amount of activity. The range of pupil reactions is from 0.6 per cent to 10.8 per cent with a median of 4.1 per cent. However, eight of the classrooms studied are included within a range of only three percentage points, from 0.6 to 4 per cent. While the pupils' main job is to respond, in some classrooms they do react and solicit to some extent.

Pupils almost never give summary reactions (*REA*). This pedagogical move for pupils occurred in only two classes and in both instances represented less than half of one per cent of total discourse.

Structuring. Pupils rarely structure. In only one class is pupil structuring greater than 1 per cent of the lines; in this class, Class 7,

TABLE 6

Percentage of Teacher Moves and Lines Devoted to Each Pedagogical Move for All Teachers Combined by Each Session and for All Sessions Combined

Pedagogical Move		*Session* I	II	III	IV	*Unit of Four Sessions*
SOL	Moves	47.6	46.3	46.3	46.0	46.6
	Lines	30.6	28.0	27.4	26.5	28.0
RES	Moves	5.1	5.1	6.6	5.7	5.5
	Lines	5.9	8.1	8.0	5.8	6.8
STR	Moves	7.3	7.8	7.3	8.9	7.7
	Lines	21.4	23.9	16.1	18.8	20.1
REA	Moves	36.0	36.7	36.7	36.8	36.5
	Lines	27.5	31.4	42.1	42.9	37.0
REA	Moves	3.0	3.0	2.5	2.1	2.7
	Lines	9.3	8.2	6.1	5.5	7.4

TABLE 7

Percentage of Pupil Moves and Lines Devoted to Each Pedagogical Move for All Pupils Combined by Each Session and for All Sessions Combined

Pedagogical Move		*Session* I	II	III	IV	*Unit of Four Sessions*
SOL	Moves	10.1	9.5	13.6	13.2	11.3
	Lines	8.7	8.0	11.8	7.5	8.7
RES	Moves	68.6	66.4	65.5	59.3	65.4
	Lines	65.6	61.2	63.0	41.3	57.5
STR	Moves	0.4	1.3	1.4	1.1	1.1
	Lines	0.8	2.1	2.3	1.0	1.5
STR-A	Moves	—	0.1	0.2	3.1	0.7
	Lines	—	5.7	4.0	27.5	9.6
REA	Moves	14.0	14.3	15.0	17.0	14.9
	Lines	20.5	17.7	16.5	20.1	18.8
REA	Moves	0.1	0.1	—	0.1	0.1
	Lines	0.2	0.1	—	0.2	0.1

pupil structuring accounts for only 2.4 per cent of the discourse. Assigned structuring (STR-A), which includes activities such as debates and reports, occurs in eight of the 15 classes; the range for the entire sample in this category is from zero to 9.8 per cent, with a median of 3.1 per cent. In only three classes is assigned structuring responsible for more than five per cent of the discourse.

A Common Pattern of Discourse

These findings suggest that in the classes under study the fundamental pedagogical pattern of discourse consisted of a teacher's solicitation followed by a pupil's response; this sequence was frequently followed by a teacher's reaction. In other words, a typical pattern started with the teacher asking a question (T/SOL), which a pupil answered (P/RES), followed by the teacher's reaction to or rating of the pupil's response (T/REA).

Other kinds of moves occurred in the classrooms and served pedagogical functions. A significant part of the discourse, for example, involved the teacher's telling the pupils about the general nature of the unit to be studied (structuring) and also some discussion among pupils (reacting); but, by and large, the basic pattern of the classroom interaction involved a question-answer sequence that was frequently followed by a rating reaction.

Stability of Pedagogical Patterns

Tables 6–13 summarize the distribution of pedagogical moves over the four class sessions included in the experimental unit. These data reveal an astonishing degree of stability over time in the pattern of discourse both for teachers and for pupils.

Tables 6 and 7 present the average percentage of lines and moves in each pedagogical category for the total sample of 15 classes. The similarity of discourse across class sessions is illustrated, for example, by the remarkably restricted range of moves concerned with teachers' solicitations (SOL), which varied from 46.0 per cent to 47.6 per cent, a difference of only 1.6 per cent. Similarly, teacher reactions (REA) varied from 36.0 per cent to 36.8 per cent, a difference of only 0.8 per cent. Pupils showed somewhat greater variability, but again the similarity across sessions is much more striking than the apparent difference. Thus the percentage of moves devoted to pupils' responding (RES) varied from 59.3 per cent to 68.6 per cent, a difference of only 9.3 per cent.

A more detailed analysis of these data is presented in Tables 8–13, which summarize the percentage of lines and moves in each

TABLE 8

Percentage of All Lines and Moves Devoted to Soliciting by Session for Teachers and Pupils in Each of the Fifteen Classes and for All Classes Combined

Class		*Teacher: Session*				*Unit of Four Sessions*	*Pupil: Session*				*Unit of Four Sessions*
		I	*II*	*III*	*IV*		*I*	*II*	*III*	*IV*	
1	Moves	29.2	30.1	30.4	29.8	29.9	0.8	1.2	2.7	2.5	1.7
	Lines	30.8	29.7	26.0	21.5	27.5	0.3	0.7	2.2	2.1	1.2
2	Moves	29.4	29.9	31.6	28.6	29.9	3.1	1.8	3.2	2.2	2.6
	Lines	20.3	22.2	28.0	13.8	20.1	3.0	0.9	1.7	1.0	1.6
3	Moves	41.8	35.1	34.5	33.8	36.6	2.7	2.5	5.2	2.1	3.1
	Lines	41.5	29.4	30.0	17.6	30.1	1.4	1.8	4.2	0.6	2.1
4	Moves	33.1	24.7	32.2	27.4	29.6	1.5	4.1	1.9	6.2	3.1
	Lines	25.1	18.4	18.1	20.4	20.7	1.0	1.9	1.3	3.2	1.8
5	Moves	26.7	21.5	25.8	22.9	24.5	5.9	11.9	7.1	14.3	9.4
	Lines	21.1	13.6	17.0	9.3	15.5	2.8	6.5	5.0	7.8	5.4
6	Moves	33.8	31.7	32.3	37.2	33.7	—	2.4	4.4	3.5	2.7
	Lines	19.0	16.5	20.9	24.3	20.2	—	0.7	2.5	1.1	1.1
7	Moves	28.4	18.2	25.5	28.8	25.7	5.3	8.5	8.3	4.1	6.6
	Lines	19.6	7.8	16.2	17.0	15.5	4.0	3.7	5.9	2.4	4.2
8	Moves	28.9	28.9	23.8	25.6	27.6	4.0	4.3	8.8	3.9	4.7
	Lines	21.4	22.8	17.3	18.3	20.4	2.1	4.0	4.7	1.5	2.9
9	Moves	32.7	23.4	30.8	31.0	29.0	1.0	3.6	1.1	—	1.5
	Lines	12.4	10.7	10.1	17.6	12.8	0.2	0.9	0.2	—	0.3

Class	Teacher: Session				Unit of Four Sessions	Pupil: Session				Unit of Four Sessions
	I	*II*	*III*	*IV*		*I*	*II*	*III*	*IV*	
10 Moves	30.2	31.3	26.7	22.7	28.3	1.3	2.0	5.6	4.6	3.1
Lines	15.3	15.5	10.5	6.4	12.0	0.5	0.8	2.7	1.0	1.2
11 Moves	32.3	35.2	34.9	24.6	32.9	1.3	1.9	2.1	8.2	2.6
Lines	22.6	22.4	33.3	11.1	23.2	0.4	0.7	1.0	1.7	0.9
12 Moves	24.2	23.7	18.1	21.4	21.5	5.3	6.4	11.8	7.3	8.0
Lines	12.7	12.9	9.8	29.2	16.0	2.6	4.2	5.7	3.3	4.1
13 Moves	32.0	30.9	28.1	32.2	30.8	3.0	2.7	8.6	3.0	4.2
Lines	37.2	30.3	21.6	28.2	28.9	1.7	1.9	5.5	2.4	3.0
14 Moves	31.7	32.2	27.4	26.0	29.8	3.1	1.3	1.6	6.5	2.7
Lines	23.1	32.0	18.9	22.2	23.8	2.0	0.5	0.7	1.8	1.3
15 Moves	19.9	26.3	28.8	20.2	24.6	12.0	5.0	3.5	11.0	7.3
Lines	12.0	17.2	19.5	9.6	14.7	10.6	3.0	2.5	5.1	5.5
$\overline{X}$ Moves	29.7	28.8	28.6	27.8	28.8	3.8	3.6	5.2	5.2	4.4
Lines	22.5	20.9	20.1	18.1	20.3	2.3	2.0	3.1	2.4	2.5

TABLE 9

Percentage of All Lines and Moves Devoted to Responding by Session for Teachers and Pupils in Each of the Fifteen Classes and for All Classes Combined

Class	Teacher: Session				Unit of Four Sessions	Pupil: Session				Unit of Four Sessions
	I	II	III	IV		I	II	III	IV	
1 Moves	0.5	1.1	2.2	2.0	1.4	34.2	30.4	29.2	24.1	30.1
Lines	0.3	1.8	1.5	2.0	1.4	19.2	20.2	19.0	12.0	18.0
2 Moves	1.2	1.1	1.6	0.9	1.2	24.7	25.6	30.0	26.3	26.6
Lines	0.7	0.5	1.9	1.0	1.0	27.4	25.1	27.6	18.3	23.9
3 Moves	2.7	2.9	1.0	1.4	2.1	22.3	25.3	25.8	24.1	24.4
Lines	4.5	5.4	3.8	0.6	3.7	15.3	19.8	19.7	18.0	18.2
4 Moves	1.8	3.0	0.9	6.7	2.8	29.5	22.9	27.1	15.1	24.6
Lines	2.0	4.3	1.5	6.8	3.7	35.2	14.6	31.0	18.5	24.8
5 Moves	6.3	10.1	5.0	2.5	5.8	23.6	15.1	17.5	14.3	17.9
Lines	10.2	21.9	5.9	1.1	9.4	16.0	11.8	15.9	13.0	14.4
6 Moves	—	2.4	5.6	4.8	3.3	29.2	25.6	27.3	28.3	27.5
Lines	—	1.5	10.3	12.0	5.9	11.2	13.7	17.3	15.1	14.3
7 Moves	3.7	8.0	7.9	4.1	5.8	24.7	11.9	21.2	26.0	21.4
Lines	3.3	6.6	14.6	4.7	7.5	20.2	6.8	12.5	12.1	13.5
8 Moves	4.0	4.1	7.5	3.9	4.4	20.4	26.9	18.4	24.4	22.9
Lines	5.4	12.7	18.3	2.9	8.8	17.0	17.6	10.2	12.4	15.0
9 Moves	1.0	3.6	2.2	—	1.7	24.8	21.3	17.6	25.6	22.5
Lines	0.2	2.4	1.1	—	0.9	6.3	5.3	4.0	7.5	5.8

Class	Teacher: Session				Unit of Four Sessions	Pupil: Session				Unit of Four Sessions
	I	II	III	IV		I	II	III	IV	
10 Moves	0.9	1.6	3.3	4.6	2.4	26.1	25.6	25.0	24.0	25.3
Lines	0.6	8.8	3.6	7.7	5.3	14.6	12.4	8.8	6.7	10.6
11 Moves	1.3	2.3	2.4	2.7	2.1	26.3	23.2	30.8	23.6	26.7
Lines	1.2	2.3	2.4	6.0	2.8	10.7	9.5	22.1	9.4	13.4
12 Moves	4.2	5.1	6.9	6.4	5.8	23.2	19.5	14.2	19.2	18.6
Lines	9.4	6.9	5.1	4.0	6.2	15.1	10.9	7.3	8.0	10.0
13 Moves	3.3	1.8	7.6	2.5	3.7	31.4	30.8	25.3	32.8	30.1
Lines	3.0	3.4	11.6	5.1	6.1	22.9	25.0	15.1	24.0	21.4
14 Moves	2.1	2.2	1.6	7.3	2.7	24.0	23.8	28.6	23.6	25.2
Lines	5.3	2.0	2.3	4.0	3.5	14.7	11.6	16.1	9.6	13.0
15 Moves	8.9	4.7	3.3	4.1	5.3	20.1	26.3	28.2	8.1	22.9
Lines	16.2	11.7	5.4	2.1	9.1	12.4	21.1	23.3	4.6	15.6
$\overline{X}$ Moves	3.2	3.2	4.1	3.5	3.5	25.8	25.1	25.1	23.4	25.0
Lines	4.3	6.0	5.9	3.9	5.0	17.3	15.5	16.7	13.1	15.6

TABLE 10

Percentage of All Lines and Moves Devoted to Structuring by Session for Teachers and Pupils in Each of the Fifteen Classes and for All Classes Combined

Class	Teacher: Session				Unit of Four Sessions	Pupil: Session				Unit of Four Sessions
	I	*II*	*III*	*IV*		*I*	*II*	*III*	*IV*	
1 Moves	2.9	2.3	1.7	4.1	2.5	—	0.5	0.7	—	0.4
Lines	7.6	10.1	3.3	7.1	7.2	—	0.4	1.0	—	0.4
2 Moves	3.1	3.9	6.1	6.3	4.8	0.8	0.4	1.8	—	0.7
Lines	9.6	11.5	13.3	10.9	11.2	1.4	0.6	0.9	—	0.8
3 Moves	5.9	9.0	6.2	6.2	7.0	—	0.4	0.5	—	0.3
Lines	14.8	11.7	5.7	8.4	10.1	—	0.8	0.1	—	0.2
4 Moves	4.6	2.6	5.6	3.9	4.1	0.3	—	—	1.7	0.4
Lines	5.1	8.2	6.1	4.2	5.9	1.3	—	—	0.8	0.6
5 Moves	4.9	5.5	6.7	3.7	5.2	—	0.9	0.7	—	0.4
Lines	20.9	12.6	19.2	7.8	15.5	—	0.8	1.0	—	0.5
6 Moves	3.1	6.1	2.5	2.8	3.7	—	0.6	—	—	0.2
Lines	24.3	27.8	7.3	5.3	16.2	—	0.2	—	—	0.04
7 Moves	5.9	11.4	6.5	10.3	7.8	—	6.3	1.8	—	1.7
Lines	14.7	45.5	17.8	23.4	24.0	—	6.8	3.0	—	2.4
8 Moves	2.7	4.3	4.8	3.9	3.7	0.5	0.3	0.7	—	0.4
Lines	9.7	7.7	7.5	9.7	8.8	0.5	0.1	0.6	—	0.3
9 Moves	13.9	14.2	13.2	11.6	13.2	—	—	—	—	—
Lines	51.3	51.9	48.8	35.3	46.6	—	—	—	—	—

Class	Teacher: Session				Unit of Four Sessions	Pupil: Session				Unit of Four Sessions
	I	*II*	*III*	*IV*		*I*	*II*	*III*	*IV*	
10 Moves	5.0	4.9	3.9	9.1	5.5	—	—	0.6	—	0.1
Lines	15.5	24.3	9.1	28.7	19.7	—	—	0.1	—	0.03
11 Moves	11.6	10.2	5.8	6.4	8.6	—	0.5	—	1.8	0.4
Lines	30.7	31.6	14.4	12.6	22.4	—	0.4	—	1.8	0.5
12 Moves	10.0	4.2	6.3	9.4	7.3	—	—	—	0.4	0.1
Lines	30.7	13.9	21.1	24.1	22.0	—	—	—	0.3	0.1
13 Moves	1.3	1.2	1.3	0.8	1.2	—	—	1.3	0.2	0.4
Lines	1.7	1.3	2.4	1.2	1.7	—	—	2.1	0.2	0.7
14 Moves	1.7	6.2	5.7	5.7	4.5	—	—	—	—	—
Lines	6.2	17.7	7.6	2.0	8.0	—	—	—	—	—
15 Moves	3.8	3.2	2.5	6.9	3.6	0.2	—	0.6	1.2	0.4
Lines	11.6	6.9	6.7	9.0	8.7	0.1	—	0.4	0.3	0.2
$\bar{X}$ Moves	4.5	4.8	4.5	5.4	4.8	0.1	0.5	0.5	0.4	0.4
Lines	15.8	17.8	11.8	12.8	14.5	0.2	0.5	0.6	0.3	0.4

TABLE 11

Percentage of All Lines and Moves Devoted to Structuring-Assigned by Session for Pupils in Each of the Fifteen Classes and for All Classes Combined

Class		Session I	Session II	Session III	Session IV	Unit of Four Sessions
1	Moves	—	—	—	—	—
	Lines	—	—	—	—	—
2	Moves	—	—	—	—	—
	Lines	—	—	—	—	—
3	Moves	—	—	—	6.9	1.2
	Lines	—	—	—	28.7	6.3
4	Moves	—	0.4	—	—	0.1
	Lines	—	17.7	—	—	4.8
5	Moves	—	—	—	5.3	1.2
	Lines	—	—	—	25.4	6.1
6	Moves	—	—	—	—	—
	Lines	—	—	—	—	—
7	Moves	—	—	—	1.4	0.2
	Lines	—	—	—	17.3	3.3
8	Moves	—	—	—	—	—
	Lines	—	—	—	—	—
9	Moves	—	—	—	—	—
	Lines	—	—	—	—	—
10	Moves	—	—	—	—	—
	Lines	—	—	—	—	—
11	Moves	—	—	—	5.5	0.7
	Lines	—	—	—	46.6	9.8
12	Moves	—	—	0.4	—	0.1
	Lines	—	—	10.3	—	3.1
13	Moves	—	—	—	—	—
	Lines	—	—	—	—	—
14	Moves	—	0.4	0.8	1.6	0.6
	Lines	—	5.2	5.1	7.3	4.3
15	Moves	—	—	—	1.7	0.2
	Lines	—	—	—	16.6	3.6
$\bar{X}$	Moves	—	0.04	0.1	1.2	0.3
	Lines	—	1.4	1.0	8.7	2.6

pedagogical category for each class in the four sessions. Once again the data reveal marked stability over time in the amount of discourse devoted by each class to a given pedagogical category. Consider, for example, the percentage of total moves in Class 1 concerned with teacher's solicitations (Table 8). For sessions 1, 2, 3, and 4, these are 29.2, 30.1, 30.4, and 29.8 respectively. For Class 2, the percentages are 29.4, 29.9, 31.6, and 28.6. For pupils' responding (Table 9), the parallel results for the four sessions of Class 1 are 34.2, 30.4, 29.2, 24.1. For Class 2, the results are 24.7, 25.6, 30.0, 26.3.

In every pedagogical category for almost all classes, the same pattern of similarity among sessions is found. Among some classes the final class session shows some deviation from the earlier sessions, probably because there were occasional debates or pupil reports in the final session; but, by and large, the amount of teacher and pupil activity in each pedagogical category for a particular class remain constant from session to session.

On the basis of these data, it seems reasonable to conclude that classes display a characteristic style of pedagogical discourse that is stable over time, at least insofar as the limited number of sessions considered in this study is concerned. While there is no basis for generalizing these findings to longer periods of time, the data strongly suggest the hypothesis that teacher-pupil interaction within various classes is characterized by particular patterns of pedagogical discourse; and notwithstanding occasional deviations, these classroom patterns of discourse remain relatively stable over time.

Substantive Meanings

In the instructions given before the experimental unit, teachers were encouraged to use the techniques they would normally follow. In spite of these instructions, the 15 teachers showed a remarkable similarity in the ratio of teacher-pupil activity and in the frequency of each pedagogical move contained in the classroom discourse. In most classes, a majority of the teachers clustered within a small range of only a few percentage points.

In contrast to the freedom permitted in using teaching techniques, the major restriction placed upon the teachers for experimental purposes involved the substantive unit of instruction on international trade. Although teachers were urged to teach in any way they chose, they were unequivocally directed and limited in the subject matter to be covered during the experimental class sessions. In view of these limitations, it is remarkable that, of all the categories of analysis, the

TABLE 12

Percentage of All Lines and Moves Devoted to Reacting (REA) by Session for Teachers and Pupils in Each of the Fifteen Classes and for All Classes Combined

Class	*Teacher: Session*				*Unit of Four Sessions*	*Pupil: Session*				*Unit of Four Sessions*
	I	*II*	*III*	*IV*		*I*	*II*	*III*	*IV*	
1 Moves	27.4	23.5	25.4	26.1	25.3	1.8	4.3	3.9	2.9	3.4
Lines	36.9	27.3	42.2	44.4	36.9	1.6	3.4	2.7	1.3	2.3
2 Moves	16.9	19.9	21.9	25.0	20.8	12.6	9.6	2.4	4.5	7.5
Lines	9.6	13.3	20.4	49.8	25.5	19.0	17.4	2.4	2.6	10.2
3 Moves	18.6	18.4	18.6	20.0	18.8	4.1	2.9	5.2	2.8	3.7
Lines	20.0	24.0	27.3	19.8	22.9	1.9	2.4	3.9	1.6	2.5
4 Moves	22.8	24.7	23.4	22.9	23.5	3.0	14.4	6.1	12.9	8.6
Lines	22.1	18.8	29.1	38.9	26.7	3.5	10.2	8.7	6.2	7.0
5 Moves	22.2	20.6	24.2	13.5	20.4	3.1	8.7	9.7	15.5	9.1
Lines	16.4	19.9	24.3	8.0	17.3	4.1	7.1	10.3	21.8	10.7
6 Moves	22.3	22.0	20.5	17.9	20.7	0.8	2.4	4.4	2.1	2.5
Lines	25.6	16.5	26.4	33.2	25.5	0.2	1.1	3.8	1.1	1.6
7 Moves	23.5	21.6	22.7	21.2	22.5	5.9	6.3	4.7	1.4	4.9
Lines	25.9	15.4	26.0	18.4	22.2	7.3	4.5	2.7	0.5	4.1
8 Moves	22.6	23.1	22.5	26.1	23.5	9.7	5.5	7.5	9.0	8.0
Lines	27.1	26.7	30.3	39.3	30.5	10.7	3.8	4.3	8.6	7.3
9 Moves	22.8	24.1	28.6	27.9	25.8	3.0	6.4	1.1	—	2.8
Lines	27.1	21.9	34.4	36.0	29.5	1.4	1.5	0.5	—	0.9

Class	Teacher: Session				Unit of Four Sessions	Pupil: Session				Unit of Four Sessions
	I	*II*	*III*	*IV*		*I*	*II*	*III*	*IV*	
10 Moves	21.2	23.6	24.4	25.3	23.4	7.7	1.6	6.7	7.1	5.5
Lines	24.7	29.2	50.7	35.4	34.7	15.0	0.6	3.2	5.1	5.9
11 Moves	22.4	21.8	18.8	20.0	20.7	0.4	—	2.4	2.7	1.3
Lines	21.8	23.1	19.3	6.6	18.2	0.4	—	2.1	2.2	1.2
12 Moves	21.6	22.0	20.1	21.8	21.3	7.9	7.6	15.6	12.0	11.2
Lines	18.3	33.1	26.6	21.9	25.3	3.8	9.0	10.5	7.1	7.9
13 Moves	21.7	23.4	19.2	23.2	22.0	2.6	4.2	5.6	3.0	3.9
Lines	21.8	23.2	31.6	33.2	27.5	1.6	3.5	4.3	3.3	3.3
14 Moves	25.1	26.9	26.2	25.2	25.9	2.1	0.4	2.4	—	1.5
Lines	25.4	27.8	36.7	23.7	28.3	1.1	0.3	1.1	—	0.6
15 Moves	22.8	24.5	25.0	15.0	23.0	10.3	7.6	5.8	19.7	9.2
Lines	28.4	24.5	33.7	5.6	24.2	7.0	5.5	4.7	28.9	10.8
$\overline{X}$ Moves	22.5	22.8	22.6	22.3	22.6	5.3	5.4	5.7	6.7	5.7
Lines	20.3	23.4	30.9	29.4	26.7	5.4	4.5	4.4	6.4	5.1

TABLE 13

Percentage of All Lines and Moves Devoted to Reacting Italicized *(REA)* by Session for Teachers and Pupils in Each of the Fifteen Classes and for All Classes Combined

Class	*Teacher: Session*				*Unit of Four Sessions*	*Pupil: Session*				*Unit of Four Sessions*
	I	*II*	*III*	*IV*		*I*	*II*	*III*	*IV*	
1 Moves	1.0	0.7	0.7	1.6	0.9	—	—	—	—	—
Lines	2.4	3.2	0.7	7.0	3.1	—	—	—	—	—
2 Moves	1.2	1.8	2.0	1.3	1.6	0.4	0.4	—	—	0.2
Lines	4.5	5.1	4.3	0.8	3.4	0.9	0.6	—	—	0.4
3 Moves	—	1.2	2.1	2.1	1.2	—	—	—	—	—
Lines	—	3.8	5.1	4.6	3.3	—	—	—	—	—
4 Moves	1.2	2.2	1.4	—	1.3	—	—	—	—	—
Lines	3.8	5.6	3.6	—	3.3	—	—	—	—	—
5 Moves	3.5	1.8	0.3	0.8	1.6	—	—	—	0.4	0.1
Lines	7.1	4.3	0.3	1.9	3.4	—	—	—	0.7	0.2
6 Moves	3.1	4.3	2.5	1.4	2.8	—	—	—	—	—
Lines	18.1	20.6	11.4	7.4	14.4	—	—	—	—	—
7 Moves	2.2	0.6	0.4	0.7	1.1	—	—	—	—	—
Lines	4.8	0.2	0.8	3.6	2.4	—	—	—	—	—
8 Moves	1.5	1.2	3.4	1.7	1.7	—	—	—	—	—
Lines	3.4	3.4	5.3	6.9	4.5	—	—	—	—	—
9 Moves	1.0	3.6	1.1	2.3	2.1	—	—	—	—	—
Lines	1.3	5.4	0.2	3.5	2.8	—	—	—	—	—

Class	Teacher: Session				Unit of Four Sessions	Pupil: Session				Unit of Four Sessions
	I	II	III	IV		I	II	III	IV	
10 Moves	1.8	1.2	3.3	2.6	2.1	—	—	—	—	—
Lines	11.7	6.1	11.2	9.2	9.4	—	—	—	—	—
11 Moves	3.0	2.8	1.4	1.8	2.2	—	—	—	—	—
Lines	11.5	8.6	5.1	1.7	6.8	—	—	—	—	—
12 Moves	2.1	1.7	0.4	0.4	1.1	—	—	—	—	—
Lines	6.8	5.4	1.0	1.2	3.3	—	—	—	—	—
13 Moves	2.6	3.3	2.2	0.8	2.3	—	—	—	—	—
Lines	8.8	10.4	5.4	1.3	6.6	—	—	—	—	—
14 Moves	3.5	0.9	3.2	1.6	2.5	—	—	—	—	—
Lines	19.0	0.9	10.1	2.6	8.5	—	—	—	—	—
15 Moves	0.7	1.8	1.1	1.2	1.2	—	—	—	—	—
Lines	1.3	10.0	3.0	3.4	4.0	—	—	—	—	—
$\overline{X}$ Moves	1.9	1.9	1.5	1.3	1.7	0.02	0.02	—	0.03	0.02
Lines	6.8	6.1	4.5	3.7	5.3	0.05	0.03	—	0.05	0.03

data for the substantive meanings covered in the classroom reveal the greatest variability among teachers. While teachers structured, solicited, and reacted for about the same proportion of lines in every classroom, they showed marked differences in the substantive material covered in the class sessions.

Substantive Meanings Dealing with International Trade

All teachers devoted a fair proportion of time to a general discussion of trade and to topics specifically related to international trade. Except for this central feature common to all classes, the substantive emphasis in each class differed from all other classes. This is illustrated by the following kinds of difference as shown in Table 14: Class 1 spent 23.5 per cent of the total discourse on imports and exports; Class 2 devoted only 5.8 per cent to this category; and Class 15 dealt with imports-exports only one half of one per cent of the time. Thus the difference between Class 1 and Class 15, two classes presumably dealing with the same substantive material, was 23 per cent of the total lines of transcript.

This is not the only difference noted in the data. Class 2, for example, devoted 27.5 per cent of the lines to a discussion of trade barriers, while Class 10 devoted only 6.4 per cent of the lines to this category—a difference of 21.1 per cent. Similarly, Class 13 devoted 28 per cent of the lines to specialization, while Class 3 devoted 4.3 per cent of the lines to this topic.

Even more striking was the difference found in the amount of time devoted to discussion of free trade. In a sense, free international trade was the major focus of the entire pamphlet. The material on general trade topics was presented in the pamphlet primarily as a way of leading up to a discussion of free trade. This was clear not only in the pamphlet that the students read but also in the teacher's manual. However, some classes, such as Class 2, emphasized trade barriers rather than free trade. Others devoted a relatively large proportion of the time to a discussion of free trade. Class 14, for example, devoted 38.4 per cent of the lines to a discussion of free trade, while Class 1 devoted only 4.7 per cent of the class discussion to this category—a difference of approximately 34 per cent!

In terms of our analysis of the pamphlet and our coding categories, a central point of the pamphlet was a discussion of the pros and cons of free trade. The teachers, given the same teaching unit to teach during the experimental class sessions, might reasonably be expected to cover at least these two areas in about the same proportions; but this was not the case. It almost seems as if the teachers were teaching a different unit on international trade. Teacher 1 focused on trade barriers (21.4 per cent) with much less of the discussion devoted to free trade (4.7 per cent). In exactly the reverse order, Teacher 5 devoted 25.9 per cent of the discussion to free trade and only 8.2 per cent to trade barriers. Teacher 10 devoted relatively little discussion to either free trade (6.2 per cent) or trade barriers (6.4 per cent). For Teacher 10's class, therefore, the unit was primarily devoted not to international free trade and problems of trade barriers, but to a general discussion of trade and international trade.

As indicated earlier, most of the classes spent a good deal of time discussing general economic principles of trade. This may well be because, for most classes, this unit was an introduction to the study of economics. But even here there were widespread differences. Class 4 devoted 50.4 per cent, over half of the discussion contained in the entire unit, to general principles of trade, while Class 7 devoted only 10.3 per cent to this category—a difference of 40 per cent. These differences may be a function of the different amounts of knowledge with which students in various classes began the unit, as well as a function of the different amounts of knowledge and interests of the 15 teachers. Nevertheless, the differences in the substantive area, particularly in relation to the similarities found in the pedagogical area, are remarkable.

Relevant and Irrelevant Substantive Meanings

The categories of related material (REL) and not trade (NTR), as distinct from specific substantive topics included in the teaching unit, also offer some interesting comparisons among teachers. Three of the teachers never discussed topics coded as "related material" (REL). These teachers were almost always on the immediate target of the subject matter contained in the teaching unit. Others devoted a good deal of the time to related material. Teacher 15, for example, frequently did not focus directly on the subject matter; 11.6 per cent of his class discussion was on related matters. Even less often on target was Teacher 12, who devoted 17.4 per cent to related material; for his class, therefore, nearly a fifth of the total discourse was somewhat off the precise substantive focus of the unit. When considered in conjunction with the 7.7 per cent of Class 12's discussion of "not trade" (NTR), it is clear that approximately one quarter of the discussion in this class was not directly concerned with international trade.

These results are in marked contrast with the results of those teachers who closely restricted the discussion to the substantive material of the unit. Three of the teachers never discussed anything other than

TABLE 14

Percentage of All Lines and Moves Devoted to Each Substantive Category and to All Substantive Categories Combined for Each of the Fifteen Classes and for All Classes Combined

Class	PFT	TRA	IMX	FSP	BAR	FOR	REL	NTR	*Total Substantive* *
1 Moves	4.4	20.1	29.0	10.7	16.6	11.5	1.4	1.7	95.4
Lines	4.7	19.3	23.5	12.0	21.4	11.3	1.4	1.7	95.3
2 Moves	9.2	26.6	8.1	15.8	19.6	7.5	2.1	5.3	94.2
Lines	12.3	23.4	5.8	12.5	27.5	7.7	1.7	5.7	96.6
3 Moves	11.4	34.8	8.7	5.4	13.1	9.6	6.8	4.9	94.7
Lines	10.8	39.5	10.9	4.3	11.5	9.6	4.7	6.1	97.4
4 Moves	6.9	52.6	7.2	6.8	10.9	8.1	—	1.2	93.7
Lines	10.1	50.4	5.4	5.9	13.2	8.1	—	1.0	94.1
5 Moves	23.7	25.1	5.5	6.7	8.5	16.0	9.5	0.2	95.2
Lines	25.9	25.7	5.6	7.9	8.2	15.3	8.9	0.5	98.0
6 Moves	18.5	19.0	16.5	26.0	12.2	—	1.5	—	93.7
Lines	21.3	23.9	15.1	21.4	10.2	—	5.2	—	97.1
7 Moves	22.1	8.7	17.2	8.8	16.5	2.7	8.9	12.8	97.7
Lines	30.4	10.3	16.3	7.1	14.1	2.7	6.3	11.7	98.9
8 Moves	19.5	21.2	10.6	23.7	13.3	8.2	—	0.1	96.6
Lines	21.9	22.3	9.5	19.1	17.3	7.5	—	0.8	98.4
9 Moves	10.4	22.5	7.1	16.4	23.1	18.8	—	—	98.3
Lines	11.9	24.1	8.1	17.0	13.8	24.4	—	—	99.3
10 Moves	5.5	42.9	8.4	23.3	4.7	4.7	5.4	—	94.9
Lines	6.2	41.8	11.0	22.9	6.4	5.4	4.4	—	98.1

Class	PFT	TRA	IMX	FSP	BAR	FOR	REL	NTR	*Total Substantive* *
11 Moves	17.4	20.8	8.6	17.2	16.0	9.0	8.4	0.4	97.8
Lines	18.7	26.5	5.7	16.3	16.5	6.7	8.3	0.2	98.9
12 Moves	7.1	44.5	1.4	0.1	13.0	5.3	10.7	12.1	94.2
Lines	8.4	45.5	0.7	0.6	11.4	5.8	17.4	7.7	97.5
13 Moves	3.0	15.1	13.2	29.6	18.4	9.0	3.4	6.3	98.0
Lines	3.6	17.7	11.7	28.0	18.8	8.4	2.0	8.7	98.9
14 Moves	28.6	26.8	15.5	10.5	9.0	—	3.6	0.1	94.1
Lines	38.4	27.2	14.5	7.0	5.9	—	4.3	0.03	97.3
15 Moves	16.8	13.1	0.8	16.3	13.5	17.4	15.8	4.5	98.2
Lines	24.5	17.2	0.5	15.0	12.1	13.8	11.6	4.3	99.0
$\overline{X}$ Moves	12.7	25.0	11.2	15.1	14.1	8.9	5.3	3.6	95.9
Lines	16.2	27.2	9.8	13.8	14.1	8.6	4.9	3.1	97.7

* Differences between totals given and 100 per cent are accounted for by moves coded NOC.

the topics presented in the pamphlet. Five other teachers devoted less than one per cent of the class discussion to topics other than international trade. Class 7, however, spent 11.7 per cent of the discussion on substantive meanings not directly related to international trade, and Class 13 devoted 8.7 per cent to such meanings.

Therefore, just as there were striking differences in the pattern of emphasis within the categories covered by the unit, such as imports-exports and specialization, there were also large differences in the degree to which teachers stayed on the immediate target of the unit. Some teachers devoted relatively large amounts of discussion to related topics, rather than to those specifically covered in the pamphlet. Others devoted a considerable proportion of time to matters that were unrelated to international trade. Thus, paradoxically, in the one area in which the research design imposed major restraints by giving the teachers a specific unit to teach, one finds the greatest differences among teachers.

Substantive-Logical Meanings

The percentage of lines contained in the substantive-logical category provides some idea of the amount of discussion devoted specifically to substantive material. Substantive entries were made, according to the context of the ongoing substantive discussion, even when the statement contained primarily instructional content. Therefore, the amount of lines contained in the substantive code does not provide an accurate measure of discourse devoted to substantive matters. Whenever there was some explicit discussion of substantive material, and only then, was an entry made in the substantive-logical category. The results summarized in Table 15 indicate that most of the classroom discussion contained entries in the substantive-logical category, and on this basis it may be inferred that by far the greatest part of the discussion in all classes involved substantive and substantive-logical meanings. There was, however, some variability among classes, indicated by a range of lines in the substantive-logical category from a low of 61.9 per cent to a high of 88.5 per cent with a median of 70.8 per cent.

Empirical Meanings

The results in Table 15 show that the largest proportion of lines concerned empirical meanings, that is, explaining and fact-stating. This is illustrated by the fact that the median percentage of lines devoted to empirical meanings was 60.3, while for evaluative meanings the median was only 7.1 and for analytic meanings only 5.0. Roughly

12 times as many lines were devoted to explaining and fact-stating as to either evaluative meanings involved in opining and justifying or the analytic meanings involved in defining and interpreting. In another substantive area, such as English literature, one might find a different pattern of substantive-logical meanings. At any rate, for the present data the proportion of lines devoted to empirical meanings ranged from a low of 44.8 per cent to a high of 73.1 per cent with a median of 60.3 per cent. It is also noteworthy that the range among teachers was not very wide. Ten of the 15 teachers are included in the range between 54 and 64 per cent of the lines concerned with empirical meanings.

Evaluative Meanings

In most classes, very little of the discourse involved evaluative meanings. In terms of proportion of total lines, the range of evaluative meanings was from 1.6 per cent to 14.4 per cent with a median of 7.1 per cent. Seven of the teachers are included within the restricted range of five to seven per cent. The largest proportion of lines in the evaluative category involves justification rather than opining. This apparently reflects the fact that opinions can be stated in relatively few words, while justifications typically involve longer statements.

But in view of the potentially controversial nature of the substantive material presented in the pamphlet, it is somewhat surprising that in the majority of classes so little of the discourse expressed evaluative meanings. A major focus of the teaching unit concerned trade policies, which inevitably involve some opinion and some justification of one's opinion about trade policies. The results, however, show that relatively little of the classroom discussion was taken up by statements made either by teachers or by pupils expressing their personal opinions about trade policies. For the most part, instead of expressing their own opinions, teachers and pupils reported opinions of other people. In light of the rather limited amount of knowledge that most students probably had in this area, the restriction in amount of evaluative meanings contained in the discourse may be a realistic reflection of what would be appropriate for this sample of students.

Analytic Meanings

The smallest proportion of the classroom discourse in terms of lines was devoted to analytic meanings, including defining and interpreting. The teachers ranged from a low of 2.9 to a high of 10.1 per cent, with a median of 5.1 per cent. The range in this area was even more restricted than that in the categories of empirical and

TABLE 15

Percentage of All Lines and Moves Devoted to Each Substantive-Logical Category and to All Substantive-Logical Categories Combined for Each of the Fifteen Classes and for All Classes Combined

Class	Analytic			Empirical			Evaluative			Not Clear	Total Substantive-Logical
	DEF	INT	*Total*	FAC	XPL	*Total*	OPN	JUS	*Total*		
1 Moves	8.3	1.7	10.0	32.9	19.7	52.6	2.3	1.4	3.7	—	66.3
Lines	6.1	1.8	7.9	23.1	33.6	56.7	2.2	4.0	6.2	—	70.8
2 Moves	4.7	0.7	5.4	15.2	30.1	45.3	2.7	4.0	6.7	—	57.4
Lines	3.4	1.5	4.9	9.8	36.7	46.5	2.7	7.8	10.5	—	61.9
3 Moves	4.6	1.2	5.8	17.7	26.0	43.7	1.0	2.0	3.0	—	52.5
Lines	3.5	0.03	3.5	10.5	43.6	54.1	0.7	4.1	4.8	—	62.4
4 Moves	9.4	0.9	10.3	16.5	26.7	43.2	1.1	1.9	3.0	0.1	56.6
Lines	8.3	1.8	10.1	12.3	42.3	54.6	0.8	4.7	5.5	0.04	70.2
5 Moves	7.8	1.8	9.6	10.3	23.0	33.3	2.9	5.9	8.8	—	51.7
Lines	6.8	1.1	7.9	6.9	37.9	44.8	1.5	12.9	14.4	—	67.1
6 Moves	8.5	2.2	10.7	13.8	41.8	55.6	1.8	0.8	2.6	—	68.9
Lines	3.4	1.4	4.8	6.3	59.9	66.2	1.4	5.3	6.7	—	77.7
7 Moves	7.7	0.7	8.4	27.8	26.5	53.4	1.5	1.5	3.0	—	65.7
Lines	5.0	0.4	5.4	20.8	41.3	62.1	1.4	4.1	5.5	—	73.0
8 Moves	4.1	0.7	4.8	25.0	32.5	57.5	3.0	3.1	6.1	0.1	68.5
Lines	2.9	0.5	3.4	17.8	43.6	61.4	3.0	8.8	11.8	0.03	76.6
9 Moves	11.9	—	11.9	16.7	50.7	67.4	0.9	2.4	3.3	—	82.6
Lines	7.0	—	7.0	6.7	63.3	70.0	0.2	11.3	11.5	—	88.5

Class	*Analytic* DEF	INT	*Total*	*Empirical* FAC	XPL	*Total*	*Evaluative* OPN	JUS	*Total*	*Not Clear*	*Total Substan-tive-Logical*
10 Moves	6.6	—	6.6	19.6	40.8	60.4	1.4	1.9	3.3	0.1	70.4
Lines	2.9	—	2.9	9.4	63.7	73.1	0.8	5.3	6.1	0.1	82.1
11 Moves	9.3	0.2	9.5	27.1	25.8	52.9	4.5	2.4	6.9	0.1	69.4
Lines	4.9	0.1	5.0	16.3	44.0	60.3	3.1	7.5	10.6	0.03	75.9
12 Moves	3.9	—	3.9	24.4	28.9	53.3	5.5	1.6	7.1	0.3	64.6
Lines	3.7	—	3.7	15.6	47.5	63.1	4.2	2.9	7.1	0.1	74.0
13 Moves	6.5	0.1	6.6	30.4	23.4	53.8	0.8	0.2	1.0	0.2	61.6
Lines	5.0	0.1	5.1	25.1	38.8	63.9	0.9	0.7	1.6	0.1	70.7
14 Moves	9.6	1.9	11.5	11.1	37.4	48.5	1.2	0.9	2.1	0.1	62.2
Lines	7.4	1.4	8.8	5.7	51.5	57.2	0.7	1.3	2.0	0.03	68.0
15 Moves	5.1	0.6	5.7	20.0	29.0	49.0	1.9	2.2	4.1	0.4	59.2
Lines	3.6	0.6	4.2	12.9	42.4	55.3	1.2	8.7	9.9	0.2	69.6
$\bar{X}$ Moves	6.9	0.8	7.7	22.0	28.8	50.8	2.1	2.1	4.2	0.1	62.9
Lines	4.9	0.7	5.6	13.6	45.9	59.5	1.6	5.9	7.5	0.04	72.8

evaluative meanings. Ten of the teachers were clustered within a range of from 3 to 5 per cent devoted to analytic meanings. The relatively low proportion of lines devoted to analytic meanings seems compatible with the nontechnical presentation in the pamphlet. Other than terms such as specialization, direct investment, and various kinds of trade barriers, the pamphlet was presented in words that most students probably could understand. Therefore, having defined a few of the major technical economic terms, there was probably little need in the classroom to spend a great deal of time on analytic meanings.

Substantive and Substantive-Logical Meanings

The cross-tabulation of substantive and substantive-logical meanings provides essentially the same picture of the classroom discourse as the separate analyses of the substantive and substantive-logical categories. For all classes the largest percentage of lines was devoted to explanation of general trade topics (TRA/XPL), which accounted for 12.3 per cent of the lines in all 15 classes. All other cross-tabulations involved less than 8 per cent of the total lines. In general, statements of personal opinion (OPN) were evenly distributed over most of the substantive categories, although justification of opinions (JUS) was highest when the substantive meanings of the discussion concerned free trade and the reduction of trade barriers. This finding is consistent with expectations based on the nature of the unit of instruction, for it is in the area of reduction of trade barriers that pro and con arguments are probably most appropriate.

Instructional Meanings

As indicated in Table 16, the median percentage of lines concerned with instructional meanings was 26 per cent, with a range from 11.6 per cent to 36.4 per cent. The greater proportion of lines involving instructional meanings is spoken by teachers. Occasionally pupils ask about assignments, examinations, or class procedures, but for the most part the instructional meanings are expressed by teachers rather than pupils.

The largest proportion of these lines involved the categories of STA (referring to statements previously made in the discourse) and ACV (referring to vocal actions). The high proportion of statements within the categories of instructional meanings accounted for by those coded STA indicates that a large proportion of the instructional meanings spoken by the teacher involved ratings of pupils' statements. One might consider these meanings as metacommunications, in that they are communications about previous communications. This reflects one of the teacher's major responsibilities, which is to comment upon the discourse in the classroom. In contrast, pupils rarely make such comments.

Statements coded ACV were primarily concerned with teachers' soliciting pupils to talk. In a sense, the large proportion of lines indicated for ACV is an over-representation of the amount of actual class time devoted to this category, for a teacher's statement simply calling the name of a student to give him permission to speak was coded ACV and given one line of credit. This means that the one line value often was coded for the teacher's saying a single word.

Other than the two categories concerned with the teacher's metacommunications coded in the STA designation and the teacher's solicitations directing the pupils to speak, coded under ACV, the great majority of lines in the instructional category was concerned with procedure (PRC), material (MAT), and assignments (ASG). Very little of the instructional content in the classroom discourse involved any of the other categories included in the system of analysis. There was, for example, rarely any discussion of the logic of the material (LOG), and rarely any discussion of language mechanics (LAM). The view that logic and the use of language are taught in every class is certainly not supported by the data.

Relatively little of the classroom discourse was focused on the categories of procedures, materials, and assignments. The classes ranged from a low of 4.6 per cent of the lines devoted to these categories to a high of 20.2 per cent, with a median of 9.9 per cent. This range, however, does not adequately represent the data, for the distribution of teachers was largely skewed toward the lower end of the distribution; that is, 13 of the 15 teachers had between 4.6 and 12 per cent of the lines devoted to these instructional categories. Of the other two teachers, one had 16.7 per cent of the lines in these areas and the other had 20.2 per cent.

The system for coding instructional content included a large variety of possible categories. They covered remarks about persons (PER), logic (LOG), physical actions (ACP), cognitive behaviors (ACC), emotional behaviors (ACE), and language mechanics (LAM). None of these categories accounted for more than one-half of one per cent of the classroom discourse in any of the classes. It would seem, therefore, that while instructional techniques unquestionably play an important part in classroom interaction, instructional meanings *per se* are infrequently the direct focus of discussion.

TABLE 16

Percentage of All Lines and Moves Devoted to Each Instructional Category and to All Instructional Categories Combined for Each of the Fifteen Classes and for All Classes Combined

Class	PRC	MAT	STA	ASG	PER	LOG	ACT	ACV	ACP	ACC	ACE	LAM	*Total*
1 Moves	1.7	3.7	22.9	0.1	0.3	0.1	0.9	9.3	0.9	3.8	0.2	0.2	44.1
Lines	2.3	3.7	11.7	1.2	0.2	0.1	0.6	4.7	0.4	2.2	0.1	0.1	27.3
2 Moves	6.3	4.7	20.0	1.3	0.1	0.1	0.5	11.5	1.4	2.7	0.1	0.4	49.1
Lines	5.1	2.7	19.4	2.1	0.1	0.04	0.3	4.5	0.6	1.0	0.04	0.1	35.9
3 Moves	8.7	9.6	14.9	4.0	2.7	—	1.9	8.8	2.4	4.4	0.03	0.3	57.7
Lines	8.1	3.9	6.5	8.2	1.2	—	1.2	3.5	1.3	2.3	0.1	0.1	36.4
4 Moves	5.2	3.3	23.1	2.6	1.1	0.3	0.3	11.0	1.4	2.8	0.5	0.4	52.0
Lines	4.5	1.8	10.3	4.4	0.5	0.1	0.1	4.9	0.8	1.3	0.2	0.2	29.1
5 Moves	6.7	3.2	24.4	1.0	0.7	0.2	0.4	13.8	1.6	5.0	—	—	52.5
Lines	7.5	2.6	10.0	1.6	0.2	0.5	0.2	5.5	0.9	2.3	—	—	31.3
6 Moves	4.8	2.3	19.7	1.2	1.2	1.2	—	8.7	0.3	2.2	—	—	41.6
Lines	7.8	0.5	6.8	2.4	0.3	0.04	—	2.8	0.1	0.6	—	—	21.3
7 Moves	6.3	7.3	22.9	1.0	—	0.2	—	9.6	0.5	1.4	0.1	0.2	49.5
Lines	6.3	3.0	10.1	1.2	—	0.2	—	4.3	0.2	0.7	0.1	0.1	26.2
8 Moves	2.5	2.2	24.9	0.4	0.5	0.1	0.4	9.4	0.5	3.5	—	—	44.4
Lines	3.2	1.8	10.2	0.9	0.3	0.1	0.2	3.6	0.3	1.5	—	—	22.1
9 Moves	5.8	0.9	21.7	0.9	0.4	—	—	4.8	0.9	1.1	—	—	36.5
Lines	4.7	0.5	4.0	0.9	0.1	—	—	0.9	0.2	0.3	—	—	11.6
10 Moves	4.4	2.4	22.2	0.6	0.6	0.3	—	6.1	0.1	2.5	—	—	39.2
Lines	4.7	1.2	7.0	1.0	0.2	0.3	—	1.6	0.03	0.7	—	—	16.7

Class	PRC	MAT	STA	ASG	PER	LOG	ACT	ACV	ACP	ACC	ACE	LAM	*Total*
11 Moves	4.4	6.0	18.6	0.6	—	—	0.1	4.9	0.5	9.7	0.1	—	44.9
Lines	5.9	3.6	6.5	1.3	—	—	0.1	1.8	0.2	3.8	0.1	—	23.3
12 Moves	2.6	3.0	19.1	2.2	0.6	—	0.1	10.6	0.4	4.0	0.1	0.4	39.5
Lines	2.2	1.4	8.1	1.0	0.3	—	0.04	4.4	0.2	1.7	0.1	0.2	19.6
13 Moves	2.0	0.9	21.7	1.2	0.3	—	0.1	12.3	2.7	2.3	—	0.1	43.6
Lines	1.7	0.7	12.4	3.0	0.2	—	0.03	6.9	2.2	1.4	—	0.1	28.6
14 Moves	4.3	6.1	24.5	3.1	0.2	0.5	0.1	8.3	0.5	2.0	0.1	0.1	49.8
Lines	5.7	4.0	9.1	7.0	0.1	0.3	0.03	2.8	0.3	0.8	0.03	0.03	30.1
15 Moves	5.0	2.3	23.3	2.0	0.1	—	1.0	9.5	1.5	3.5	0.5	0.3	49.0
Lines	6.6	1.0	11.8	2.2	0.1	—	0.6	4.6	1.1	1.6	0.2	0.1	29.9
$\overline{X}$ Moves	4.3	3.6	21.9	1.4	0.5	0.1	0.4	9.7	1.9	3.4	0.1	0.2	46.9
Lines	5.0	2.1	9.7	2.5	0.2	0.1	0.2	3.8	0.6	1.5	0.1	0.1	26.0

TABLE 17

Percentage of All Lines and Moves Devoted to Each Instructional-Logical Category and to All Instructional-Logical Categories Combined for Each of the Fifteen Classes and for All Classes Combined

Class		FAC	XPL	DEF	OPN	JUS	INT	NCL	PRF
1	Moves	9.5	0.5	—	0.4	0.1	0.8	—	4.4
	Lines	7.3	0.3	—	0.8	0.1	0.5	—	4.9
2	Moves	13.3	0.4	—	2.1	0.1	1.5	—	7.9
	Lines	9.7	0.2	—	1.6	0.1	0.8	—	4.0
3	Moves	24.8	1.2	—	1.2	1.0	2.4	—	9.8
	Lines	13.8	2.2	—	0.8	1.6	1.8	—	10.9
4	Moves	12.4	0.5	—	1.3	0.4	1.9	—	10.6
	Lines	8.6	0.4	—	0.8	0.4	1.2	—	7.4
5	Moves	18.1	0.1	—	0.4	—	0.4	—	12.0
	Lines	13.8	0.1	—	0.6	—	0.2	—	6.3
6	Moves	11.2	0.7	—	0.8	—	2.0	—	5.8
	Lines	8.5	1.3	—	0.8	—	0.7	—	3.6
7	Moves	11.0	1.4	—	0.3	0.1	2.8	—	6.9
	Lines	9.0	1.7	—	0.1	0.1	1.6	—	3.5
8	Moves	8.9	0.3	—	0.5	0.3	2.8	—	6.6
	Lines	5.9	0.7	—	0.4	0.2	1.4	—	3.7
9	Moves	8.4	—	—	0.7	0.2	—	—	3.7
	Lines	5.4	—	—	0.2	0.4	—	—	1.2
10	Moves	8.6	0.6	—	1.0	0.1	2.4	—	4.5
	Lines	6.1	1.0	—	0.6	0.03	0.8	—	1.6
11	Moves	16.5	—	—	0.4	—	0.8	—	3.9
	Lines	13.2	—	—	0.1	—	0.7	—	2.7
12	Moves	11.7	—	—	1.1	0.1	1.1	—	6.2
	Lines	6.5	—	—	0.5	0.2	0.5	—	2.9
13	Moves	6.7	0.4	—	0.7	—	1.1	—	7.5
	Lines	4.6	0.3	—	0.5	—	0.7	—	7.6
14	Moves	11.9	—	—	0.5	0.1	1.1	—	8.7
	Lines	9.6	—	—	0.4	0.1	0.6	—	10.7
15	Moves	13.5	0.4	—	0.7	0.6	2.1	—	7.1
	Lines	9.5	0.3	—	0.4	2.2	1.5	—	4.5
$\bar{X}$	Moves	12.0	0.4	—	0.8	0.2	1.5	—	7.2
	Lines	8.6	0.5	—	0.6	0.4	0.9	—	5.1

TABLE 17 (continued)

Percentage of All Lines and Moves Devoted to Each Instructional-Logical Category and to All Instructional-Logical Categories Combined for Each of the Fifteen Classes and for All Classes Combined

QAL	RPT	ADM	POS	NEG	NAD	PON	AON	DIR	*Total*
1.6	12.6	4.5	5.5	1.4	0.6	0.3	0.1	—	42.3
0.8	6.2	2.2	2.9	0.7	0.3	0.2	0.03	—	27.2
2.5	5.1	8.2	3.9	0.7	0.5	0.4	—	0.1	46.7
1.0	2.2	3.3	12.6	0.3	0.2	0.1	—	0.04	36.1
1.0	6.1	1.9	3.4	0.3	0.4	0.8	0.1	0.1	54.5
0.3	2.3	0.6	1.4	0.1	0.1	0.2	0.04	0.04	36.2
2.0	4.5	7.9	7.0	0.8	1.1	0.4	0.3	—	51.1
1.0	1.8	3.1	3.3	0.4	0.6	0.2	0.2	—	29.4
4.4	1.4	6.6	8.5	1.8	0.9	0.8	0.5	0.2	56.1
1.8	0.6	2.4	3.5	0.7	0.3	0.4	0.4	0.1	31.2
2.2	9.3	3.8	1.3	1.0	1.3	0.3	—	—	39.7
1.1	3.0	1.1	0.3	0.3	0.7	0.1	—	—	21.5
2.3	8.6	4.8	5.5	1.4	0.7	—	—	—	45.8
1.0	3.8	2.0	2.4	0.6	0.3	—	—	—	26.1
5.1	4.6	5.7	5.9	1.2	0.9	0.5	—	0.1	43.4
2.2	1.8	2.2	2.3	0.4	0.6	0.2	—	0.1	22.1
1.7	2.6	11.7	5.8	0.7	0.7	0.2	—	—	36.4
0.3	0.6	2.1	1.1	0.1	0.2	0.04	—	—	11.6
4.9	5.6	3.4	4.7	1.4	1.6	—	—	—	38.8
1.8	1.4	1.0	1.3	0.4	0.7	—	—	—	16.7
1.8	9.9	2.5	4.5	0.5	0.4	0.4	—	—	41.6
0.7	3.2	0.9	1.4	0.1	0.1	0.1	—	—	23.2
3.0	7.8	2.2	5.8	0.6	1.8	0.3	—	—	41.7
1.2	3.2	0.9	2.6	0.3	0.7	0.1	—	—	19.6
2.4	12.6	4.2	5.5	1.0	0.8	0.2	—	—	43.1
1.4	7.0	2.3	3.1	0.5	0.5	0.1	—	—	28.6
4.2	4.5	8.5	4.8	1.4	0.6	0.2	—	—	46.5
1.5	1.8	2.6	1.7	0.7	0.2	0.1	—	—	30.0
3.7	5.5	5.3	7.2	0.4	1.2	0.3	0.1	—	48.1
1.7	2.5	2.3	3.7	0.2	0.8	0.2	0.1	—	29.9
2.9	7.3	5.2	5.5	1.0	0.9	0.3	0.1	0.03	45.3
1.2	2.9	2.0	2.9	0.4	0.4	0.1	0.04	0.02	26.0

TABLE 18

Percentage of All Lines and Moves in Each Category of Rating Reaction for Each of the Fifteen Teachers and for All Teachers Combined

		POSITIVE				NEGATIVE			
Teacher		POS	ADM	RPT	*Total*	QAL	NAD	NEG	*Total*
1	Moves	5.4	4.5	7.9	17.8	1.5	0.6	1.4	4.5
	Lines	2.8	2.2	3.9	8.9	0.8	0.3	0.6	1.7
2	Moves	3.5	7.9	1.9	13.3	2.0	0.4	0.4	2.8
	Lines	12.4	3.2	0.7	16.3	0.9	0.1	0.1	1.1
3	Moves	2.9	1.5	5.0	9.4	0.9	—	0.01	0.9
	Lines	1.2	0.5	1.9	3.6	0.3	—	0.04	0.3
4	Moves	6.1	7.8	2.4	16.3	1.5	0.7	0.6	2.8
	Lines	2.9	3.1	1.0	7.0	0.8	0.4	0.3	1.5
5	Moves	7.7	6.6	0.8	15.1	2.5	0.5	0.6	3.6
	Lines	3.3	2.4	0.3	6.0	1.1	0.2	0.2	1.5
6	Moves	1.2	3.5	6.7	11.4	2.2	1.2	0.8	4.4
	Lines	0.3	1.0	2.0	3.3	1.1	0.7	0.2	2.0
7	Moves	4.9	4.5	6.3	15.7	1.8	0.4	1.3	3.5
	Lines	2.1	2.0	2.8	6.9	0.9	0.2	0.5	1.6
8	Moves	5.4	5.5	2.8	13.7	4.0	0.8	0.8	5.6
	Lines	2.1	2.1	1.1	5.3	1.8	0.6	0.3	2.7
9	Moves	5.6	11.5	1.5	18.6	1.7	0.4	0.7	2.8
	Lines	1.0	2.0	0.4	3.4	0.3	0.1	0.1	0.5
10	Moves	4.7	3.2	3.6	11.5	4.5	1.5	1.4	7.4
	Lines	1.3	1.0	0.9	3.2	1.7	0.7	0.4	2.8
11	Moves	4.0	2.5	7.8	14.3	1.8	0.2	0.4	2.4
	Lines	1.2	0.9	2.5	4.6	0.7	0.1	0.1	0.9
12	Moves	5.1	2.0	3.9	11.0	1.9	1.2	0.3	3.4
	Lines	2.4	0.8	1.6	4.8	0.7	0.5	0.1	1.3
13	Moves	5.3	4.2	4.3	13.8	2.3	0.7	0.8	3.8
	Lines	3.0	2.3	3.1	8.4	1.3	0.5	0.4	2.2
14	Moves	4.5	8.5	3.3	16.3	4.2	0.6	1.2	6.0
	Lines	1.7	2.7	1.1	5.5	1.5	0.2	0.7	2.4
15	Moves	6.4	5.2	3.5	15.1	2.7	0.9	0.2	3.8
	Lines	3.4	2.2	1.5	7.1	1.2	0.6	0.1	1.9
$\bar{X}$	Moves	5.1	5.1	4.4	14.6	2.4	0.7	0.7	3.8
	Lines	2.8	1.9	1.7	6.4	1.0	0.3	0.3	1.6

Instructional-Logical Meanings

As one would anticipate from the analysis of instructional meanings, the instructional-logical meanings are expressed primarily by teachers rather than the pupils. Of the various categories considered in the instructional-logical category (Table 17), fact-stating (FAC) accounted for the largest percentage of lines (8.6 per cent for all 15 classes). The next most frequent category in the instructional-logical category was performing (PRF), which accounted for 5.1 per cent. This reflects the teachers' relatively frequent directive statements concerned with instructional content, such as directing a pupil to speak or to perform some other classroom action. Aside from the rating subcategories in the instructional-logical meanings, none of the other categories accounted for more than 1 or 2 per cent of the classroom discourse.

Rating Reactions

Rating reactions clearly are part of the teacher's role and *not* part of the pupil's role in the classroom. This is supported by the fact that for pupils none of the categories of rating reactions accounted for more than 1 per cent of the lines in any classroom, and for most rating categories pupils' statements accounted for less than 1 per cent of the lines. Thus, pupils do not react by rating the moves of either the teacher or other pupils.

Negative reactions. Among the teachers, negatively oriented ratings (Table 18) clearly play much less of a part than positively oriented evaluations. The distinct negative reactions such as "no" and "not right," coded in the category NEG, accounted for less than 1 per cent of the lines in all classrooms. The negatively oriented reactions coded under NAD (not admitting) also accounted for less than 1 per cent of the lines. Thus, the definitely negative reactions made by the teachers were relatively rare in our sample of classroom discourse. Somewhat less directly negative reacting is represented by the qualifying category of reaction (QAL), but even this category accounted for relatively little of the discourse. Eight of the 15 teachers had less than 1 per cent of their lines in this category. The severely restricted range is indicated by a low of 0.3 and a high of only 1.8 per cent, with a median of 1 per cent in the qualifying category.

Positive reactions. Statements in the positive category (POS) by the teachers did not account for a very large proportion of the lines.

The portion was greater, however, than that contained in any of the negatively reacting categories. The teachers ranged from 0.3 to 12.4 per cent of their lines in this category, with a median of 2.1 per cent. This distribution was distinctly skewed toward the lower end, with 14 of the 15 teachers having less than 4 per cent of their lines devoted to directly positive reactions. Therefore, while teachers offered almost no negative reactions, they also made relatively few clear-cut positive reactions.

Admitting reactions (ADM), which represent a degree of positive rating somewhat less explicit than those coded in the POS category, accounted for less than 4 per cent of the lines in each of the classes. They ranged from 0.5 to 3.2 per cent, with a median of 2 per cent in the admitting category. A similar pattern was found for the repeat category of rating reactions (RPT), with a low of 0.3 and a high of 3.9, and a median of 1.5 per cent. As in the admitting category, all 15 teachers had less than 4 per cent of the total lines in this category of reactions.

If all of the positively oriented reactive categories (POS, ADM, and RPT) are considered together, obviously a somewhat larger proportion of lines is included in these reactive categories. In terms of the total amount of classroom discourse, however, these reactive categories still play a relatively minor quantitative role, with a low of 3.2 per cent, a high of 16.3 per cent, and a median of only 5.5 per cent. The high of 16.3 per cent represents a most unusual class in terms of the distribution of teachers in our sample; 12 of the 15 teachers were within the range of 3 to 7 per cent of the lines in the positively oriented reactive categories, with only three teachers (1, 2, and 13) above 7 per cent. This does not necessarily imply that positive reactions play an insignificant role in the learning process, but it does mean that quantitatively little of the discourse is directly concerned with this kind of reaction.

Summary

1. The teacher-pupil ratio of activity in terms of lines spoken is approximately 3 to 1; in terms of moves, this ratio is about 3 to 2. Therefore, regardless of the unit considered, teachers are considerably more active than pupils in amount of verbal activity.

2. The pedagogical roles of the classroom are clearly delineated for teachers and pupils. Teachers are responsible for structuring the lesson, soliciting responses from pupils, reacting to pupils' responses, and, to some extent, summarizing aspects of the discourse. The pupil's

primary task is to respond to the teacher's solicitations. Occasionally pupils react to preceding statements, but these reactions are rarely evaluative. Pupils do not overtly rate teachers' statements, and they rate other pupils' responses only when the teacher asks them to do so. There are deviations from this pattern, but they are infrequent. By and large, pupils do not solicit responses from the teacher about substantive meanings. When pupils do solicit, the solicitations usually concern instructional matters, such as asking for clarification of an assignment or explanation of a classroom procedure. Pupils do not spontaneously structure the discourse; their structuring moves are almost always in fulfillment of specific assignments made by the teacher and usually involve debates or reports.

3. In most classes, structuring accounts for about 10 per cent of the lines spoken; soliciting, responding, and reacting each accounts for between 20 and 30 per cent of the lines; assigned structuring and summarizing reactions account for a relatively small proportion of the discourse. Teachers vary somewhat from this pattern; but the distribution of the variation is fairly restricted, with most teachers clustering within a few percentage points of each other for any given category of analysis. Moreover, teachers tend to be remarkably stable over class sessions in their pattern of discourse, so that one can reasonably speak of a teacher's pedagogical style as an internally consistent and temporally stable dimension of behavior.

4. In approximately two-thirds of the moves and three-fourths of the lines, speakers referred to or talked about substantive material; that is, the subject matter of international trade. Of all the categories of analysis, classes varied most widely in the substantive meanings expressed. This finding was not anticipated in view of the fact that the major restriction imposed on the teachers by the research procedure was the specification of the particular substantive meanings to be covered.

5. By far the largest proportion of the discourse involved empirical meanings. This includes fact-stating and explaining, which accounted for between 50 and 60 per cent of the total discourse in most of the classrooms studied. Analytic (defining and interpreting) and evaluative (opining and justifying) meanings were expressed much less frequently, each of them accounting for less than 10 per cent of the discourse in any class. Thus most of the experimental unit was devoted to stating facts and explaining principles and problems of international trade, while considerably less of the discourse was concerned either with defining terms or with expressing and justifying personal opinions about economic issues.

6. Approximately one-fourth of the lines of the discourse involved instructional meanings, and almost all of these were expressed by teachers rather than pupils. A large part of these meanings might be viewed as "metacommunication," in that they involved teachers' comments about pupils' preceding comments. Other instructional categories that occurred with relative frequency concerned statements about procedures, materials, and assignments. All other instructional categories accounted for very little of the discourse.

7. Paralleling the instructional category, the analysis of instructional-logical meaning indicated that the most frequent statement in this area involved teachers stating facts, usually about procedures, assignments, and other instructional matters. A substantial proportion of statements in this area also dealt with teachers directing pupils to perform various actions; and almost all of the remaining instructional-logical entries involved some form of rating reaction by the teacher.

8. Teachers rarely expressed clear-cut negative reactions to pupils' responses. In general, rating reactions did not account for a large part of the discourse in terms of percentage of total lines spoken; but when teachers did rate, their reactions were almost always at least moderately positive. If the teacher reacted negatively, it was usually in terms that, in one way or another, qualified the pupil's response rather than totally rejected it. In every instance, however, the ratio of positive to negative ratings was strongly weighted in the positive direction.

CHAPTER FOUR

THE SOLICITING AND RESPONDING MOVES

THE PRELIMINARY ANALYSIS in terms of pedagogical moves and teaching cycles led to the conclusion that the core of classroom discourse is the response-expectant soliciting move followed by the expectancy-fulfilling responding move. This central soliciting-responding pattern is called the *soliciting-responding act.* The chapter presents the conceptual framework developed for the description of the soliciting-responding act, the system for analysis, and the results of the analysis.

Conceptual Framework

The question to be answered by empirical observation of the soliciting-responding act is "Does the person addressed by the solicitor present the expected responding move?" In order to answer this question, one must be able to answer two prior questions: "Who solicits whom?" and "What action is expected?"

The Soliciting Move

To observe soliciting is to observe (1) who solicits whom; (2) what the solicitor indicates he expects the other person to do; and (3) the manner in which the solicitor uses words to make his expectation known. The analysis of the soliciting move takes into account these three aspects of the move.

In the classroom the speaker of the soliciting move is either the teacher, a pupil, or some other person who is not a member of the class. The "what" of the soliciting move is the solicitor's expectation, which serves to restrict the field of reference. The restriction of reference is referred to as the indicative meaning of the move. The indicative meaning includes the solicitor's indication of the person who is expected to perform, dimensions of the activity to be performed, and the occasion for the performance. The "how" of the soliciting move is considered to be the stylistic meaning of the move and includes dimensions of the speaker's manner of presenting the indicative meaning.

The indicative meaning. The meaning common to all soliciting moves is the functional meaning; that is, in each move the words and their structure indicate that the speaker is directing some person to perform some activity at some time. When one calls for the performance of an activity, he gives some indication of the limits within which he expects the performance to fall; the solicitor sets the limits for acceptable behavior. The limits are perhaps most obvious when the speaker commands a person to perform a physical act, e.g., "Close the window!"

The indicative meaning of the soliciting move is analyzed in terms of five major limiting elements of an activity: (1) the nature of the task and the type of behavior it requires; (2) the logical process activity, which indirectly provides clues about the range of possible answers; (3) the information process activity; (4) the occasion for the performance; and (5) clues regarding terms appropriate to the responding move. These dimensions reflect both the limits presented by the solicitor and the activity he directs the person to perform within the set of limits.

1. *The task.* In the classroom there are two fundamental types of tasks that one may direct a person to perform: a substantive task and an instructional task. In calling for the performance of a substantive task, one directs the agent to deal with the knowledge that is the focus of study. In calling for the performance of an instructional task, one directs the agent to deal with matters related to the management and maintenance of the social context within which substantive knowledge is pursued.

In order to respond to a soliciting move, regardless of the type of task called for, the agent must perform some type of behavior. In the classroom there are two basic types of behavior: linguistic behavior and non-linguistic behavior. The solicitor indicates whether the agent is to perform a task that requires the use of language or is to perform a task that requires the use of objects or symbols other than verbal ones. The type of behavior called for can, therefore, be described in terms of the objects one needs in order to perform the activity. These objects are classified in two broad categories: linguistic objects and non-linguistic objects.

In this sense, words as written marks and as spoken sounds are considered symbols that one uses to signify meaning. In other classrooms with different subject matter, the results of intellectual activity could be signified by symbols other than words, such as musical notes, color and line, movement, and the like. Words, then, are "physical entities serving as tokens of intellectual signification" (16:63). When the solicitor directs the agent to use words, he indicates whether language is to be used in oral or in non-oral form.

When the solicitor directs the agent to perform a substantive task, he requires the agent to use language. The agent is to present information in propositional form; for example, the solicitor may ask for a definition of trade, reasons for trade, or data about imports and exports.

When the solicitor directs the agent to perform an instructional task, he may direct the agent to perform a linguistic act or a non-linguistic act. He may, for example, request information about an assignment or a test or he may direct the agent to close the door or to move a desk.

2. *The logical process activity.* The indication of the logical process or extra-logical process that the agent is to use in responding is one of the principal means by which the solicitor specifies the limits within which an acceptable reply will fall.

When the solicitor calls for the performance of a substantive task, he implicitly indicates the logical process he expects the respondent to use in dealing with the substantive topic under discussion. Three types of logical process are identified in the discourse: analytic processes (defining and interpreting), empirical processes (fact-stating and explaining) and evaluative processes (opining and justifying).* For example, when a teacher asks, "What does 'trade' mean?" he is asking the respondent for a definition (analytic process). When a pupil asks, "Why does most trade take place between highly developed countries?" he is calling for an explanation (empirical process). When a teacher asks, "Why do you think the U.S. should increase its trade with the U.S.S.R.?" he is asking the student to justify his point of view or opinion (evaluative process).

In contrast with substantive tasks that involve only logical processes, instructional tasks may involve either the logical processes indicated in the preceding paragraph or extra-logical processes, such as performing, directing, and repeating. The logical processes are applicable when the solicitor calls for information regarding instructional matters; for example, a pupil might ask the teacher to indicate what material will be covered in an examination, or the teacher might ask a

*** See pp. 22–26 for descriptions of the logical processes.**

pupil to explain why he has not completed his assignment on time. Both of these solicitations call for information. On the other hand, the extra-logical processes are applicable when the solicitor does not call for specific information about instructional matters, but (a) calls for the performance of a physical act, such as collecting papers or distributing tests; or (b) asks the agent to repeat something he previously has said; or (c) indicates that the agent is free to choose the information he will present. In the latter case, the solicitor directs the agent to speak (for example, "John?" or "Any other comment?"), but does not specify what information the agent is to present; the information presented by the agent in these cases will, of course, have logical significance, but no specific logical process is expected by the solicitor.

3. *The information process activity.* In addition to indicating the nature of the task, the type of behavior, and the logical process activity, the solicitor indicates the information process activity necessary for the performance of the expected responding move. This activity refers to the operation the agent is to perform with the information presented in the soliciting move.

The solicitor, for example, may direct the agent to assign a truth function to the information presented in the soliciting move. The soliciting move "Do we need products from other countries?" is the meaningful equivalent of "X: we need products from other countries?". In this instance, "X" represents the truth function: "It is the case that . . ." or "It is not the case that. . . ." Actually, the respondent replies by saying "Yes" or by saying "No," e.g., "Yes" = "It is the case that we need products from other countries." The information process involved here is referred to as *assigning a truth function.*

The solicitor may, on the other hand, present a series of alternatives and expect the respondent to select one or more of those alternatives, e.g., "Do we import more than one-half, one-half, or less than one-half of our consumer goods?" The respondent selects the appropriate information and presents it as the responding move. The information process involved here is *selecting from stated alternatives.*

As a third alternative, the solicitor may expect the agent to use the information in the soliciting move in constructing a responding move. To the soliciting move, "Why do we trade?" the respondent presents the following responding move: "We trade because we need goods and services." The respondent assumes as true what the solicitor says and extends its propositional meaning by presenting information of the logical significance expected; that is, he assumes we trade and offers an explanation as to why we trade. The solicitor may also expect the agent to construct a responding move by converting a command for action into action. The information process involved here is *constructing a response.*

In some cases the solicitor indicates that he expects the agent both to assign a truth function for and to extend the information in the soliciting move. The process in such instances is described as *assigning/constructing.* When the teacher, for example, says "Do you have a question?" he not only expects a "Yes" or "No" but also expects the pupil to continue by giving the question if the answer is "Yes." In practice, the respondent frequently constructs his move and thereby implies the truth function; i.e., he asks his question without saying "Yes."

Finally, the solicitor may present alternatives yet be ambiguous as to whether he expects the respondent to select from the alternatives or to assign a truth function to the stated alternatives. The teacher could say "Shall we trade or fade?" and the pupil says, "Yes," indicating that the stated alternatives are all inclusive, that is, "It is true that we shall either trade or fade." On the other hand, he could also select one of the alternatives: "We shall trade."

4. *Occasion for the expected responding move.* The concepts of time and place are useful in analyzing the meaning of directives. By varying the precision with which one indicates when and where an agent is expected to perform, one can significantly limit the actions an agent may perform. The indication of the time and the place for the expected performance is considered as an indication of the occasion for the anticipated responding move.

5. *Clues regarding terms.* When the speaker presents the soliciting move, the linguistic structure of the words he uses tends to emphasize certain terms that may be considered key terms. These key terms may be used to identify the topic of the soliciting move. If the solicitor expects the respondent to present additional information about the topic, he implicitly indicates the logical significance of that information, as previously discussed. He may also provide special clues regarding terms appropriate to the responding move. The complete or propositional meaning of the soliciting-responding act can be determined only when one combines the content meaning of the soliciting move and the content meaning of the responding move it elicits (6:354). The soliciting move "Why do we trade?" and the responding move "Because we need certain goods and services" when combined yield the statement "We trade because we need certain goods and services." In this soliciting move the solicitor presents a propositional function; that is, when the respondent replaces the information placeholder "why" with specific information, one may determine the propo-

sitional meaning of the soliciting-responding act. While the specific meaning of a propositional function, such as why, what, when, where, how, or who, depends on its use in a given move, the propositional functions when given meaning in context tend to specify the type of information appropriate to the responding move.

The solicitor may offer more direct clues to the terms by citing terms that he expects the agent to use or by citing terms that he expects the agent to exclude from the responding move. He may, for example, cite terms by saying, "Tell me why nations trade and state your reply in terms of the three factors of production." He could exclude terms by saying, "What state is the largest producer of consumer goods? Don't tell me New York or Connecticut." By referring to information previously admitted to the discourse, the solicitor could cite terms that parallel in essential characteristics those that he expects in the responding move—for example, "What other minerals, in addition to bauxite, do we import?"

Finally, when the information process is assigning a truth function, the solicitor may explicitly suggest the truth value he expects by providing leading expressions, for example, "You do think we ought to increase our exports, don't you?"

The stylistic meaning. The stylistic meaning of a soliciting move refers to the speaker's manner of presenting the indicative meaning; that is, "how" the solicitor makes his expectations known. In observing the stylistic meaning of the move, the purpose is to describe aspects of the form or structure of this functional unit of speech.

Authors of textbooks on teaching methods sometimes discuss the form or style that questions in the classroom ought to have. Underlying this concern is apparently the assumption that teachers do ask "questions" and that the asking of questions is or should be useful for accomplishing educational objectives. This assumption has frequently led to prescriptive statements; the most often noted prescriptions can be summarized as follows: (1) keep them brief and make them specific and (2) present problems and do not overstructure (10:99). Evidence to support either of these prescriptions is generally lacking. One is in doubt about the relation between the form of speech units, as an element of stylistic meaning, and the anticipated and/or unanticipated outcomes of the teaching process.

In this study it is assumed that form communicates a type of meaning and that form can vary as a function of other elements of meaning in the soliciting move. In short, variations in form are meaningful. The purpose at this stage of inquiry is to establish concepts adequate for description. One may begin by attempting to observe those aspects of method most frequently mentioned in prescriptive statements: length, mode, composition, and construction.

In observing the stylistic meaning of the soliciting move, one is concerned, therefore, with the following questions: (1) What is the length of the teacher's moves and of the pupil's move? (2) Is the length of a move related to the task solicited? (3) How are soliciting moves presented—as interrogatives, commands, or statements? (4) How many and what types of activities do teachers and pupils call for in a move?

By using a standard length of line when typing the protocols of classroom discourse, we were able to determine the amount of discourse spoken by the teacher and by the pupils and also the amount of discourse devoted by each speaker to each of the pedagogical moves. With the identification of the speaker and the task of each soliciting move, it is possible to relate speaker, task, and length of move to determine the differences between teacher and/or pupil substantive moves and teacher and/or pupil instructional moves.

Since the soliciting move is a functional unit of speech, it is not presented exclusively in any one grammatical mood; that is, not all "questions" function as directives and not all directives are "questions." It may be the intention of the speaker that the agent consider the directive as an inquiry. On the other hand, he may intend that it be taken as a command. The way in which the speaker intends the directive to be taken is the mode of the presentation.

When one solicits, he may call for the performance of one or more tasks. In the framework of this analysis, he may call for the performance of one substantive task or two substantive tasks; one instructional task or two instructional tasks; or one substantive task and one instructional task. The type and number of tasks called for are analyzed in terms of the combination of primary activities the solicitor directs the agent to perform; namely, the logical process activity and the information operation. This aspect of the stylistic meaning of the move is referred to as the composition of the move.

Relationships of Soliciting and Responding Moves

The concept of the soliciting-responding act combines the functional meaning of the soliciting move and the functional meaning of the responding move. In the soliciting move the solicitor intends to elicit a subsequent act. Through the indicative meaning of the move, the solicitor specifies the limits within which the agent addressed is expected to perform the subsequent act. The soliciting move is, therefore, the initiatory response-expectant move. In the responding move, on the other hand, the respondent attempts to fulfill the expectation specified by the solicitor; the responding move is reflexive in nature and bears a reciprocal relation to the soliciting move.

When the soliciting move does in fact elicit a responding move—that is, when the intent is fulfilled—the soliciting move has both intentional meaning and consequential meaning. The solicitor both intends to elicit and does elicit subsequent action. When the soliciting move does not elicit the intended response, the move has only intentional meaning.

The responding move, in like manner, has both intrinsic meaning and relational meaning. What the respondent says has intrinsic meaning as a unit of speech that makes some contribution to the discourse. In this sense, the move may or may not fulfill the complete expectation of the soliciting move that elicited it. What the respondent says has relational meaning to the extent that the move reflects the expectation of the solicitor.

In the analysis of the soliciting move and of the responding move as separate moves, one is concerned with the intentional meaning of the soliciting move and with the intrinsic meaning of the responding move. In analyzing the intentional meaning of the solicitation, one asks, "What action does the solicitor intend to elicit?" In analyzing the intrinsic meaning of the responding move, one asks, "What does the respondent say?"

In the analysis of the relationships of the soliciting move and the responding move in the soliciting-responding act, one is interested in the consequential meaning of the soliciting move and the relational meaning of the responding move; that is, in the relation between the intended response and actual response. In analyzing the consequential nature of the solicitation, one asks, "Does the soliciting move elicit the intended response?" In analyzing the relational meaning of the responding move, one asks, "How does what the respondent says relate to what the solicitor intended to elicit?" In this research, the analysis of the soliciting-responding act is in terms of the relational meaning of the response; that is, one examines the extent to which the responding move reflects the intentional meaning of the soliciting move.

System for Analysis of Soliciting and Responding Moves

The first three parts of this section describe the categories used in the analysis; the fourth part reports the results of the reliability test of the system.

Persons Involved in the Soliciting-Responding Act

The soliciting move is the initiatory maneuver in an anticipated interaction. The persons involved in the interaction are the solicitor and the agent addressed by the solicitor.

1. *The solicitor.* The solicitor is the person who presents the oral directive to another person in order to elicit a responding move.

1.1. *The teacher*

1.2. *A pupil*

1.3. *Any other speaker*

2. *The agent solicited.* The agent is the person(s) addressed by the solicitor. He is expected to perform the activity specified by the solicitor.

2.1. *The teacher*

2.2. *All pupils*

2.3. *Any one pupil* (No contextual or verbal clue given.)

2.4. *One specified pupil* (One pupil named before expectation is made known.)

2.5. *One selected pupil* (Expectation made known, then pupil selected as agent.)

The Indicative Meaning of the Soliciting Move

The indicative meaning of the soliciting move includes the solicitor's indication of (1) the nature of the performance in terms of the pedagogical task expected and the type of behavior expected; (2) the primary activities he directs the agent to perform; and (3) the clues he gives the agent regarding the terms in which an acceptable responding move is to be phrased.

1. *The pedagogical task.* In the classroom there are two basic types of task: the substantive task and the instructional task. The solicitor indicates the task or tasks he expects the agent to perform.

1.1. *The substantive task.* If the solicitor directs the agent to perform a task that requires the agent to deal with the subject matter under study, then he directs the agent to perform a substantive task.

Examples

T/SOL: Why are imports to the U.S. so important?

T/SOL: What has happened to our foreign investments in the last fifteen years?

1.2. *The instructional task.* If the solicitor directs the agent to perform a task that requires the agent to tend to some aspect of the management of the classroom or the social context within which the subject matter is pursued, then he directs the agent to perform an instructional task.

Examples

T/SOL: Joyce, listen instead of talking.

T/SOL: Which shall I give you first, the assignment or the test?

2. *The type of behavior expected.* Two categories are established for the description of the types of behavior called for: linguistic and non-linguistic.

Coding of this aspect of the soliciting move does not require a separate set of categories. The data are derived from the categories used for description of the logical or extra-logical process activity. Oral responding moves involving defining or fact-stating, for example, are linguistic acts. The closing of a door and the distribution of texts, on the other hand, are physical acts, the performance of which do not require the use of language. These latter moves, therefore, are coded as "extra-logical: performance non-linguistic."

3. *The primary activities.* The two primary activities are (a) the logical process activity to be used in dealing with the information solicited or the extra-logical process activity related to the completion of a physical act and (b) the information process activity which refers to the solicitor's indication of how he expects the agent to use the information presented in the soliciting move.

3.1. *The logical process activity.* The logical process activity called for in the soliciting move component will be one of the following logical modes: the analytic mode, the empirical mode, the evaluative mode, or the extra-logical mode.

For those logical processes included in the original analysis system, complete definitions are given in Appendix A.

3.11 *The analytic mode*
  3.111 *Defining*
  3.112 *Interpreting*

3.12 *The empirical mode*
  3.121 *Fact-Stating*
  3.122 *Explaining*

3.13 *The evaluative mode*
  3.131 *Opining*
  3.132 *Justifying*

3.14 *The extra-logical mode.* The solicitor does not call for verifiable information but calls for the completion of a physical act that can be observed but not verified; or the solicitor indicates that the agent is free to choose the information he will present. In the latter case, the information presented by the agent will have logical significance, but no specific logical meaning is expected by the solicitor.

3.141 *Perform oral.* To perform orally is to speak. The solicitor directs the agent to speak but does not specify the information the agent is to present.

Examples

T/SOL: Any other comment? (Indicates that the agent is free to choose logical process.)

P/SOL: How much coffee does the U.S. actually import? (Agent chooses to solicit a fact.)

3.142 *Language performance: non-oral.* To perform with language in a non-oral form is to read, write, hear, or think, but not to speak.

Examples

T/SOL: Please turn to page 21 and look at that chart for a few minutes. (Solicitor directs agent to read.)

T/SOL: Put that down in your notes. (Solicitor directs agent to write.)

3.143 *Non-language performance.* To perform without language is to complete a physical act that does not involve writing, reading, speaking, cogitating, or listening.

Examples

T/SOL: Pass in your books.

T/SOL: All right, class, settle down back there.

3.144 *Directing.* To direct is to seek direction from the agent. In the directive itself, there is no indication of a specific object to be evaluated. The solicitor does not indicate the logical process activity expected.

Examples

T/SOL: What ought we do today?

T/SOL: How shall we handle this problem?

P/SOL: How do we go about our debates?

3.145 *Repeating.* To repeat is to restate the substance of some vocal action that has already been entered into the discourse. A solicitation that requests a repetition does not solicit information but solicits the act of "repeating."

Examples

T/SOL: Pardon?

T/SOL: Repeat that so John can hear you.

3.15 *Logical process unclear.* The logical process is unclear when the wording of the move or the meaning of the move is ambiguous.

Example

T/SOL: You spent the money in America, but the salesman /missed/, would he?

3.2. *The information process activity.* The information process activity refers to the solicitor's indication of how he expects the agent to use the information presented in the soliciting move when responding as directed.

3.21 *Assigning a truth function* (A). The solicitor directs the agent to affirm, to accept, to agree with, to deny, or to disagree with information presented in the soliciting move. The solicitor indicates that a sufficient response to the solicitation is either a "Yes" or a "No," which means "It is the case that . . ." or "It is not the case that. . . ."

Examples

P/SOL: Is that a machine tool?

T/SOL: Do we operate under a high tariff system today?

T/SOL: Is trading in both cases based on the same principle?

P/SOL: Are the figures recent?

3.22 *Selecting* (S). The solicitor directs the agent to select one or more alternatives and indicates that a sufficient response is, or represents, the choice of one or more of the alternatives presented. The exclusive disjunction must be stated or clearly implied.

Examples

T/SOL: Now, portfolio investments are mostly long term or short term?

T/SOL: Is it a matter of dealing between people or is it a matter of dealing between governments?

T/SOL: Do we find the greatest flow of trade between developed and underdeveloped countries, between two underdeveloped countries or do we find the greatest flow of trade between two developed countries?

3.23 *Constructing* (C). The solicitor directs the agent to construct a response if he neither presents alternatives for the agent to choose among nor directs the agent to assign a truth function for information presented in the soliciting move, but does direct the agent to extend the information presented in the soliciting move as the basis for a response. All commands, most directives involving nonlinguistic behavior, and most directives with information-placeholders require the construction of a response.

Examples

T/SOL: Differentiate between domestic and international trade.

T/SOL: Most trade is carried on through the medium of what?

T/SOL: Put the newspapers away!

3.24 *Constructing/Assigning* (C/A). The solicitor directs the agent both to assign a truth function to information presented and to construct an additional aspect of the response; the solicitor indicates that providing a truth function is appropriate but not sufficient as a response.

Example

T/SOL: Does anyone have a good definition of trade?

3.25 *Selecting/Assigning* (S/A). The solicitor's direction is ambiguous as to whether the agent is to assign a truth function to a set of alternatives or is to select one alternative.

Examples

T/SOL: Do you think we ought to lower our tariffs or forget world trade?

P/RES: Ycs.

4. *Clues regarding appropriate terms.* The solicitor may indicate that the responding move is to be stated or is not to be stated in terms of particular substantive concepts; he may refer to previous statements admitted in the discourse and direct the agent to provide information that parallels in essential detail that other information; or he may provide clues indicating whether the agent is to affirm or negate information presented in the solicitation. He may also use an information placeholder, or propositional function, that gives a clue about the range of alternatives or type of information appropriate for a response. By referring to the terms of the response in one or more of these ways, the solicitor provides clues to the agent that may be useful in responding to the directive.

4.1. *Terms cited.* The solicitor cites terms when he indicates to the agent that the response is to be phrased in specific terms.

Example

T/SOL: Now, tell me why there is trade. Try to answer in terms of factors of production.

P/RES: Because countries don't have the same natural resources.

4.2. *Terms excluded.* The solicitor excludes terms when he indicates to the agent that certain concepts are not to be used in constructing a response to the directive.

Examples

T/SOL: Aside from natural resources, why do countries trade?
P/RES: Some countries don't have the kind of workers they need.
T/SOL: What states have very little manufacturing? Don't tell me New York.
P/RES: Arizona.

4.3. *Terms of a parallel nature.* The solicitor calls for terms of a parallel nature when he indicates that the response is to be similar in essential detail to the information previously presented in the discourse. Frequently, the solicitor directs the agent to use terms that parallel those already used or to make an observation about a phenomenon similar to one already made. The clue to parallelism is usually "some other," "another," or "something else."

Examples

T/SOL: Now give me *another* reason why we have some raw materials being traded.
T/SOL: How *else* might one invest American capital abroad?

4.4. *Leading.* The solicitor provides a leading clue when he directs the agent to assign a truth function and provides a suggestion as to the specific response acceptable to or expected by the solicitor. Examples of leading clues are "don't we," "isn't it," and "shouldn't we."

Examples

T/SOL: We import great quantities of tin, *don't we*?
P/RES: Yes.
T/SOL: We ought to join the Common Market in order to keep up our markets, *shouldn't we*?
P/RES: I guess so.

4.5. *Propositional functions.* Propositional functions are words used in soliciting moves as placeholders for the information the agent is directed to present. Since usage determines the specific meaning of a word, a propositional function does not have a unique meaning, but it does have a limited range of meanings that serve as clues to the agent.

1. What	*What* is tin?
2. What about, how about	*What about* Red China? *How about* natural resources?
3. What type of, sort of, kind of	*What kind of* material do we import? *What sort of* products does Ghana sell? *What kind of* trade do we specialize in?

4. How, in what manner-way	*How* do banks enter into the problem? *In what way* does a country put a tariff on?
5. Why, for what purpose-cause-reason, what is the purpose-cause-reason	*Why* do nations trade? *What's the purpose* of the investment, aside from making profits?
6. Who, whom	*Who* was greatly interested in infant industries? *Who* makes the machines that make the machines? The tariff is put on to protect *whom*?
7. When, at what time	*When* were you in Canada?
8. Where, at what place	*Where* else, besides Africa, are diamonds found? *Where* do you have the greatest trade occurring?
9. How much-many, to what degree-extent, how X	The difference between our imports and exports is about *how much*? *How many* people are unemployed in the U.S. today? *How effective* was the shark repellent?
10. Which	*Which* country is the grey country?
What X	*What country* in the world has the highest capital investment?
Preposition-what-X	The majority of our tin comes *from what country*?
Whose X	*Whose business* does it protect?
What is the X that . . .	*What is the country that* has a marked difference in its economic system?

5. *The occasion for the solicited performance.* The solicitor indicates when and where he expects the agent to perform the activity. The solicitor may indicate that the action is to be performed immediately or at some future time; he may indicate that he expects action within the classroom or at some other place. (Since the meanings of the terms are self-evident, the definitions developed for coders are not given here.)

5.1. *Immediate and Within the Classroom*
5.2. *Immediate and Outside the Classroom*
5.3. *Future of This Class Session and Within Classroom*
5.4. *Future Class Session and Within Classroom*
5.5. *Future Study Unit and Within Classroom*
5.6. *Future After Class and Outside Classroom*
5.7. *Future-Unspecified and Within Classroom*
5.8. *Future-Unspecified and Outside Classroom*

The Stylistic Meaning of the Soliciting Move

Stylistic meaning refers to the speaker's manner of presenting the indicative meaning; that is, "how" the solicitor makes his expectation known. The stylistic meaning of the soliciting move includes the length of the presentation in terms of the number of lines, the mode in which the directive is presented, the composition of the move in terms of the number and combination of tasks and primary activities presented, and the construction of the move.

1. *The length of the presentation.* The length of the presentation is determined by the number of lines of typescript included in the move. Standard line is a 4.5-inch segment of the typescript.

2. *Mode of presentation.* Mode of presentation refers to grammatical concepts of purpose-mood of the soliciting move. The grammatical concepts have been adapted to the pedagogical context under study.

2.1. *The imperative mode.* The mode of presentation is imperative if the solicitor presents the solicitation as a command that is to be obeyed. Imperatives usually begin with an action word but may begin with a word that refers to the solicitor (I) or with the indication of the agent.

Examples

T/SOL: Make a generalization based on these two figures.

T/SOL: I want you to stop this talking immediately.

T/SOL: So put that down in your notes.

2.2. *The interrogative mode.* The mode of presentation is interrogative if the solicitor presents the solicitation as an inquiry to which the agent is to respond. The response is "sought after," but not "demanded." Interrogatives are not propositions, but are often quasi-statements in which a propositional function is to be replaced or for which a truth function is to be determined.

Examples

T/SOL: What would be another argument in favor of trade barriers?

T/SOL: Isn't that a variation?

T/SOL: Our production went up about how much?

2.3. *The declarative mode.* The mode of presentation is declarative if the solicitor presents the solicitation as a complete assertion or as a partial assertion to be completed by the agent. The assertion or partial assertion is a solicitation because in the pedagogical context it serves to elicit a response from the agent. In the partial assertion, the solicitor's pause in speech indicates to the agent that he is to complete the assertion.

Examples

T/SOL: It can also be due to factors that we haven't mentioned at all.

T/SOL: Two of the biggest things that we import in this country we do produce ourselves.

T/SOL: Of course, we discussed the great exception to this rule yesterday.

3. *Construction of the move.*

3.1. *Elliptical.* A solicitation is elliptical when words necessary for comprehending what performance is called for or for comprehending what information is to be used in responding to the directive are not stated; such information may be understood by the agent from the context in which the directive is spoken. There are two types of elliptical directives: Type 1—solicitations that include only the agent and the general nature of the expected response, such as "Yes?" and/or a proper name; and Type 2—solicitations containing something other than "Yes?" and/or a proper name.

Examples

T/SOL: Yes? (Type 1)
P/SOL: Don't you think we ought to lower our tariffs?

T/SOL: Why? (Type 2)
P/RES: Because we don't use that much cobalt in a year.

3.2. *Conditional.* A solicitation is conditional when the solicitor indicates that the agent is to consider the information presented in the solicitation as providing the antecedent of a hypothetical or a specified state of affairs, as distinct from an unspecified or general state of affairs. Since the conditional is not limited to the hypothetical, logical process activities other than explaining may be indicated.

Examples

T/SOL: If we were to trade with Red China, what products would we exchange?
P/RES: Probably rice and machines.

T/SOL: Assuming all countries had the same factors of production, what would be the case?
P/RES: There wouldn't be any trade.

3.3. *Completion.* A solicitation is completion in form when the solicitor inverts the solicitation, placing the propositional function at the end of the solicitation; or when the solicitor does not ask either for a truth function or for a propositional function and pauses to indicate that the agent is to provide the information necessary for the completion of the information presented in the solicitation.

Examples

T/SOL: Now, for example, when Roosevelt was President he initiated a program for the relief of what?

T/SOL: The greater demand will be issued for those products, thus creating a higher . . .

P/RES: Income for the people who make them.

T/SOL: And finally one other very important factor in production today and that is the role of . . .

P/RES: The government.

3.4. *Interlarded information.* A solicitation contains interlarded information when the mode of presentation is interrogative or imperative and additional information is presented in the declarative mode. Usually this information is related to the expected performance, but occasionally it is not.

Examples

T/SOL: Is there anyone who doesn't have a book with him? *I thought we had enough to go around.*

T/SOL: What is the term that we use, America's program for its investment in a foreign country or towards its exports with a foreign country? *It's just a nice catchall term that we use.*

4. *The composition of the move.* The composition of the move is described in terms of the number and the various combinations of logical activities and information activities called for in the solicitation. (See pp. 89–91).

Reliability Test

Three members of the research staff participated in the reliability test. Five classes were selected at random from the complete list of 15 classes. From the five classes, two sessions were selected from each, yielding a total of 10 randomly selected class sessions. Randomly selected groups of moves from the beginning, the middle and the end of the 10 class sessions were identified in order to establish a balanced sample of over 5 per cent of the 5,135 soliciting moves.

The three coders were divided into teams, one of which consisted of two coders and the other of a single coder. Assignment of coders to teams was rotated so that all possible permutations of pairs and singles were compared. Following the procedure for the coding of all other protocols, one member of the pair coded a given sample; the other member reviewed the coding; then both members of the pair arbitrated any disagreements. The single coder coded the sample and reviewed his own coding.

After each of the ten samples had been coded independently by the two teams, the codings were compared and the percentage of agreement among coders for each dimension of meaning was computed. As shown in Table 19, the overall agreement among coders is 97.1 per cent and the range is from 96.1 per cent to 99.0 per cent.

Results of Analysis of Soliciting and Responding Moves

For the most part, the data are summarized here for all classes combined over the four sessions to provide a comprehensive view of the soliciting and responding moves in the discourse. In some instances, data are presented for each of the classes for purposes of comparison among the classes.

TABLE 19

Percentage of Agreement among Coding Teams for Each Major Category in Content Analysis of Soliciting Components

Category	*Per Cent of Agreement*
Total	97.1
Persons Involved	96.4
Indicative Meaning	99.0
Stylistic Meaning	96.1

Role of the Soliciting Move in the Discourse

The soliciting move accounts for about one-third of all moves spoken in the 15 classes. The median percentage for all classes is 32.5 per cent, with a high of 39.8 per cent in Class 3 and a low of 29.2 per cent in Class 12.

One might expect the 345 pupils to solicit more often than the 15 teachers. One of the rules of the teaching game, however, is that the teacher is the chief solicitor: the teacher speaks 86.9 per cent of all soliciting moves in the 15 classes.

Differences in roles of the teacher and the pupil are apparent when the percentage of the teacher's discourse and the percentage of the pupil's discourse devoted to soliciting are considered. The data summarized in Table 20 clearly demonstrate that the soliciting move

TABLE 20

Percentage of the Teachers' and Pupils' Moves and Lines Devoted to Soliciting for Each of the Fifteen Classes and for All Classes Combined

	Teacher		*Pupil*	
Class	*Moves*	*Lines*	*Moves*	*Lines*
All Combined	46.6	28.0	11.3	8.7
1	49.0	34.8	4.1	4.6
2	51.3	34.2	6.5	4.2
3	55.7	42.7	9.1	6.9
4	48.4	34.1	7.9	4.5
5	42.4	26.1	22.6	14.1
6	51.9	24.4	7.5	6.2
7	40.4	21.5	18.5	15.0
8	44.8	27.9	12.2	10.7
9	40.5	13.9	5.4	4.7
10	45.5	14.7	8.3	6.5
11	49.4	31.6	7.8	3.4
12	36.7	16.7	18.7	14.9
13	51.4	40.7	10.4	10.4
14	44.7	32.9	8.1	6.3
15	42.5	24.2	17.6	13.1

plays a more prominent role in the teacher's discourse than it does in the pupils' discourse. Soliciting moves account for 46.6 per cent of the teachers' moves, but only 11.3 per cent of the pupils' moves. The picture is approximately the same when these data are considered in terms of percentage of lines: whereas 28.0 per cent of all lines spoken by the teacher involve soliciting, only 8.7 per cent of the lines by the pupil involve soliciting.

The Component

The analysis of the soliciting move is in terms of the components of the move. A component includes one task (substantive or instructional) and one set of primary activities (logical process activity or information process activity). The 5,135 soliciting moves are the equivalent of 5,377 soliciting move components, of which the teacher speaks 4,695 and the pupil speaks 682. The larger number of components reflects the fact that 242 soliciting moves are two-component moves. In other words, 96.3 per cent of all soliciting moves call for a single task, which is related either to the subject matter or to instructional matters; only 4.7 per cent call for two different tasks, whether substantive or instructional or both.

The Solicitor and the Task

The fundamental limiting factor presented to the agent by the solicitor is the indication of the task to be performed. The task may either be a substantive one, related directly to the subject matter under study, or an instructional one, related to the social-managerial aspects of the classroom. Table 21 presents the distribution of the soliciting components in terms of solicitor and the task the solicitor expects the agent to perform.

TABLE 21

Distribution of Soliciting Components by Speaker and Speaker-Task for Each of the Fifteen Classes and for All Classes Combined

		Teacher			*Pupil*		
Class	*Total*	*Total*	*Substantive*	*Instructional*	*Total*	*Substantive*	*Instructional*
All Combined	100.0	87.3	53.7	33.6	12.7	8.3	4.4
1	100.0	95.0	66.7	28.3	5.0	3.3	1.7
2	100.0	92.3	53.5	38.8	7.7	4.0	3.7
3	100.0	92.5	39.9	52.6	7.5	3.9	3.6
4	100.0	91.0	52.7	38.3	9.0	3.3	5.7
5	100.0	73.6	26.5	47.1	26.4	20.1	6.3
6	100.0	93.3	65.0	28.3	6.7	5.1	1.6
7	100.0	79.8	50.0	29.8	20.2	14.4	5.8
8	100.0	86.0	55.4	30.6	14.0	11.2	2.8
9	100.0	95.6	78.5	17.1	4.4	3.8	0.6
10	100.0	90.4	69.7	20.7	9.6	8.1	1.5
11	100.0	93.1	65.5	27.6	6.9	2.8	4.1
12	100.0	73.1	40.5	32.6	26.9	16.9	10.0
13	100.0	88.1	54.3	33.8	11.9	7.2	4.7
14	100.0	92.3	61.0	31.3	7.7	2.9	4.8
15	100.0	77.8	43.4	34.4	22.2	15.5	6.7

In general, the speaker of the soliciting component is more likely to be a teacher than a pupil, and the task called for by the solicitor is more likely to be substantive than instructional. The teacher is the speaker of 87.3 per cent of all soliciting move components and the pupil is the speaker of only 12.7 per cent. Both the teacher and the pupil more often solicit the performance of a substantive task than they solicit the performance of an instructional task. In 62 per cent of the 5,377 components the solicitor indicates that he expects the agent to perform a substantive task, while in 38 per cent he expects the performance of an instructional task. In only two of the 15 classes do the solicitors—teachers or pupils—expect more instructional than substantive tasks, and in these two classes they expect at least 44 per cent of the performances to be substantive in nature.

In order of observed frequency, the distribution for speaker and task is teacher-substantive, teacher-instructional, pupil-substantive, and pupil-instructional components. Teacher-substantive task components represent 53.7 per cent of all soliciting components, and teacher-instructional task components account for 33.6 per cent of all soliciting components. Pupil-substantive task components account for 8.3 per cent of all soliciting components, and pupil-instructional task components represent 4.4 per cent of all soliciting components. This pattern of distribution is altered somewhat in Classes 3 and 5, in which teacher-instructional components as a percentage of all components is greater than the percentage observed for teacher-substantive components. In three classes (4, 11, and 14) the percentage of pupil-instructional components is greater than the percentage of pupil-substantive components, but in these instances the difference is not more than two percentage points. It is accurate to say, therefore, that the combination of speaker and task observed for all classes combined is also representative of the individual classes.

In analyzing the soliciting components of the 15 classes in terms of speaker and task, one finds that teacher-substantive components constitute a relatively high percentage of all components and exhibit fairly wide variation from class to class. The teachers tend to monopolize the use of the soliciting components but vary in the extent to which they expect the performance of a substantive rather than an instructional task. Pupil-instructional components, on the other hand, constitute a relatively small number of all soliciting components and show little variation from class to class. Classes vary somewhat more in the extent to which pupils solicit the performance of substantive tasks.

The median for the teacher-substantive components as a percentage of all soliciting components is 54.3 per cent. The range is 52 percentage points, from a high of 78.5 per cent in Class 9 to a low of 26.5 per cent in Class 5. In only four classes do teacher-substantive components account for less than 50 per cent of all components. The median for the teacher-instructional task components as a percentage of all components is 31.3 per cent. The range is 35.5 percentage points, from a high of 52.6 per cent in Class 3 to a low of 17.1 per cent in Class 9.

The median for pupil-substantive task components as a percentage of all components is 5.1 per cent and the range is 17.3 percentage points, from a high of 20.1 per cent in Class 5 to a low of 2.8 per cent in Class 11. For the pupil-instructional components as a percentage of all components, the median for the 15 classes is 4.1 per cent. The range of 9.4 points, from a high of 10 per cent in Class 12 to a low of 0.6 per cent in Class 9, is the most restricted range observed.

In summary, the analysis of the soliciting move components in terms of the speakers and of the tasks they call for reveals that the teacher is the primary solicitor and that substantive tasks are more frequently expected than instructional tasks. Considering teachers and pupils as groups, both teachers and pupils call for the performance of a substantive task in about 60 per cent of their components and call for the performance of an instructional task in about 40 per cent of their components. Teacher-substantive components generally account for the majority of components, followed in order of frequency by teacher-instructional components, pupil-substantive components, and pupil-instructional components.

The Solicitor and Agent

The solicitor's indication of the agent is a significant aspect of the soliciting component. As indicated in Table 22, when the teacher is the solicitor, he usually expects *one* pupil to present the responding move, rather than several pupils or all pupils in unison. When the pupil is the solicitor, he ordinarily expects the teacher to respond, rather than one or more of his fellow pupils: the pupil directs 83.3 per cent of his soliciting components to the teacher.

The expected interaction pattern, established by the solicitor's verbal clues regarding the responding agent, varies in relation to the nature of the task. When the teacher expects all pupils to perform, the task is most likely to be instructional: the teacher directs 14.7 per cent of his instructional task components to all pupils. In contrast, he directs only 0.2 per cent of his substantive task components to all pupils.

The teacher's manner of designating the one pupil he expects to

TABLE 22

Distribution of Soliciting Components by Agent for Speaker and Speaker-Task

	Speaker of Soliciting Component											
	Teacher						*Pupil*					
	Total		*Substantive*		*Instructional*		*Total*		*Substantive*		*Instructional*	
Agent	%	*f*	%	*f*	%	*f*	%	*f*	%	*f*	%	*f*
Total	100.0	4695	100.0	2889	100.0	1806	100.0	682	100.0	446	100.0	236
Teacher	—	—	—	—	—	—	83.3	568	85.9	383	78.4	185
Pupil	94.2	4423	99.8	2883	85.3	1540	16.3	111	14.1	63	20.3	48
Specified	51.3	2410	38.6	1115	71.8	1295	11.3	77	9.2	41	15.3	36
Selected	19.9	935	29.2	844	5.0	91	0.3	2	—	—	0.8	2
Any	23.0	1078	32.0	924	8.5	154	4.7	32	4.9	22	4.2	10
All Pupils	5.8	272	0.2	6	14.7	266	0.4	3	—	—	1.3	3

perform is also related to task. When the task is substantive, the teacher presents 38.6 per cent of the directives to a specific individual; but when the task is instructional, he presents 71.8 per cent of the components to a specific individual. When the task is substantive, therefore, the teacher tends to leave the specification of agent somewhat more open in terms of verbal clues than he does when the task is instructional. When a pupil is to perform a substantive task, the teacher is more likely to select a pupil or to permit any one pupil to perform than he is to specify an individual pupil.

When the pupil directs his solicitation to the teacher, the task is more likely to be substantive than instructional. When a pupil addresses another pupil, the task is also more likely to be substantive than instructional.

In identifying the agent, the teacher and the pupil are alike in two respects: both generally expect one agent to respond and both expect the interaction to be between teacher and pupil, even though theoretically the pupil can initiate pupil-pupil interaction.

Logical Process Activities

Indication of the logical process or extra-logical process that the agent is to use in responding is one of the principal means by which the solicitor specifies limits within which an acceptable reply will fall. Viewing the logical processes as a whole, regardless of task, analytic processes (defining and interpreting) account for 10.7 per cent of the soliciting components, empirical processes (fact-stating and explaining) for 59.1 per cent, evaluative processes (opining and justifying) for 4.9 per cent, and extra-logical processes for 25.2 per cent.

Logical processes with substantive tasks. As indicated in Table 23, of the three logical modes, the empirical mode is expected in 80.2 per cent of the soliciting components that call for the performance of a substantive task: the solicitor expects fact-stating in response to 37 per cent of the substantive task directives and explaining in reply to 43.2 per cent. In contrast, the solicitor expects a type of analytic meaning in the responding move to 14.4 per cent of the components (defining in 13.1 per cent and interpreting in 1.3 per cent), and the evaluative mode in only 5.2 per cent (opining in 3.7 per cent and justifying in 1.5 per cent). The ratio of expected responding components with empirical meaning to those with evaluative meaning is 15 to 1. This ratio is of considerable interest in view of the fact that trade policies, which inevitably involve opining and justifying opinions, might reasonably be considered of central importance in discussions of international trade, the topic under study in the classes observed.

TABLE 23

Distribution of Soliciting Components by Logical Activity for Task and Task-Speaker

Logical Process	*Substantive Task*						*Instructional Task*					
	Total		*Teacher*		*Pupil*		*Total*		*Teacher*		*Pupil*	
	%	*f*	%	*f*	%	*f*	%	*f*	%	*f*	%	*f*
Total	100.0	3335	100.0	2889	100.0	446	100.0	2042	100.0	1806	100.0	236
Analytic	14.4	483	15.7	454	6.5	29	4.5	91	3.6	64	11.4	27
DEF	13.1	438	14.2	411	6.1	27	.1	1	.1	1	—	—
INT	1.3	45	1.5	43	.4	2	4.4	90	3.5	63	11.4	27
Empirical	80.2	2674	79.5	2298	84.3	376	24.6	503	20.9	378	53.0	125
FAC	37.0	1235	36.1	1044	42.8	191	23.8	486	20.4	368	50.0	118
XPL	43.2	1439	43.4	1254	41.5	185	.8	17	.5	10	3.0	7
Evaluative	5.2	172	4.7	135	8.3	37	4.7	95	3.5	63	13.5	32
OPN	3.7	123	3.5	100	5.2	23	4.4	89	3.2	58	13.1	31
JUS	1.5	49	1.2	35	3.1	14	.3	6	.3	5	.4	1
Extra-Logical	—	—	—	—	—	—	66.2	1353	72.0	1301	22.1	52
PRO	—	—	—	—	—	—	38.4	783	42.7	771	5.1	12
PLG	—	—	—	—	—	—	11.1	227	12.4	224	1.3	3
PNL	—	—	—	—	—	—	4.9	101	5.2	94	3.0	7
RPT	—	—	—	—	—	—	11.6	237	11.5	208	12.3	29
DIR	—	—	—	—	—	—	.2	5	.2	4	.4	1
NCL	.2	6	.1	2	.9	4	—	—	—	—	—	—

The data in Table 23 also indicate that both the teacher and the pupil in a majority of their substantive task components call for information with empirical meaning: the teacher expects the pupil to reply to 36.1 per cent of his components with a statement of fact and to 43.4 per cent with an explanation. Similarly, the pupil expects 42.8 per cent of the responding moves to be statements of fact and 41.5 per cent to be explanatory statements. The pupil tends to call for replies with evaluative meaning more frequently than does the teacher: the pupil expects responding moves with evaluative meaning to 8.3 per cent of his components, while the teacher calls for evaluative statements in only 4.7 per cent of his components. In contrast, the teacher is more likely to call for statements with analytic meaning than is the pupil: while the teacher expects analytic statements in the replies to 15.7 per cent of his components, the pupil expects analytic statements in only 6.5 per cent of his components. Both the teacher and the pupil expect defining more frequently than they expect interpreting.

Logical and extra-logical processes with instructional tasks. In contrast to substantive tasks that involve only logical processes, instructional tasks may involve either logical processes or extra-logical processes, such as repeating, performing, and directing. When the solicitor calls for the performance of an instructional task, he expects 66.2 per cent of the responding moves to involve extra-logical processes and 33.8 per cent to involve logical processes.

Components in which the solicitor expects the performance of an oral activity, but does not call for the presentation of specific information, account for 38.4 per cent of all instructional task components. In such cases the solicitor, most frequently the teacher, calls the name of the agent (e.g., "John") and expects him to determine the nature of his own move. Almost 15 per cent of the teacher's soliciting components are of this type, and with it he controls the flow of class discussion by designating which pupils shall speak and in what order. Directing a person to perform with language in a non-oral form (such as reading and writing) and directing a speaker to repeat a statement each account for slightly more than 11 per cent of the instructional task components.

Of the instructional task components that call for tasks involving logical processes, most expect a reply with empirical meaning and most of these expect factual statements. Speakers infrequently call for instructional tasks with analytic or evaluative meaning, and even more rarely do they call for explanations of instructional matters.

The differences between the teacher's and the pupil's instructional

TABLE 24

Distribution of Soliciting Components by Information Activity for Task and Task-Speaker

Information Activity	*All*		*Substantive Task*						*Instructional Task*					
			Total		*Teacher*		*Pupil*		*Total*		*Teacher*		*Pupil*	
	%	*f*	%	*f*	%	*f*	%	*f*	%	*f*	%	*f*	%	*f*
Total	100.0	5377	100.0	3335	100.0	2889	100.0	446	100.0	2042	100.0	1806	100.0	236
Assign	18.4	988	19.1	630	12.5	360	60.5	270	17.5	358	13.3	240	50.0	118
Select	1.8	101	2.3	77	2.0	58	4.3	19	1.1	24	0.8	14	4.3	10
Construct	73.8	3968	73.0	2438	79.2	2287	33.9	151	75.0	1530	79.2	1431	41.9	99
Construct/Assign	6.0	320	5.6	190	6.3	184	1.3	6	6.4	130	6.7	121	3.8	9

task directives are much more pronounced than their differences in substantive task directives. While the teacher calls for tasks with extra-logical meaning in 72.0 per cent of his instructional task components, the pupil calls for such tasks in only 22.1 per cent of his instructional task components. On the other hand, the pupil calls for fact-stating in 50.0 per cent of his instructional task components, but the teacher calls for fact-stating in only 20.4 per cent of his instructional task components. These data indicate that the pupil generally expects specific factual information about instructional matters such as assignments and materials, while the teacher usually expects extra-logical performances such as oral activity, repeating, and directing. Another difference between the teacher and the pupil is that the pupil tends to call for interpretations of and opinions about instructional matters more frequently than does the teacher.

The Information Process Activity

In addition to indicating the logical process activity, the solicitor also specifies the information process activity necessary for the performance of the expected responding move. Table 24 summarizes the data regarding the operations the agents are expected to perform with the information presented in the soliciting move.

Constructing a response on the basis of information presented (C) is the information process called for most frequently: in 73.8 per cent of the soliciting components the speaker directs the agent to construct a responding move that completes or extends the information in the soliciting component. In 18.4 per cent of the components, the speaker directs the agent to assign a truth function (A) to the information presented; that is, to state whether the information given is true or false. The ratio of constructing processes to assigning processes is 4:1. The constructing/assigning process, in which the agent is expected to assign a truth function and/or to construct a response, accounts for only 6 per cent of the total soliciting components. In only 1.8 per cent of the soliciting components does the solicitor expect the agent to select one or more of the stated alternatives (S). The information process of selecting/assigning (S/A) was not observed in the protocols.

When one considers the substantive task components and the instructional task components separately, the percentages for the various information process activities are very much the same, as shown in Table 24. The difference in any instance is no larger than 1.8 percentage points.

The slight differences observed when relating information process and task are in contrast to the greater variability when relating information process and speaker. The teacher and the pupil differ markedly in their use of the information processes. The differences between the teacher and the pupil are highlighted when one considers the substantive task directives and the instructional task directives by the teacher and by the pupil. Of the teacher's substantive task components, 79.2 per cent call for the constructing operation (C), but the pupil expects the constructing operation in only 33.9 per cent of his substantive task components. In contrast, the pupil calls for assigning a truth function (A) in 60.5 per cent of his substantive directives, while the teacher calls for assigning a truth function in only 12.5 per cent of his substantive components. The pupil's directives thus tend to involve questions that can be answered "Yes" or "No," while the teacher's directives expect respondents to construct their own replies. For the selecting from alternatives process (S) and the constructing/assigning process (C/A) the differences between the teacher and the pupil are less pronounced.

For instructional task directives, the picture is very much as it is for substantive directives. Whereas the teacher expects the respondent to construct a reply (C) in 79.2 per cent of his instructional components, the pupil expects the agent to do so in only 41.9 per cent of his components. But when it comes to assigning a truth function (A), the pupil expects this operation in 50.0 per cent of his components, whereas the teacher expects an answer of "Yes" or "No" to only 13.3 per cent of his directives. The differences for selecting from alternatives (S) and constructing/assigning (C/A) are again not so great.

The Speakers, the Tasks, and the Primary Activities

Having analyzed the soliciting components in terms of the speakers (teacher and pupil), the tasks (substantive and instructional), and the primary activities (logical process and information process), one can gain an overview of the soliciting components by considering these factors in relation to each other. Table 25 provides an overview of the 25 principal *component types* defined in terms of speaker, task, logical process, and information process. The 25 most frequent component types account for 90.5 per cent of all soliciting components; the top 10 component types include 74 per cent of all components, while the next 15 component types account for only an additional 16.5 per cent.

Of the top 25 component types, the teacher speaks 19 and the pupil speaks 6. In 15 of the component types the speaker specifies a substantive task and in 10 he specifies an instructional task. The information process of constructing (C) accounts for 14 of the top 25

TABLE 25

The Twenty-Five Most Frequent Soliciting Component Types

Rank	% of SOL Components	f	Soliciting Component Type: Speaker	Task	Logical Activity	Information Activity
1	19.9	1070	Teacher	Sub	Explaining	Construct
2	14.3	770	Teacher	Sub	Fact-Stating	Construct
3	14.2	764	Teacher	Inst	Perform Oral	Construct
4	6.5	350	Teacher	Sub	Defining	Construct
5	4.1	223	Teacher	Inst	Perform Lang.	Construct
6	3.9	208	Teacher	Inst	Repeating	Construct
7	3.4	182	Teacher	Inst	Fact-Stating	Assign
8	3.2	172	Teacher	Sub	Fact-Stating	Assign
9	2.6	140	Pupil	Sub	Fact-Stating	Assign
10	1.9	103	Teacher	Sub	Explaining	Assign
11	1.7	94	Pupil	Sub	Explaining	Construct
12	1.7	94	Teacher	Inst	Perfrm No/Lang.	Construct
13	1.6	84	Pupil	Sub	Explaining	Assign
14	1.3	71	Teacher	Sub	Fact-Stating	C/A
15	1.3	69	Teacher	Sub	Explaining	C/A
16	1.3	68	Pupil	Inst	Fact-Stating	Assign
17	1.3	68	Teacher	Inst	Fact-Stating	Construct
18	1.1	58	Teacher	Sub	Opining	Assign
19	1.0	52	Teacher	Inst	Interpreting	Construct
20	.9	47	Teacher	Inst	Opining	Assign
21	.7	36	Pupil	Sub	Fact-Stating	Construct
22	.7	36	Pupil	Inst	Fact-Stating	Construct
23	.7	35	Teacher	Sub	Opining	Construct
24	.6	33	Teacher	Sub	Interpreting	Construct
25	.6	32	Teacher	Sub	Defining	C/A

component types, while assigning a truth function (A) accounts for 8 and constructing/assigning (C/A) accounts for 3. The information process of selecting (S) is so infrequently used that it is not included in the top 25 component types.

Of the top 10 component types, the teacher speaks 9 and the pupil speaks 1. In 6 of the top 10, the speaker calls for the performance of a substantive task and in 4 he calls for the performance of an instructional task. The information process activity is constructing (C) for the first 6 component types and is assigning a truth function (A) for the remaining 4 of the top 10. The teacher's 9 most frequent

TABLE 26

Percentage of Soliciting Components with Clues for Task and Task-Speaker

Clue	*Substantive Task*						*Instructional Task*					
	Total		*Teacher*		*Pupil*		*Total*		*Teacher*		*Pupil*	
	%	*f*	%	*f*	%	*f*	%	*f*	%	*f*	%	*f*
F-Word	68.8	2294	73.8	2131	36.5	163	16.7	342	15.2	274	28.8	68
Cite Term	0.7	25	0.8	24	0.2	1	0.1	1	0.1	1	—	—
Exclude Term	1.9	65	2.2	63	0.4	2	0.3	6	0.3	6	—	—
Parallel Term	10.0	333	11.4	329	1.0	4	1.6	33	1.7	30	1.3	3
Leading	5.8	193	2.8	82	24.9	111	2.4	49	2.2	40	3.8	9
Total Number of Soliciting Components	—	3335	—	2889	—	446	—	2042	—	1806	—	236

component types account for 81.9 per cent of the teacher's components.

Perhaps most revealing is the fact that the first 4 component types account for 54.9 per cent of all soliciting components. The teacher speaks all 4 component types; in all 4 the teacher specifies that the information process activity is to be constructing (C); in 2 of the 4 he expects the empirical process activity; and in 3 of the 4 he expects the performance of a substantive task.

Clues Regarding Appropriate Terms

The speaker of a soliciting move frequently gives clues regarding terms that are appropriate for the responding move. The clue most frequently given is the propositional function word, or F-word (e.g., "*What* do you think?"). The solicitor presents an F-word in 49.0 per cent of all soliciting components. The next most frequently observed clue is a clue to parallelism, which the solicitor presents in 6.8 per cent of all components. The solicitor presents a leading expression indicating which truth function is expected (e.g., "Don't you think that . . .") in 4.5 per cent of all components. Seldom does the solicitor present those clues most directly related to the terms of the expected response—citing terms and excluding terms: the speaker cites terms in only 0.5 per cent of the components and excludes terms in only 1.3 per cent of the components.

Clues regarding appropriate terms are given more frequently in components that call for substantive tasks than in those that call for instructional tasks: 87 per cent of all clues appear in substantive directives, while only 13 per cent appear in instructional directives. Furthermore, it is usually the teacher rather than the pupil who offers clues: the teacher presents 89.2 per cent of all clues observed in the discourse.

The data summarized in Table 26 indicate that the teacher and the pupil differ greatly in their use of the various clues. For the teacher-substantive components, 73.8 per cent contain an F-word, but for the pupil-substantive components, only 36.5 per cent contain an F-word. The reverse relationship is observed when the task is instructional: the pupil uses an F-word in 28.8 per cent of his instructional components, but the teacher uses an F-word in only 15.2 per cent of his instructional components. Neither teacher nor pupil frequently uses the leading expression when the task is an instructional one, but the pupil does provide a lead for 24.9 per cent of his substantive components, while the teacher offers a lead in only 2.8 per cent of his substantive components. The pupil offers clues less often than the teacher. However, the pupil does offer clues more often than does

TABLE 27

Distribution of Propositional Function Words by Task and Task-Speaker

Propositional Function Word	Total		Substantive Task						Instructional Task					
			Total		Teacher		Pupil		Total		Teacher		Pupil	
	%	*f*	%	*f*	%	*f*	%	*f*	%	*f*	%	*f*	%	*f*
All Combined	100.0	2636	100.0	2994	100.0	2131	100.0	163	100.0	342	100.0	274	100.0	68
What	46.3	1219	43.5	997	44.8	955	25.8	42	64.9	222	69.3	190	47.1	32
What About	2.4	64	2.3	52	1.9	41	6.7	11	3.5	12	2.9	8	5.9	4
What Type	3.8	101	4.4	101	4.7	100	.6	1	—	—	—	—	—	—
How	7.4	195	8.0	183	7.2	153	18.5	30	3.5	12	3.3	9	4.4	3
Why	17.1	451	19.0	437	18.6	397	24.6	40	4.1	14	4.0	11	4.4	3
Who	3.2	84	2.8	64	2.6	56	4.9	8	5.8	20	7.3	20	—	—
When	.6	16	0.5	12	.5	11	.6	1	1.2	4	.4	1	4.4	3
Where	3.6	94	3.4	78	3.2	68	6.1	10	4.7	16	3.3	9	10.3	7
How Much	3.3	88	3.3	75	3.1	65	6.1	10	3.8	13	2.2	6	10.3	7
Which	12.3	324	12.8	295	13.4	285	6.1	10	8.5	29	7.3	20	13.2	9

the teacher when the task is an instructional one; the pupil presents 33.9 per cent of his instructional tasks with a clue, while the teacher presents only 18.9 per cent with a clue.

Propositional function words. Table 27 presents data showing the frequency with which the teacher and the pupil use F-words in relation to the task called for. The most frequently used F-word is the general "what" (e.g., *What* do you suggest?): "what" is used in 46.3 per cent of all soliciting components that include F-words. The teacher uses "what" in 44.8 per cent of the substantive task directives in which he presents an F-word, "why" in 18.6 per cent, and "which" in 13.4 per cent. In contrast, the pupil uses "what" in 25.8 per cent of the substantive task directives in which he presents an F-word, "how" in 18.5 per cent, and "why" in 24.6 per cent. The pupil relies less heavily on the general "what" than does the teacher in substantive directives; instead, he is somewhat more likely to use "why" and "how."

That "what" is the primary F-word is even more apparent when one considers their use in the instructional directives. The teacher uses "what" in 69.3 per cent of all of his instructional components that include an F-word, and the pupil uses "what" in 47.1 per cent of all his instructional components that include an F-word.

The Type of Behavior and the Occasion

Each soliciting move is presented to one or more persons in the class and is designed to elicit some type of behavior that is to occur at some designated time and place.

The data show that the solicitors expect linguistic behavior in response to 98.1 per cent of the 5,377 soliciting components. It is only with an instructional task that the speaker may call for non-linguistic behavior, such as setting up classroom equipment or distributing materials. He does so in only 5 per cent of the instructional task directives. The teacher speaks almost all of the components to which a non-linguistic responding move is appropriate. In contrast, the pupil speaks only 7 such moves, and he never addresses one to the teacher.

The solicitors indicate that they expect 87.7 per cent of responding moves to be presented immediately and expect 98.1 per cent of the responding moves to occur within the classroom. The pupil never expects the teacher to defer action or to act outside the classroom. Furthermore, the pupil never expects a fellow pupil to defer action, and in only one of his 682 solicitations does he expect a fellow pupil to act outside the classroom. The teacher is more likely to expect deferred action and action outside the classroom, and the majority of deferred/out-of-class expectations are teacher's instructions about assignments.

Stylistic Meaning

Stylistic meaning, which describes the action of the solicitor and not the anticipated action of the agent, refers to the solicitor's manner of presenting the indicative meaning; that is, "how" he makes his expectation known.

Length of solicitations. The mean length of soliciting moves in terms of lines of typescript is 1.9. This contrasts with the mean length of 9.1 lines for structuring, 3.5 lines for reacting, and 2.0 lines for responding. Teacher soliciting moves tend to be longer than pupil soliciting moves: the mean number of lines in teacher soliciting moves is 1.9 lines, while the mean for the pupil is 1.5. The teacher substantive directive averages 2.0 lines, while the average teacher instructional directive is 1.7 lines.

Mode of presentation. The solicitor may present the soliciting component as a request, as a command, or as an assertion to which the agent is expected to respond. The data indicate that the teacher presents 65.5 per cent of his soliciting components as a request for action, while the pupil presents 90.6 per cent of his components as a request. On the other hand, the teacher expresses the solicitation as a command for action when he presents 29.8 per cent of his components, but the pupil presents only 7.6 per cent of his components as a command. Clearly, the major mode is the request, and the teacher is freer to command action than is the pupil.

In terms of speaker and task, the solicitors use the command chiefly with the instructional task, and the teacher uses the command to a greater extent than does the pupil. The teacher presents 4.6 per cent of his substantive task components as commands, while the pupil presents only 1.4 per cent of his substantive task components as a command. When the task is an instructional one, however, the teacher presents 70 per cent of the components as a command, but the pupil presents only 19.5 per cent as a command.

The speakers present 3 per cent of all soliciting moves as assertions; that is, the solicitors present 163 of the components as statements intended to be taken as calls to action. This finding suggests the limitation in considering all response-expectant moves as "questions."

Construction of component. The teacher, rather than the pupil, is likely to use special constructions in presenting the soliciting move. The teacher presents half of his instructional tasks in an elliptical manner and over 10 per cent of his substantive tasks in a conditional context, in an incomplete manner, and/or with interlarded information. The pupil's use of special constructions exceeds the teacher's use in only one respect: the pupil more frequently presents his substantive tasks in a conditional context than does the teacher.

The greatest difference between the teacher and the pupil is their presentation of components in an incomplete manner. The use of this construction suggests that the speaker did not initially intend to solicit, but changed his intent after he had begun to speak. The data indicate that the pupil infrequently solicits in this way, and the teacher seldom does when the task is an instructional one. When the teacher presents a substantive task, however, he presents 12.3 per cent as incomplete (for example, "We usually import very little of our foodstuffs, instead we generally . . .").

Interlarding information is more frequent with substantive tasks, and the teacher interlards information twice as often as does the pupil. Paralleling this observation is the fact that it is the teacher who frequently amplifies the nature of the primary activities; 17 per cent of all teacher components are amplified by rephrasing or clarifying. That amplification is more frequently observed with substantive tasks than with instructional tasks might indicate that the teacher is more certain of the response he wants to elicit when he talks about instructional matters than when he talks about the subject matter under study.

The use of the incomplete construction, interlarding, and amplifying by the teacher suggests he does not think out his solicitations so carefully as does the pupil, who generally must seek permission before he speaks. In other words, the pupil thinks out his move, seeks permission to make the move, and then speaks. The data seem to indicate that in many instances the teacher does not think carefully about the move before speaking, but attempts to formulate his expectation as he speaks.

Composition of the move. Only 242, or 4.7 per cent, of all soliciting moves are two-component moves. The teacher speaks all but 7 of the two-component moves. When the teacher speaks these moves, he usually expects one of the tasks to be substantive in nature and frequently expects both tasks to be substantive. When the teacher presents more than one task in a move, he most frequently expects the same information process for both tasks but expects the performance of two different logical process activities. In such two-component moves, the information process is usually constructing and the logical process activities are generally fact-stating and explaining.

The Responding Move

Responding moves account for about 30 per cent of all moves spoken in the discourse. The median percentage is 27.6 for the 15 classes, from a high of 33.6 per cent in Class 13 to a low of 23.5 per cent in Class 5. As indicated in Table 28, the responding move plays

TABLE 28

Percentage of the Teachers' and Pupils' Moves and Lines Devoted to Responding for Each of the Fifteen Classes and for All Classes Combined

	Teacher		*Pupil*	
Class	*Moves*	*Lines*	*Moves*	*Lines*
All Combined	5.5	6.8	65.4	57.5
1	1.8	1.6	76.1	76.0
2	2.2	1.6	67.1	62.8
3	3.2	5.2	70.2	59.9
4	4.4	5.7	65.2	64.2
5	9.9	15.3	42.7	36.7
6	4.1	6.0	77.6	80.3
7	9.2	10.5	58.9	47.9
8	6.8	11.5	59.4	55.3
9	2.1	0.9	80.6	80.8
10	4.0	7.0	66.7	55.9
11	2.8	3.5	80.9	51.6
12	10.5	9.0	44.6	37.4
13	6.0	8.3	75.1	73.8
14	3.6	4.1	74.2	62.2
15	9.2	14.9	55.4	44.1

a more significant part in the pupil's discourse than it does in the teacher's discourse; responding moves account for 65.4 per cent of the pupil's moves but only 5.5 per cent of the teacher's moves. In every class the pupil speaks as least three-fourths of all responding moves.

The chief significance of the responding move is that it serves to fulfill the expectation of the soliciting move. By relating dimensions of the responding move to dimensions of the soliciting move that elicited it, one can determine to what extent the responding move actually fulfills the expectation of the soliciting move. Congruence, a measure of the observed reciprocity that exists between the responding move and the soliciting move, is observed for the task and for the two primary activities—the logical process activity and the information process activity.

Task congruence. The task the solicitor expects the agent to perform is either a substantive task or an instructional task. As indicated in Table 29, the respondent usually performs a task that is consistent with the expectation of the solicitor: in 92 per cent of the 4,705 responding components, the respondent performs a task expected by the solicitor. In 3.3 per cent of the responding components the respondent ignores a task specified by the solicitor in a two-task solicitation, and in 1.9 per cent of the responding components the respondent performs a task not anticipated by the solicitor. In only 2.8 per cent of the responding components does the respondent perform a task that is incongruent with the expressed expectation of the solicitor.

The teacher occasionally performs tasks not anticipated by the solicitor. The unsolicited task added by the teacher is usually an instructional one: 42 of the 47 tasks the teacher adds are instructional in nature. In contrast, pupils occasionally perform tasks that are incongruent with the expressed expectation of the solicitor or ignore the task. The pupil as respondent ignores 137 substantive tasks and 17 instructional tasks; in addition, he speaks 52 substantive responding components and 49 instructional responding components that are incongruent with the solicitor's expectation.

Logical process congruence. The logical process activity, as one of the primary activities specified by the solicitor, is directly related to the task. When the respondent does not perform a task consistent with the solicitor's expectation, the respondent cannot perform the task-related logical process. Since 8 per cent of the responding components represent tasks that are inconsistent with the solicitor's expectation, in 92 per cent of the responding move components there is a logical process activity that is congruent with the expectation of the solicitor.

There are four types of logical process congruence: primary, ascending modal, descending modal, and implicit congruence. Primary congruence indicates that the respondent uses the logical process within each of the three modes according to the solicitor's expectation; for example, the solicitor expects fact-stating and the respondent answers with a factual statement, or the solicitor expects explaining and the respondent replies with an explanation. Ascending modal congruence indicates that the respondent uses the more complex process within a given logical mode; for example, the solicitor expects fact-stating, but the respondent replies with explaining. In the case of descending modal congruence, the reverse is the case: the solicitor expects the more complex process within a given logical mode (e.g., explaining), but the respondent uses the less complex (e.g., fact-stating). Implicit congruence indicates that the solicitor did not specify a particular logical process activity, but left the choice to the respondent.

Modal logical incongruence indicates that the respondent uses a

TABLE 29

Distribution of Responding Components According to Task and Logical Activity Congruence

Task and Logical Process Activity Congruence	*Teacher and Pupil*		*Teacher Responding Component*				*Pupil Responding Component*			
			Substantive		*Instructional*		*Substantive*		*Instructional*	
	%	*f*	%	*f*	%	*f*	%	*f*	%	*f*
Total	100.0	4705	100.0	356	100.0	218	100.0	3548	100.0	583
Task										
Incongruent	2.8	131	3.9	14	7.3	16	1.5	52	8.4	49
Ignored	3.3	156	.5	2	—	—	3.9	137	2.9	17
Added	1.9	89	1.4	5	19.3	42	.6	20	3.8	22
Logical Process Activity										
Primary Congruence	84.0	3951	77.2	275	69.3	151	86.0	3054	80.8	471
Ascending Modal Congruence	3.8	181	12.7	45	2.8	6	3.6	126	.7	4
Descending Modal Congruence	1.2	56	2.6	9	—	—	1.2	43	.7	4
Implicit Congruence	1.8	87	.3	1	.4	1	2.2	78	1.2	7
Modal Incongruence	1.2	54	1.4	5	.9	2	1.0	38	1.5	9

logical mode different from that expected by the solicitor; for example, the solicitor expects opining or justifying (evaluative mode) and the respondent answers with fact-stating or explaining (empirical mode).

The data in Table 29 show that there is primary congruence between the expected and the observed logical process activity in 84 per cent of the responding move components. Primary congruence is highest in the pupil-substantive task responding components and is lowest in the teacher-instructional task responding components, where the percentages are 86 and 69.3 respectively.

In general, neither the teacher nor the pupil as respondent tends to use the more complex process when the less complex process will suffice. Ascending modal congruence accounts for only 3.8 per cent of all responding move components. Although in terms of frequencies ascending congruence is most often observed in pupil-substantive responding moves, ascending congruence accounts for a larger percentage of teacher-substantive task responding components. Ascending congruence is seldom related to an instructional task.

Descending modal congruence (1.2 per cent) is less frequently observed than is ascending modal congruence (3.8 per cent). As with ascending modal congruence, descending modal congruence accounts for a larger percentage of the teacher-substantive responding components (2.6 per cent), but is most frequently observed with the pupil-substantive task components (43 components, 1.2 per cent).

Modal logical incongruence, in which the respondent's logical mode is different from that expected by the solicitor, occurs in only 54, or 1.2 per cent, of the 4,705 responding components. Pupil responses account for 47. Implicit congruence accounts for 87, or 1.8 per cent, of all responding move components; of these, almost all occur with pupil-substantive task components.

Information process congruence. The analysis of the soliciting move components shows that the teacher, as the chief solicitor, most frequently expects the constructing process, and the pupil most frequently expects the assigning process. In terms of the responding move, the teacher is expected to assign truth functions and the pupil is expected to construct.

The data included in Table 30 indicate that the teacher and the pupil use the expected information process in 87.0 per cent of the responding components, while 7.7 per cent of their responding components are incongruent with the soliciting components that elicited them.

The teacher uses the expected information process in 75.8 per cent of his substantive components and in 61.9 per cent of his in-

TABLE 30

Distribution of Responding Components According to Information Activity Congruence

Information Activity Congruence	*Teacher and Pupil*		*Teacher Responding Component*				*Pupil Responding Component*			
			Substantive		*Instructional*		*Substantive*		*Instructional*	
	%	*f*	%	*f*	%	*f*	%	*f*	%	*f*
Total	100.0	4705	100.0	356	100.0	218	100.0	3548	100.0	583
Congruent	87.0	4096	75.8	270	61.9	135	90.3	3203	83.7	488
Assigning	11.6	548	40.5	144	28.9	63	6.7	236	18.0	105
Selecting	1.5	72	2.5	9	3.2	7	1.3	47	1.5	9
Constructing	68.6	3228	31.7	113	27.5	60	76.4	2711	59.1	344
Construct/Assigning	5.3	248	1.1	4	2.3	5	5.9	209	5.1	30
Incongruent	7.7	363	21.9	78	18.8	41	5.3	188	9.6	56
Assigning	6.3	295	19.8	70	15.7	34	4.5	157	5.8	34
Selecting	.7	35	1.9	7	2.3	5	.5	18	.9	5
Constructing	.2	9	—	—	.4	1	.1	5	.5	3
Construct/Assigning	.5	24	.2	1	.4	1	.2	8	2.4	14
Ignored	3.4	157	.8	3	—	—	3.9	137	2.9	17
Assigning	1.2	55	—	—	.4	1	.1	5	.5	3
Selecting	.1	3	—	—	—	—	.1	3	—	—
Constructing	1.8	85	—	—	—	—	2.1	73	2.1	12
Construct/Assigning	.3	14	.2	1	—	—	.3	11	.3	2
Component Added	1.9	89	1.5	5	19.3	42	.5	20	3.8	22

structional components. In contrast, the pupil uses the expected information process in 90.3 per cent of his substantive components and in 83.7 per cent of his instructional components.

The incidence of information process incongruence is 21.7 per cent for the teacher's substantive components and 18.6 per cent for his instructional components. In contrast, 5.3 per cent of the pupil's substantive-task components and 9.6 per cent of the pupil's instructional-task components are incongruent.

The percentage of congruence is highest for the teacher in substantive responding components in which the information process is constructing: all of the teacher's substantive-constructing components, which account for 19.7 per cent of all teacher responding components, reflect basic congruence. Similarly, the percentage of congruence is highest for the pupil in substantive-task components in which the information process is constructing: 97.2 per cent of the pupil's substantive-constructing components reflect operational congruence. Such components account for 67.5 per cent of all pupil responding components.

The percentage of incongruence is highest when the processes are selecting and assigning. When the expected information process is assigning a truth function, both teachers and pupils present one-third of their response components with incongruent processes. When the expected information process is selecting, the teacher does not fulfill the expectation in 42.8 per cent of the responding components, and the pupil does not fulfill the expectation in 28 per cent of the responding components.

Observation of the congruence between responding components and the soliciting components warrants the conclusions that the teacher performs the expected information process less often than the pupil; the teacher does so most frequently when the anticipated process is assigning or selecting.

Summary

Summarized below are the principal results of the analysis:

1. Reflexive moves are more numerous than initiatory moves; nevertheless, the initiatory soliciting move is the most frequently made move. In each of the 15 classes about one-third of all moves are soliciting moves.

2. The teacher is the chief solicitor; he speaks 86.9 per cent of all soliciting moves. For the teacher, 46.6 per cent of his moves are solicitations, while for the pupil only 11.3 per cent are solicitations.

3. The teacher and the pupil expect the performance of a substantive task in about 60 per cent of their moves and the performance of an instructional task in approximately 40 per cent of their moves. In no class do the speakers expect less than 45 per cent of responding moves to involve a substantive task.

4. The solicitor seldom presents more than one task in the solicitation; when he does, one of them is usually a substantive task. In the two-task move, the solicitor usually expects two different logical process activities but the same information process activity for both tasks. The logical processes are most often stating and explaining, and the information process is usually constructing.

5. The solicitor generally expects the respondent to act immediately within the classroom. In few moves does the solicitor indicate that he expects either delayed action or action outside the classroom.

6. The solicitor most frequently expects the respondent to give information with empirical meaning. When the task is substantive, the solicitor more often expects explaining than fact-stating. The solicitor infrequently expects responses with analytic meaning or evaluative meaning; however, he expects responses with analytic meaning more frequently than he expects responses with evaluative meaning. With instructional tasks, the teacher generally expects extra-logical meanings, while the pupil expects fact-stating.

7. The information processes in order of observed frequency for all speakers are constructing, assigning a truth function, constructing/assigning, and selecting from stated alternatives. The teacher and the pupil differ sharply in their use of the information process: the teacher expects the constructing operation much more frequently than does the pupil, while the pupil calls for assigning a truth function much more frequently than does the teacher.

8. The clue the solicitor most frequently gives to indicate the terms appropriate for the responding move is the propositional function word. The most frequently observed function word is "what." The second most frequent clue the solicitor gives is the clue to parallel terms. The solicitor rarely cites terms or indicates that certain terms are to be excluded from the responding move.

9. When the teacher solicits, he usually expects one pupil to respond; when the pupil solicits, he usually expects the teacher to respond. The intended interaction, regardless of who solicits, is almost always between teacher and pupil, rather than between pupil and pupil.

10. The solicitor almost always expects the respondent to use language in performing the specified task. While the teacher may

sometimes call the performance of actions that do not involve language, the pupil almost never does so.

11. The length of the average soliciting move is about one and one-half lines of typescript. The teacher's moves are generally longer than the pupil's, and the substantive task moves are longer than the instructional task moves.

12. The solicitor usually presents the soliciting move as a request rather than as an assertion or as a command. The teacher is freer to command action than is the pupil.

13. The respondent performs the task expected by the solicitor in 92 per cent of the responding moves. He generally performs the logical process activity and the information process activity related to the task as expected. The pupil in making responding moves to substantive task solicitations performs most often as expected, while the teacher in response to instructional task solicitations shows the lowest rate of congruence. In terms of the logical processes, the pupil tends to shift from one logical mode to another and thereby present logically incongruent responses, while the teacher is likely to shift from one process to another but stay within the mode in those moves that are not primarily congruent. With the information processes in those moves that are not primarily congruent, both respondents, but especially the teacher, are likely to ignore the processes of selecting from alternatives and assigning a truth function.

CHAPTER FIVE

THE STRUCTURING MOVE

THE STRUCTURING MOVE is an initiatory move; it sets the context for classroom behavior by launching or halting-excluding interaction between teacher and pupils and by indicating the nature of the interaction. As an initiatory maneuver, the structuring move is not called out by anything in the immediate classroom situation except the speaker's notion of what should be said or taught. Like soliciting, also an initiatory move, the structuring move conveys *directive meaning.* However, unlike solicitations, which explicitly direct the person(s) addressed to respond, structuring moves implicitly direct classroom activities by setting the context for the behavior of teacher and pupils.

The first section of this chapter presents the conceptual framework underlying the analysis of structuring moves; the second section outlines the system for analysis derived from the conceptual framework; and the third section presents a description of structuring moves in the 15 classes studied.

Conceptual Framework

Two concepts were fruitful in suggesting categories of analysis with which to describe the functions of structuring moves: (1) the notion of the sub-game as a segment of the teaching game and (2) the concept of directive meaning.

The Sub-Game in the Classroom Game

Just as a football game consists of four quarters of play and a baseball game of nine innings, the classroom game is made up of segments which are designated "sub-games." In this research, the unit on international trade is viewed as a classroom game. Within this game, there are sub-units or sub-games, each of which is identified primarily by the type of activity that is the focus of attention during a given period of play. Student debates, class discussions, viewing films, pupil reports, and taking examinations are examples of activities that compose sub-games.

In carrying out the function of setting the context for classroom interaction, speakers of structuring moves may set the context for the entire classroom game and/or one or more of the sub-games. For example, on the first day of a unit of work the teacher may structure the game as a whole by announcing the topic for the unit and indicating the nature of the subject matter to be studied. Or the teacher may structure a sub-game by announcing a debate, a field trip, or a pupil report. On occasion, the teacher may in a single move structure both the game as a whole and one or more sub-games.

Directive Meaning

The notion of directive meaning as developed by Wellman provides the framework for studying the directive functions of structuring moves. According to Wellman, "Any sentence which directs action or tells someone to do something may be said to have directive meaning" (21:228). For Wellman, directive meaning has three basic features: indication, quasi-comparison, and prescription-prohibition. Indication refers to the agent who is to perform the action, the object involved in the action, and the time reference. For example, in the sentence "John, please paint the kitchen door tomorrow," John, the door, and tomorrow are the agent, the object, and the time reference respectively. Quasi-comparison specifies the action to be performed; in the example just cited, painting is the action to be performed. Prescription-prohibition, the central feature of directive meaning, refers to prescribing or prohibiting the performance of an action.

Structuring moves may be said to express directive meaning as it is interpreted by Wellman. The central feature of directive meaning, prescription-prohibition, parallels the central feature of structuring: speakers of structuring moves get activities under way, halt activities, and on occasion exclude activities before they get under way. The student chairman who says "Our next topic for discussion is the Common Market" performs the function of *launching* discussion on the topic of the Common Market. Because in actual classroom discourse it is difficult to distinguish between the functions of excluding activities and halting activities, we combined these two functions into one function and labeled it *halting-excluding*. The teacher who says, "That's the end of our time for debate" performs the function of halting-excluding. These two functions, launching and halting-excluding, are the central features of structuring as directive discourse.

Wellman's other features of directive meaning also apply to structuring. Speakers launch and halt-exclude such classroom events as debating, reporting, voting, and collecting homework. These performances, labeled *activities,* parallel Wellman's features of quasi-comparison. Speakers also indicate the *agent* who is to perform these activities. The agent may be the teacher, a pupil, some combination of these classroom participants, or some outside person. Furthermore, speakers frequently make reference to a *time* factor in connection with the activities, either the *beginning point* (i.e., when the game or sub-game is to get under way) or the *duration* (i.e., how long the game or sub-game is to continue).

Speakers may also indicate the *topic* for discussion or for study and the *cognitive process* for dealing with that topic. For example, a teacher might say, "Let's discuss why the Common Market was organized." In this case the teacher announces the topic of Promoting Free Trade (PFT) and the logical process of explaining (XPL).

Although Wellman's concept of *method* also applies to structuring, the specific categories for this dimension differ from Wellman's categories and are unique to structuring. Examination of the protocols revealed that there are three methods by which speakers carry out the functions of launching and halting-excluding. First, a speaker might simply announce to the class the topic for discussion (e.g., "Let's now go into the Common Market") and then proceed to entertain questions about it; in this instance, the speaker launches the discussion by *announcing.* On the other hand, a speaker might begin a discussion of the Common Market by tracing its historical development and analyzing its purposes, without explicitly announcing his topic; in this case, the speaker launches by *stating propositions* about the subject. Or a speaker might launch a discussion on the Common Market both by announcing the topic and by tracing its historical development; in this case the speaker launches by *announcing and stating propositions.*

The dimensions of function, method, activity, topic, cognitive process, agent, beginning point in time, and duration of time describe the directive features of structuring moves. Three other dimensions of structuring, although not included in Wellman's concept of directive meaning, merit attention because they describe significant features of classroom discourse: reason-giving, instructional aids, and regulations.

Explaining by giving reasons for an event or state of affairs (XPL) is one of the cognitive processes used in dealing with substantive material; this includes, for example, giving explanations of why countries engage in international trade and why Europeans established the Common Market. In the analysis of structuring moves, there is yet another kind of reason-giving that is pedagogically significant. The concept of reason-giving as it relates to structuring is concerned not with substantive explanations but rather with reasons for the game or sub-game and their various dimensions. For example, a speaker may give reasons why he is launching a certain topic or why he is halting a pupil report.

Examination of the protocols reveals that classroom activities often involve the use of instructional aids such as charts, graphs, newspaper articles, textbooks, and films. Frequently the speaker of a structuring move uses or calls for the use of instructional aids such as these, and we therefore included categories to describe them.

Regulations, the third additional dimension, refers to the rules governing classroom behavior. In directing classroom behavior, the speaker of a structuring move often gives regulations regarding the scope of the topic under study, time sequence, administration, and the "mental associations" to be made. Scope specifies what shall be included in the subject matter for discussion; time sequence refers to the order in which announced activities are to occur; administration refers to the use of materials, the roles of participants, and other aspects of classroom management; and "mental associations" refers to what the participants are to do mentally as the activities proceed, such as keeping certain facts in mind and drawing connections between ideas.

The concept of game/sub-game and the concept of directive meaning establish the conceptual framework for the analysis of structuring moves. The features of directive meaning are viewed as dimensions of the game/sub-game and are described with each game/sub-game identified. As indicated previously, within a single structuring move a speaker may structure the entire game and/or one or more sub-games. When two or more sub-games are structured within a single structuring move, each sub-game is described in a component in terms of the dimensions indicated above.

System for Analysis of Structuring Moves

Content Analysis System: Structuring Move and Game/Sub-Game

1. *The structuring move* is one of four pedagogical moves that describe in functional terms the verbal maneuvers of the teacher and the pupil in playing the classroom game of teaching. Structuring moves serve the pedagogical function of setting the context for subse-

quent behavior in the classroom by (a) launching or halting-excluding interaction between pupils and teachers and (b) indicating the nature of the interaction in terms of the dimensions of time, agent, activity, topic and cognitive process, regulations, reasons, and instructional aids. Structuring moves may set the context for the entire classroom game and/or one or more sub-games. Each game or sub-game identified in a structuring move is coded as a component of the structuring move. Structuring moves are initiatory moves that do not elicit a response, are not in themselves direct responses, and are not called out by anything in the immediate classroom situation except the speaker's notion of what should be said or taught.

The postscript -A is added to a structuring move (STR-A) when the move is a result of an assignment, such as student reports or debates. The postscript serves to distinguish moves of this kind from structuring moves that have not been previously assigned.

2. *The game and sub-game* are the basic units for describing the structuring move. The verbal behavior of the classroom is viewed as a language game that is composed of smaller sets of actions called sub-games. A sub-game is a set of actions with regulations performed by agents during a given period of time and presumably carried out for certain reasons. The various sub-games together constitute the game as a whole.

For this research, the game is the unit of study on international trade. Examples of sub-games are: a formal debate of two teams of pupils for part of a class session, the viewing of a twenty-minute film on the Common Market by the entire class, and a class discussing foreign investments for an entire session.

Examples

T/STR: Let's now discuss direct investment overseas by Americans. (One sub-game)

T/STR: After we have our debate by the two terms, I shall open the floor for questions, and then I'll let you vote on the issue. (Three sub-games whose activities are debating, questioning from the floor, and voting)

T/STR: Today we begin our unit on trade. We'll be working on it for the entire week. As you know from our discussion in current events, this is a most important topic today. . . . (This move structures for the entire game of international trade)

Content Analysis System: Dimensions of the Game/Sub-Game

Ten dimensions of the game/sub-game are included in the analysis of the structuring move: (1) function; (2) method; (3) activity; (4)

agent; (5) topic; (6) cognitive process; (7) time; (8) regulation; (9) instructional aid; and (10) reason-giving. Within each component these ten dimensions are identified when they appear and are coded according to the rules of analysis described in Appendix B.

1. *Function.* The speaker performs the function of launching or halting-excluding the game/sub-game.

1.1. *Launching.* Structuring moves that launch start the game or sub-game on a specified course. The speaker may launch the activity, agent, substantive topic, instructional topic, and cognitive process. He may also indicate the time, regulations, instructional aids to be used, and reasons for the game/sub-game or for one of the dimensions of the game/sub-game.

Examples

T/STR: Now then, could we talk about the importance of investments. In your text they make quite a point of the relationship—and very justly so—of the relationship between trade imports and investment. Because after all money is exported just like anything else in many respects.

T/STR: This topic of the Common Market will be covered in a film which we'll show in just a few minutes.

T/STR: Well, let me try to steer you in the right direction, Jane. Let me by asking you perhaps a question or two.

P/STR: I want to ask a question.

1.2. *Halting-excluding.* To halt-exclude a game or a sub-game is to set it outside the limits of the activities of the class. The speaker may halt-exclude the dimensions of activity, topic, and cognitive process.

Examples

T/STR: Let's leave out all the products and articles connected with the difference between an area that can and an area that cannot. Let's take something like beef cattle. Now cattle can be raised in large parts of the world. We can raise them in the U.S. We can raise them in Argentina. We raise them in most of Europe.

T/STR: This is the end of our time for debate between the two sides.

T/STR: I think for strategic reasons this would be a good point for us to break.

2. *Method.* Method refers to the way the speaker carries out the functions of launching and halting-excluding. There are two basic methods: announcing and stating propositions. A speaker may use one or both methods in launching and halting-excluding.

2.1. *Announcing.* To announce is to name or give notice about one or more dimensions of the game or sub-game: beginning point in time, duration of time, agent, activity, substantive topic, instructional topic, cognitive process, regulations, instructional aids, and reasons.

Examples

T/STR: Now let's take the importance of foreign investment. And of course we're speaking here in general. We just want to clarify it in our own minds.

T/STR: . . . For tomorrow we'll take the fourth and last chapter and then on Friday you will see just what this week has earned on this question of international trade.

T/STR: Perhaps now in the minute or two that we have left, we might talk about one of the important aspects of world trade and that is tariffs.

T/STR: Finally, let's discuss the differences and similarities between foreign and domestic trade.

2.2. *Stating propositions.* To state propositions is to deal with the subject matter under study by using analytic, empirical, or evaluative language. For description of these logical processes see pp. 22–26.

Examples

T/STR: And we listened to Dr. Nkrumah who runs Ghana and agreed to build this dam for them. The idea was that at the bottom of the dam there would be a complete aluminum smelter and factory so that Ghana could turn out finished aluminum products . . . .

P/STR-A: Most of you probably know that South America—most of the South American countries are one-profit economies. You've learned also that this—this isn't very ambitious for a country—'cause the great industrial nations like the United States or West Europe, they are dependent on them providing progress . . . .

2.3. *Announcing and stating propositions.* To announce and state propositions is to combine the two methods described above in launching or halting-excluding a game or sub-game.

Examples

P/STR-A: I am going to report on the Balance of Payments. (Announcing) In the past few years the gold supply of the U.S. has steadily decreased due to . . . . (Stating proposition)

T/STR: Now, export control. (Announcing) By export control we mean the government can say to a businessman, "You can't send cloth to China." (Stating proposition)

3. *Activity.* Activity refers to oral and non-oral performances carried on by the teacher and pupils.

3.1. *General oral activity.* The speaker indicates that the activity will be oral but does not specify the type of oral activity. Words such as talk, leads into, raise, discuss, take up, go into, come back to, move into are indications that the activity will be oral.

Examples

T/STR: Now then could we talk about the importance of investments . . . .

T/STR: . . . then we're going to move into some of the problems presented by this overall pattern of world trade.

3.2. *Questioning-answering.* The speaker indicates that the activity will be asking questions and answering questions.

Examples

P/STR: I want to ask you a question.

T/STR: Let me steer you in the right direction—since this is your report, I will ask you questions about it.

3.3. *Reporting.* The speaker indicates that the activity will be a report addressed to the class by one or several participants.

Examples

T/STR: Linda, I know your report is ready and I'm going to let you give it for all of the class in a minute.

T/STR: This naturally leads us to another area that we pick up—I think we have another group—series of projects tomorrow—reports on the Common Market.

3.4. *Debating.* The speaker indicates that the activity will be debating pro and con on a particular resolution by two or more class participants. Debating includes the presentation of position, rebuttal, and summary of position.

Example

T/STR: All right, today we have scheduled a debate. Now I hope the debate will last all period and I think the issue is controversial enough to go on for more than a period . . . .

3.5. *Viewing/listening to audio-visual device.* The speaker indicates that the activity will be viewing and/or listening to a film, phonograph record, film strip, television, radio, or other audio-visual device.

Example

T/STR: We have a film. I'm going to show only part of it, not the total film. The film deals with the Common Market.

3.6. *Holding a panel discussion.* The speaker indicates that the activity will be a formal panel discussion.

Example

T/STR: . . . the next day looking at Mr. Kennedy's trade program—his new tariff program, as well as taking a look at your panel.

3.7. *Following up a formal presentation.* The speaker indicates that the activity will be a discussion based on a formal presentation of a report, debate, film, or the like. The following-up activity means that there will be "comments from the floor" following the presentation.

Example

T/STR: . . . After the general debate, I will ask each of the sides to summarize their points of view and then we will entertain questions from the floor.

3.8. *Reading and/or reading and note taking.* The speaker indicates that the activity will be silent or oral reading and/or reading and taking notes.

Example

T/STR: I'm going to read from the book a paragraph concerning the similarities of domestic and international trade . . . . "Trade takes place between countries . . . ."

3.9. *Taking an examination.* The speaker indicates that the activity will be taking an examination or test.

Example

T/STR: This announcement may shock you but part of this course is to see just what after a week of classroom discussion you have learned if anything. So tomorrow you will be tested as a post-war, I guess would be right, as a post-test to compare with the results of the pre-test of last Friday . . . .

3.10. *Writing.* The speaker indicates that the activity will be writing, other than taking a test, such as filling out a routine questionnaire, taking notes, or writing a composition.

Example

T/STR: Now then, we'll take a few minutes to fill out that little card sent down from the office. I hope you all know your dad's phone number at work.

3.11. *Voting.* The speaker indicates that the activity will be voting on a particular issue. Voting may be by show of hands, by written ballot, or by voice.

Example

T/STR: . . . After all of that is over I will ask the members of the class to vote on the strength of the evidence presented—not on any foregone conclusion or other ideas but on the strength of the evidence presented which argument you thing is better. So I will ask you to vote for a side.

3.12. *Giving instructions.* The speaker indicates that the activity will be the giving of instructions to the participants regarding class assignments, class procedures, or general school business.

Example

T/STR: And after you copy down the titles, I will tell you how I would suggest you go about this.

3.13. *Meeting in small groups.* The speaker indicates that the activity will be a small group discussion or committee work on a specified topic.

Example

T/STR: International relations—you people are still, I hope, working as committees. If you notice on the board as you came in, or maybe it was erased, the other class—the committees are operating, and they are meeting during this period.

3.14. *Taking attendance.* The speaker indicates that the activity will be the taking of attendance orally or by some written means.

Example

T/STR: . . . Before I do anything else, let me take the attendance.

3.15. *Reviewing.* The speaker indicates that the activity will be review of previous classwork.

Example

T/STR: Let us review for just a second, before we continue with the material here, what we covered yesterday. Having established the relationship . . . .

3.16. *Taking field trip.* The speaker indicates that the activity will be a field trip by members of the class as part of their class work.

Example

T/STR: On Monday we'll be going to see the City Council. Jack is in charge of bus fares and is ready to collect from each of you as soon as you can get together your funds.

3.17. *Non-language routine.* The speaker indicates that the activity will be some non-language routine such as collecting texts, distributing graded homework papers, or cleaning up the room.

Example

T/STR: The summaries will be picked up at the end of the period.

4. *Agent.* Agent refers to the principal performer(s) of the activity of the game/sub-game.

4.1. *Teacher and all pupils.* The speaker indicates that the agent will be the teacher and all the pupils.

Example

T/STR: Before we get into other things, let's talk about the quota for just a moment as this is, or can be, much more severe than a tariff.

4.2. *All pupils.* The speaker indicates that the agent will be all the pupils of the class.

Example

T/STR: . . . So tomorrow you will be tested as a post-war, I guess would be right, as a post-test to compare with the results of the pre-test of last Friday . . . .

4.3. *Some pupils.* The speaker indicates that the agent will be several pupils.

Example

T/STR: This naturally leads us to another area that we pick up. I think we have another group—series of projects tomorrow—reports on the Common Market.

4.4. *Pupil.* The speaker indicates that the agent will be one pupil.

Examples

T/STR: Linda, I know your report is ready and I'm going to let you give it for all of the class in a minute.

P/STR-A: I'll give you a definition of the Balance of Payments. The Balance of Payments is actually a table of all the economic transactions which a country's citizens and businesses and governments have with the rest of the other countries during a certain year.

4.5. *Teacher.* The speaker indicates that the agent will be the teacher.

Example

T/STR: I'm going to read from the book a paragraph concerning the similarities of domestic and international trade . . . .

4.6. *Teacher and pupil.* The speaker indicates that the agent will be the teacher and one pupil.

Example

T/STR: Let me steer you in the right direction—since this is your report, I will ask you questions about it.

4.7. *Teacher and some pupils.* The speaker indicates that the agent will be the teacher and several pupils.

Example

T/STR: Now while the boys are working on the affirmative, I'll work with the girls on the negative and then we'll switch.

5. *Topic.* Topic refers to the subject matter of the discourse. There are two types of topic, substantive and instructional.

5.1. *Substantive topic.* Substantive topics refer to the subject matter under study by the class. See pp. 21–22 for the categories of substantive topics.

5.2. *Instructional topic.* Instructional topic refers to matters pertaining to classroom management, assignments, materials, and procedures. See pp. 26–29 for the categories of instructional topics.

6. *Logical process.* Logical process refers to the cognitive activities involved in dealing with the topic under study. See pp. 22–26 for description of logical processes.

7. *Time.* This category refers to the beginning point and the duration of the game/sub-game.

7.1. *Beginning point.* Beginning point refers to the time the game or sub-game is to commence.

7.11 *Present.* The speaker indicates that the game or sub-game will begin immediately.

Example

T/STR: Perhaps now in the minute or two that we have left we might talk about one of the important aspects of world trade and that is tariffs.

7.12 *Future—this session.* The speaker indicates that the game or sub-game will begin some time in the future during the session under way.

Example

T/STR: The summaries will be picked up at the end of the period.

7.13 *Future—other sessions.* The speaker indicates that the game or sub-game will begin during a subsequent session of the unit of study.

Example

T/STR: It's actually carried out under huge, under monetary controls systems within each of the countries. We'll get into this more on Wednesday.

7.14 *Future—unspecified.* The speaker indicates that the game or sub-game will begin at an unspecified time in the future during the current unit of study.

Example

T/STR: . . . and we'll come back to tariffs later when we talk about tariff history and policy of the U.S. or rather survey it rapidly.

7.15 *Future—out of class.* The speaker indicates that the sub-game will begin sometime in the future during the unit, but outside of class rather than during a class session.

Example

T/STR: Now what you will be doing at home tonight is reading these four chapters on international trade and tomorrow we'll . . . .

7.16 *Future—extra unit.* The speaker indicates that the sub-game will begin some time during a future unit of study.

Examples

T/STR: . . . and next week we will discuss more of them.

T/STR: We want to take the remaining few minutes here to just briefly look at the policy toward underdeveloped areas without going into them specifically, which we will do at a later date [this is near the end of the last session of this unit].

7.2. *Duration.* Duration refers to the length of time the game/sub-game is to continue.

7.21 *Unit.* The speaker indicates that he is structuring for the entire unit of study, which, for this research, is a series of four sessions on international trade.

Examples

T/STR: Now what we're going to do this week is to study the topic "international trade" . . . .

T/STR: All right now, this is basically the outline we'll be following, oh for the rest of the week on our unit on international trade. As you see, Topic I: The Nature and Importance of Trade, this is what we'll . . . .

7.22 *Sessions.* The speaker indicates that the game or sub-game will continue for more than one session during the unit of study.

Example

T/STR: . . . For the rest of the week [three more days] I hope that you will be doing all of the talking and that I will merely ask questions designed to stimulate discussion of the different chapters that we will take up.

7.23 *Session.* The speaker indicates that the game or sub-game will continue for an entire session during the unit of study.

Example

T/STR: . . . Now what I want to do this period in the way of introduction is to relate this topic of international trade with some of the work we've already covered in class . . . .

7.24 *Segment.* The speaker indicates that the sub-game will continue for a part of a session during the unit of study. The speaker indicates the duration explicitly or through the context of the discourse.

Example

T/STR: Perhaps now in the minute or two that we have left we might talk about one of the important aspects of world trade and that is tariffs.

7.25 *Unspecified.* The speaker does not specify how long the game or sub-game will continue and the context of the discourse gives no clue about the duration.

Examples

T/STR: . . . and we'll come back to tariffs later when we talk about tariff history and policy of the U.S. or rather survey it rapidly.

T/STR: Now what you will be doing at home tonight then is reading these four chapters on international trade and tomorrow we'll . . . .

8. *Regulations.* Regulations refer to the rules by which the game or sub-game is played. The regulations fall under the general headings of scope, time sequence, mental associations, and administration.

Scope refers to the breadth of the topic under study; i.e., what shall be included in the subject matter under discussion. *Time sequence* refers to the order in which the game/sub-games are to occur; e.g., if two sub-games are launched at the same time, which is to begin first. *Mental associations* refer to what the participants are to do mentally as the game/sub-game proceeds; e.g., the participants are to "take mental notes" and draw connections between ideas. *Administration* refers to the use of certain materials, the role of participants, and other technical aspects of the game/sub-game.

Examples

T/STR: As we look at our papers that we prepared for today, we have here in a more formal way some of the things we discussed before lunch, only we are getting to more specific details. For example, question one wants to know what is domestic trade and why is it necessary, if so . . . . (scope)

T/STR: . . . Now there are a series of questions that I wanted to be answered on the basis of those two films. Basically, number one, the first one, "The Living Circle." (time sequence)

T/STR: . . . so as I explain our imports follow along on that chart and keep in mind the relation to exports and foreign investments. Now the U.S. imports . . . . (associations)

T/STR: So that you'll have a test on this tomorrow and that will be conducted by Dr. Brown and not me . . . you of course should not be alarmed by the fact that there will be a test. This will certainly count on your grade. (administration)

9. *Instructional aids.* This category refers to the materials used in playing the game/sub-game.

9.1. *Textbook for the unit of study.*

Example

T/STR: Can we speak of multilateral trade. Multilateral Trade. And I think the diagrams in the text clearly show you how this works.

9.2. *Charts; graphs; tables.*

Example

T/STR: Now, take population itself on the graph I have right up here is to help you to analyze population. You see you can speak of China with 700 million people, around 650 million people, but the employment, the use of these people . . . .

9.3. *Maps; globes.*

Example

T/STR: Let's look at the world and see if we can get some over-simplification. It has been described as a ball which if you cut in half, a ball that oh at certain parallels, you get a sharp distinction. Now for argument's sake, I have cut this globe at 30° parallel.

9.4. *Books other than textbooks: magazines, dictionaries, encyclopedias, other reference materials.*

Example

T/STR: . . . Adam Smith put this out in a large degree in his book, *The Wealth of Nations,* in 1776 in which he was talking about specialization for example in the manufacture of pins . . . .

9.5. *Films; film strips; recordings.*

Example

T/STR: . . . Now there are a series of questions that I wanted to be answered on the basis of those two films. Basically, number one, the first one, "The Living Circle."

9.6. *News media such as newspapers, radio, and television*

Example

T/STR: Last night on the news, you know that organization that sends Negroes up to Washington . . . .

9.7. *Field trips; interviewing people out of class.*

Example

T/STR: . . . And then allow you to give your individual reports based on personal interviews hoping that as you report on your personal interviews some of the things that we have been talking about for the last three or four days—and even before—will have more meaning to us . . . .

9.8. *Homework papers and assignments; notes on readings and class discourse.*

Example

T/STR: As we look at our papers that we prepared for today, we have here in a more formal way some of the things we discussed before lunch, only we are getting down to more specific details.

For example, question one wants to know what is domestic trade and why is it necessary, if so . . . .

9.9. *Classroom-prepared material such as an outline, dittoed or mimeographed sheets, writings on the chalkboard.*

Example

T/STR: Someone mentioned the word profit before. Maybe it was me. I think perhaps we can illustrate one of the reasons as to why we trade by an example on the board.

9.10. *Other resources, both human and material.*

Example

T/STR: . . . but you go down on Route 1 to North Bergen. What do you see? A great big red, white, and blue sign "Buy American. Protect Your Job."

10. *Reason.* Reason refers to justification or explanation for the game/sub-game or for one or more of the dimensions of the game/sub-game.

Examples

T/STR: Let's go back to Cuba because that was the most outstanding example recently.

T/STR: This whole story of cars is interesting. Let's take a look at sports cars. The U.S. could probably build all the cars it needs if it wanted to.

T/STR: Now we say that there are certain factors that enter into the question of production. And this concept that we are getting into is a very important one.

Coding Procedure

The following procedure was used in coding the data: (a) each of the 60 protocols was first coded by one coder; (b) this initial coding was then reviewed by a second person who noted his disagreements with the first coder; (c) finally, these disagreements were arbitrated by two coders, one being the original coder and the second a coder who had not been involved in coding the protocol.

Reliability Test

Three members of the research staff participated in the reliability test. Two protocols were selected at random from each of five randomly selected classes. Randomly selected groups of nine structuring moves each from the beginning, middle, and end of the sessions were taken from the ten protocols. This yielded a random, balanced sample of over 10 per cent of all structuring moves. The three coders were divided into teams, one of which consisted of two coders and the other of a single coder. Assignment of coders to the two coding teams was rotated so that all possible permutations of pairs and singles were compared. Following the general procedure for analysis, one member of the pair coded a given sample; the other member reviewed the coding; then both members of the pair arbitrated disagreements between initial coder and the reviewer. The single-member "team" performed each step in the coding procedure by himself.

After each of the ten samples had been coded independently by the two teams, the codings of the teams were compared and the percentage of the agreement between teams in terms of frequency for each major category was computed. The results as presented in Table 31 indicate a consistently high degree of reliability for all major categories of analysis: agreement ranged from 86 to 100 per cent.

TABLE 31

Percentage of Agreement among Coding Teams in the Content Analysis of Structuring Components

Category	*Per Cent of Agreement*
Number of Components in Move	96.6
Function	100.0
Method	99.1
Activity Announced	96.6
Agent Announced	98.3
Duration of Time	97.4
Beginning Point in Time	97.4
Substantive Topic Announced	94.1
Instructional Topic Announced	100.0
Logical Process Announced	92.3
Substantive and Substantive-Logical Meanings Stated	99.1
Reason-Giving	98.6
Regulations	89.8
Instructional Aids	86.4

Results of Analysis of Structuring Move

This section presents a description of structuring moves in the classrooms studied. The data are presented in terms of the role of structuring moves in the discourse and in terms of the various dimensions of directive meaning conveyed in structuring moves. For the most part, the data are summarized for all 15 classes combined over the four sessions; in some instances, for purposes of comparison among classes, data are presented for each of the 15 classes.

Role of Structuring Moves in the Discourse

As indicated in Chapter Three, structuring moves represent a smaller proportion of the discourse in the 15 classrooms than any of the other three types of moves: structuring accounts for only 5.5 per cent of all moves and 18.1 per cent of all lines spoken. Although the teacher, the pupil, and audio-visual devices speak structuring moves, the teacher controls the structuring move: the teacher is responsible for 86 per cent of the structuring moves, while the pupil speaks only 12 per cent, and audio-visual devices account for 2 per cent.

Teacher's role. Although the teacher speaks 86 per cent of all structuring moves, structuring moves account for only a small proportion of the moves by the teacher. The data in Table 32 indicate that

TABLE 32

Percentage of the Teachers' and Pupils' Moves and Lines Devoted to Structuring for Each of the Fifteen Classes and for All Classes Combined

	Teacher		*Pupil*	
Class	*Moves*	*Lines*	*Moves*	*Lines*
All Combined	7.7	20.1	1.8	11.1
1	4.5	9.7	1.3	1.7
2	7.5	17.1	1.7	2.0
3	10.2	14.2	4.4	21.9
4	6.7	10.0	1.7	13.4
5	8.8	24.4	3.4	15.7
6	6.1	20.1	0.5	0.2
7	11.9	33.4	5.4	20.4
8	6.2	11.7	0.7	1.0
9	18.3	50.4	—	—
10	8.8	24.1	—	—
11	12.7	30.0	3.2	38.9
12	12.5	32.0	0.5	12.0
13	1.8	2.4	1.0	2.4
14	7.3	11.1	2.3	22.9
15	6.2	14.3	1.6	10.8

TABLE 33

Frequency Distribution of Moves and Speakers Following Teacher, Pupil, and Audio-Visual Device Structuring Moves

Prior Structuring Move and Speaker	*Total*	*Following Move and Speaker*											
		T/STR	P/STR	P/STR-A	A/STR	T/SOL	P/SOL	T/RES	P/RES	T/REA	T/NOC	P/NOC	*None*
Total	854	38	2	4	1	641	56	—	2	63	—	7	15
T/STR	737	37	2	2	1	618	30	—	1	2	—	7	14
P/STR	62	—	—	—	—	13	21	1	—	26	—	—	—
P/STR-A	42	—	—	2	—	9	5	—	—	25	—	—	—
A/STR	13	1	—	—	—	1	—	—	—	10	—	—	1

the median percentage of teacher moves devoted to structuring is 7.5 per cent, with a high of 18.3 per cent in Class 9 and a low of 1.8 per cent in Class 13. Eight teachers are clustered between 6.1 and 8.8 per cent.

If these data are considered in terms of lines spoken, structuring accounts for a much greater percentage of the teacher's discourse. This is to be accounted for by the fact that structuring moves are generally longer than other types of moves. (The mean length of structuring moves is 9.1 lines of typescript, in contrast to 3.5 lines for reacting, 2.0 lines for responding, and 1.9 lines for soliciting.) The median percentage of lines devoted to structuring is 17.2 per cent, with a wide range from 50.4 per cent in Class 9 to 2.4 per cent in Class 13. The two teachers at the extremes of the distribution are markedly different from the other 13 teachers, who range from 33.4 to 9.7 per cent.

Pupil's role. Structuring accounts for a smaller proportion of pupil activity than of teacher activity. As indicated in Table 32, the median percentage of pupil moves devoted to structuring is 1.6 per cent, with a range from 5.4 per cent in Class 7 to zero in Classes 9 and 10. Self-initiated structuring represents only 1 per cent of all pupil moves, and assigned structuring moves (STR-A), which include activities such as reporting and debating assigned by the teacher, account for less than 1 per cent. In two classes there is no pupil structuring whatsoever, and in only eight classes are there assigned structuring moves.

If these data are considered in terms of percentage of lines, the picture is somewhat different. The median percentage of pupil lines devoted to structuring is 10.8 per cent, with a range from 38.9 per cent in Class 11 to zero in Classes 9 and 10. Class 11 is considerably different from the other classes, in that pupils in this class devote almost two-fifths of their lines to structuring. This difference is to be accounted for by the fact that lengthy pupil reports and debates, classified as STR-A, are assigned by the teacher in this class.

Relation to other moves. According to the system for analysis, any type of move may follow a structuring move in the discourse. The data in Table 33 indicate, however, that certain types of move tend to follow structuring moves by the teacher and by the pupil. For example, after the teacher structures, the probability is nine to one that the teacher will speak the following move. Furthermore, the following move is most likely to be a teacher solicitation: 83.9 per cent of the moves following a teacher structuring move are teacher solicitations. In contrast, after the pupil structures, the probability is only three in ten that the pupil will speak the following move; but the most common pupil move following a pupil structuring move is a solicitation. It is the teacher who is more likely to speak after the pupil structures, and most frequently the following teacher move is a reaction: teacher reactions follow 49.0 per cent of all pupil structuring moves. In summary, a teacher solicitation tends to follow a teacher structuring move, and a teacher reaction tends to follow a pupil structuring move.

Single- and Multiple-Component Moves

According to the system for analysis, speakers may structure the game as a whole and/or one or more sub-games in a structuring move, and each game or sub-game is described in a component of the move. Single-component moves (i.e., moves that present one set of directives for the entire game or a single sub-game) are by far the most common; 85 per cent of the structuring moves are one-component moves, and the teacher speaks 85 per cent of these moves. Fifteen per cent of the structuring moves are multiple-component moves that present more than one set of directives, and virtually all of these are spoken by the teacher.

Function and Method

Speakers of structuring moves set the content for classroom interaction by performing two basic functions: launching and halting-excluding the game or sub-games. Data in Table 34 indicate that speakers perform the function of launching much more frequently than they perform the function of halting-excluding. In 95.4 per cent of all structuring components, speakers launch the game or sub-games; in contrast, in only 4.6 per cent do the speakers halt-exclude the game or sub-games.

Launching is primarily the function of the teacher rather than the pupil. Of all structuring components, 85.2 per cent are launching components spoken by the teacher. In contrast, only 10.2 per cent are launching components spoken by the pupil. The range for the teacher is from a high of 96.8 per cent in Class 6 to a low of 73.5 per cent in Class 13, with a median of 86.2 per cent. The range for the pupil, on the other hand, is from 23.6 per cent in Class 13 to zero in Classes 9 and 10, with a median percentage of 11.8 per cent.

To halt-exclude is strictly a function of the teacher; in no class does the pupil perform this function. When the teacher does halt or exclude a sub-game, he usually does so in a multiple-component move in which he also launches a new sub-game. More frequently, however, the teacher does not explicitly halt or exclude sub-games; rather, he signals the end of one sub-game by launching a new sub-game.

TABLE 34

Percentage Distribution of Structuring Components According to Function and Speaker for Each of the Fifteen Classes and for All Classes Combined

		Teacher		*Pupil*	
Class	*Total*	*Launching*	*Halting-Excluding*	*Launching*	*Halting-Excluding*
All Combined	100.0	85.2	4.6	10.2	—
1	100.0	86.2	—	13.8	—
2	100.0	85.7	4.2	10.1	—
3	100.0	78.0	5.5	16.5	—
4	100.0	84.0	6.0	10.0	—
5	100.0	80.4	4.1	15.5	—
6	100.0	96.8	—	3.2	—
7	100.0	76.5	6.4	17.1	—
8	100.0	90.2	3.8	6.0	—
9	100.0	89.0	11.0	—	—
10	100.0	91.0	9.0	—	—
11	100.0	88.1	1.0	10.9	—
12	100.0	94.6	2.7	2.7	—
13	100.0	73.5	2.9	23.6	—
14	100.0	88.1	—	11.9	—
15	100.0	82.9	5.3	11.8	—

Speakers perform the function of launching by using one of three methods: announcing, stating propositions, or announcing and stating propositions. As shown in Table 35, the most frequent method is announcing; that is, giving public notice about one or more dimensions of the game or sub-game. Speakers launch by announcing in 45.2 per cent of all structuring components, by announcing and stating propositions in 34.1 per cent, and by stating propositions in only 16.1 per cent.

The teacher and the pupil differ in the methods by which they launch. While the teacher launches by announcing in 46.9 per cent of his components, the pupil launches by this method in only 31.1 per cent of his components. Whereas launching by stating propositions occurs in only 12.3 per cent of the teacher's components, the pupil launches by this method in 49.1 per cent of his components. While

TABLE 35

Distribution of Structuring Components by Function and Method of Structuring for Teacher and Pupil

Function and Method	Total		Teacher		Pupil	
	%	f	%	f	%	f
Total	100.0	1033	100.0	927	100.0	106
Launching	95.4	986	94.9	880	100.0	106
Announcing	45.2	468	46.9	435	31.1	33
Announcing and Stating Propositions	34.1	352	35.7	331	19.8	21
Stating Propositions	16.1	166	12.3	114	49.1	52
Halting-Excluding	4.6	47	5.1	47	—	—

the teacher uses the method of announcing and stating propositions in 35.7 per cent of his components, the pupil uses this method in only 19.8 per cent of his components.

The data also indicate that the pupil uses a different method in announcing self-initiated structuring moves than he uses in announcing assigned structuring moves. In pupil self-initiated structuring the most common method is announcing, while in assigned structuring the most frequent method is stating propositions.

Activity

In structuring the game or a sub-game, the speaker usually announces the type of activity (e.g., general oral activity, debating, reporting, questioning-answering) in which participants are to engage. In 61.7 per cent of all components the speaker announces an activity. The range of activities announced in the classrooms studied is indeed limited, as shown in Table 36. General oral activity, which accounts for 61.4 per cent of all activities announced, is by far the most common. Speakers indicate that the activity will be general oral in nature (i.e., will involve "talking") by using such cues as "Let's now discuss . . . ," or "Let's go into . . . ," or "Let's take up . . . ." Inspection of the protocols reveals that general oral activity most often is a verbal interchange between the teacher and pupils, usually involving soliciting and responding, with the teacher playing the most active role. The data show that the other types of activity account for much smaller percentages. Reporting and questioning-answering, which account for only 8.5 per cent and 7.7 per cent respectively, are the second and

TABLE 36

Distribution of Structuring Components by Activity Announced for Teacher and Pupil

Activity Announced	*Total*		*Teacher*		*Pupil*	
	%	f	%	f	%	f
Total	100.0	637	100.0	598	100.0	39
General Oral	61.4	391	65.1	389	5.1	2
Reporting	8.5	54	7.0	42	30.7	12
Questioning-Answering	7.7	49	4.3	26	59.0	23
Reviewing	3.9	25	4.2	25	—	—
Taking Examination	3.8	24	4.1	24	—	—
Debating	2.7	17	2.8	17	—	—
Non-language Routine	2.5	16	2.7	16	—	—
Reading	2.2	14	2.3	14	—	—
Following Up Presentation	2.0	13	2.0	12	2.6	1
Viewing/Listening to Audio-Visual Devices	1.5	10	1.7	10	—	—
All Others	3.8	24	3.8	23	2.6	1

third most frequently announced activities. Actually, questioning-answering accounts for a much larger percentage of the activities, since, as already indicated, general oral activity turns out to be essentially a soliciting-responding interchange. Thus, three types of activity—general oral, reporting, and questioning-answering—account for three-fourths of all activities announced. None of the other types of activity accounts for more than 3.9 per cent.

Announcing activities is clearly the responsibility of the teacher, as indicated by the fact that he announces 93.4 per cent of all activities. General oral activity, accounting for almost two-thirds of the activities the teacher announces, is the most frequent. The pupil limits his very infrequent announcing of activities to announcing reporting and questioning-answering. In announcing the latter, he usually follows a standard procedure: he first structures by announcing "I have a question," and then proceeds to address his solicitation directly to the teacher.

Agent

In launching the game or a sub-game, the speaker usually designates the agent(s) who are to participate in the activity announced. In only 6 per cent of the structuring components in which activities are announced are the participants not specified. This is in accordance with expectations, since the various types of classroom activities by their very nature call for the involvement of certain participants; for example, debating usually involves some pupils in the class, taking an examination involves all pupils, and questioning-answering and general-oral activity ordinarily involve the teacher and all pupils.

Table 37 illustrates this pairing of activities and agents. Since general oral activity is the activity that occurs most frequently, it is not unexpected that the teacher and all pupils are designated the participants in two-thirds of the components in which activities are announced. In contrast, in only one-fifth of the components are pupils without the teacher announced as the participants for such activities as debating, reporting, and taking examinations—all of which are pupil activities assigned by the teacher. It is therefore clear that teachers not only participate directly in most classroom activities, but also take responsibility for planning and assigning those activities

TABLE 37

Frequency Distribution of Structuring Components According to Activity and Agent Announced

		Agent					
Activity	*Total*	*Teacher and all Pupils*	*All Pupils*	*One or More Pupils*	*Teacher*	*Other*	*None*
Total	637	415	55	64	36	29	38
General Oral	391	363	2	—	—	2	24
Reporting	54	—	—	34	20	—	—
Questioning-Answering	49	22	—	—	—	27	—
Reviewing	25	15	—	—	—	—	10
Taking Examination	24	—	24	—	—	—	—
Debating	17	—	—	15	—	—	2
Non-language Routine	16	—	13	1	2	—	—
Reading	14	2	6	2	4	—	—
Following Up Presentation	13	6	4	1	1	—	1
Viewing/Listening to Audio-Visual Devices	10	6	—	3	—	—	1
All Others	24	1	6	8	9	—	—

in which they do not take an active role. In none of the classes are outside speakers announced as participants.

Announcing Topic and Logical Process

In three-fourths of all structuring components speakers announce the substantive or instructional topics that are to be studied or discussed in the game or sub-game. Almost all of the 769 examples of announcing a topic deal with the subject matter of international trade. Only nine topics deal with instructional matters such as examinations and routine classroom management problems. It is the teacher's responsibility to announce the topics for study or discussion, as indicated by the fact that the teacher announces 95 per cent of all topics.

It is not uncommon for a speaker to launch the game or a sub-game by announcing a topic, without specifying the activity to be engaged in; this occurs in 22 per cent of all structuring components. More frequently, in 52 per cent of the components, a topic is announced along with an activity—for example, a debate on the Common Market, a general oral discussion on Canadian-United States trade, or an examination on the unit of international trade.

TABLE 38

Frequency Distribution of Structuring Components According to Substantive Topic Announced for Each Class and for All Fifteen Classes Combined

Class	TRA	FSP	IMX	FOR	BAR	PFT	REL	NTR
Total	289	69	61	63	103	127	30	18
1	17	4	1	—	1	3	1	—
2	23	8	1	3	13	6	2	2
3	13	6	4	5	6	2	—	1
4	27	2	3	10	12	18	1	—
5	15	3	11	1	3	17	—	—
6	20	—	12	2	9	26	1	7
7	19	6	7	14	15	5	7	1
8	28	16	8	5	5	9	6	—
9	16	4	3	2	7	7	—	—
10	25	1	—	1	8	3	5	3
11	19	2	3	4	3	6	1	1
12	23	10	1	2	5	4	4	—
13	22	2	4	3	2	2	—	—
14	14	2	2	8	11	18	2	1
15	8	3	1	3	3	1	—	2

As shown in Table 38, trade (TRA), the most general of all topics included in the unit on international trade, is announced most frequently: in almost two-fifths of the components in which a topic is announced, the speaker indicates that trade (i.e., general economic principles of trade) will be the focus of attention. This finding is in line with results showing that trade was the topic most frequently discussed in the classrooms studied. In contrast with the data reported in Chapter Three (pp. 41–86) in which promoting free trade (PFT) ranked fourth among the substantive topics discussed, promoting free trade ranks second among the topics announced. The difference is to be explained by the fact that most of the debates, films, and reports deal with problems relating to the promotion of free trade, and these activities are usually announced in structuring moves.

Classes show marked differences in the substantive topics announced. For example, in Class 15 the topic "trade" is announced only 8 times, while in Class 8 it is announced 28 times. Promoting free trade is announced 26 times in Class 6, but only once in Class 15. Similarly, barriers to trade (BAR) is announced as the topic only once in Class 1, but 15 times in Class 7. These findings are consistent with results reported in Chapter Three which indicate that classes showed marked differences in the substantive material covered in the class sessions.

In about 20 per cent of the components in which the speaker announces a topic, he also specifies the logical process to be used by participants in dealing with the topic. This is illustrated in the following example from one of the protocols:

> T/STR: Well, now that we've got the facts on the Common Market, let's now take up the reasons why we should or should not join.

In this instance, the teacher announces the topic "promoting free trade" and indicates that the class will consider reasons for and against our joining the Common Market; that is, the discussion will involve giving reasons for opinions on the issue (logical process: justifying). The teacher and not the pupil is primarily responsible for announcing logical processes.

Time: Beginning Point and Duration

In launching the game or a sub-game, the speaker gives an indication of its beginning point (i.e., whether it is to get under way immediately or at some future time) and its duration (i.e., whether it will continue for the unit, session[s], or segment of a session). Data presented in Table 39 indicate that in 80 per cent of all launching components, speakers launch sub-games to begin immediately and to continue for only a segment of a session. This means that, for the most part, classes are structured as they move along from sub-game to sub-game within a session. In only 6 per cent of the launching components do speakers launch a sub-game to begin later in an ongoing session. This means that only infrequently are participants given advance notice regarding sub-games that will take place subsequent to the ongoing sub-game.

While both the teacher and the pupil launch sub-games for the present (although, as previously reported, launching is primarily the teacher's responsibility), only the teacher launches for the future. Never does the pupil announce a sub-game that will begin at some future time, not even later during an ongoing session.

TABLE 39

Frequency Distribution of Launching Components According to Beginning Point in Time and Duration

Beginning Point in Time	*Duration*					
	Total	*Segment*	*Session*	*Sessions*	*Unit*	*Unspecified*
Total	986	868	37	3	16	62
Present	818	787 *	14	2	15	—
Future	168	81	23	1	1	62
Future This Session	60	59	—	—	1	—
Future Other Session	62	21	23	1	—	17
Future Unspecified	46	1	—	—	—	45

* Includes all 106 pupil components.

In only 14 structuring components spoken at the beginning of class sessions do teachers launch sub-games for these sessions. These 14 components are spoken by only 10 teachers. Interestingly enough, there are more instances of teachers structuring subsequent sessions: 23 teacher components, usually spoken near the end of a session, launch sub-games for the following day's session. All but 3 of the teachers launch for at least one subsequent session in this manner. Sixteen structuring components that launch the game as a whole for the duration of the entire unit occur in the discourse, and these 16 components are spoken by 11 of the 15 teachers. It is interesting to note that in one class (Class 10) the teacher structures neither for the unit as a whole, nor for any one of the four sessions; structuring in this class is confined to launching sub-games for segments within the class sessions.

Regulations

The data indicate that it is the teacher's responsibility to cite regulations regarding the scope, time sequence, mental associations, and administration of the game and sub-games. Of the 247 structuring components in which regulations are given, 243 are spoken by the teacher. The teacher thus cites regulations in about one-fourth of his structuring components. It is clearly not the job of the pupil to set forth regulations that participants must follow in playing the classroom game.

Instructional Aids

The teacher uses or calls for the use of instructional aids in one-third of his components. In contrast, the pupil uses or calls for the use of instructional aids in over one-half (57.5 per cent) of his components. The high percentage for the pupil is to be accounted for by the fact that the coding rules specify that in assigned structuring components (STR-A) homework is to be coded if no other instructional aid is specifically mentioned. Inspection of the coded protocols reveals that homework is coded in 22 of the 42 assigned structuring components by the pupil. Without these, the percentage for the pupil is 36.8, which is similar to the percentage for the teacher.

The data indicate that the most commonly used resource is the textbook, which is mentioned in one-fourth of all components in which the speaker specifies instructional aids. Reliance on the textbook is much greater than the data suggest, for "text" is coded only when the speaker explicitly calls for its use. Material such as dittoed outlines, the blackboard, charts, graphs, maps, and films are also occasionally used by the teacher, but aside from the textbook the pupil refers only to homework, news media, and other printed references.

Reason-Giving

The data indicate that it is clearly the teacher's job to give reasons for the game or sub-game and their various dimensions: the teacher speaks 212 of the 221 components in which reasons are cited. The median percentage of teacher structuring components that cite reasons is 23.9, with a range from 50.0 per cent for Teacher 6 to 9.9 per cent for Teacher 12. There seems to be a slight tendency for teachers who structure more frequently to cite reasons proportionately less often than teachers who do not structure as often.

Summary

Summarized below are the principal results of the analysis:

1. Structuring moves represent a smaller proportion of the discourse than any of the other three types of moves: structuring accounts for only 5.5 per cent of all moves and 18.1 per cent of all lines spoken.

2. Structuring moves play a more significant part in the teacher's discourse than they do in the pupil's discourse. Structuring accounts for 7.7 per cent of the teacher's moves and only 1.8 per cent of the pupil's moves. In terms of lines, structuring accounts for 20.1 per cent of the teacher's discourse and 11.1 per cent of the pupil's discourse.

3. Although any type of move may follow a structuring move, in the actual discourse certain types of move tend to follow the structuring moves. A teacher soliciting move tends to come after a teacher structuring move and a teacher reacting move tends to come after a pupil structuring move.

4. Eighty-five per cent of the structuring moves are one-component moves (i.e., moves that structure one set of directives for the game or a sub-game), of which the teacher speaks 85 per cent. Multiple-component moves represent the remaining 15 per cent, and virtually all of these are spoken by the teacher.

5. Speakers perform the function of launching much more frequently than they perform the function of halting-excluding. In 95.4 per cent of all structuring components speakers launch the game or sub-game, while in only 4.6 per cent speakers perform the function of halting-excluding. For the teacher, the most common method for launching is announcing; for the pupil it is stating propositions. Launching is primarily the function of the teacher, while halting-excluding is exclusively a function of the teacher.

6. In structuring the game or a sub-game, the speaker usually announces the type of activity in which participants are to engage. Three types of activities—general oral, reporting, and questioning-answering—account for three-fourths of all activities announced.

7. The speaker usually announces the agent(s) who are to take part in the activity announced. The teacher and all pupils are designated the agents in two-thirds of components in which activities are announced.

8. In three-fourths of the structuring components speakers an-

nounce the topics that are to be studied or discussed. Virtually all topics announced are substantive rather than instructional. The most frequently announced topic is trade, and the second most frequently announced is promoting free trade. In about 20 per cent of the components in which the speaker announces a topic, he also specifies the logical process with which participants are to deal with the topic.

9. Most structuring components (about 75 per cent) launch sub-games to begin immediately and to continue for only a segment of a session. For the most part, classes are structured as they move along from sub-game to sub-game. Although both the teacher and the pupil launch sub-games for the present, this is primarily the teacher's responsibility. On occasion, teachers structure a sub-game or series of sub-games for a class session. About two-thirds of the teachers structure the game as a whole at the outset of the first session of the unit.

10. It is the teacher's job to cite regulations and give reasons for dimensions of the game or sub-game. Both the teacher and the pupil use or call for the use of instructional aids. The text, blackboard, and teacher-prepared material such as dittoed outlines are the instructional resources most frequently used.

CHAPTER SIX

THE REACTING MOVE

IN THE THEORETICAL VIEW of classroom teaching as a language game, reacting is a reflexive move that is occasioned, but not directly called out, by a preceding move; the occasioning move may be a soliciting, responding, or structuring move or a preceding reacting move. For example, rating by a teacher of a pupil's responding move is designated as a reacting move; that is, the student's responding move is the occasion for the teacher's reaction but does not elicit it.

This chapter reports our investigation of the distinctive functions of reacting moves in pedagogical discourse and the ways in which teachers and students carry out these functions in the classroom. The first two sections describe the conceptual framework and the system for analysis derived from this framework; the third section presents a description of the reacting moves in the 15 classes studied.

Conceptual Framework

Reacting as a Reflexive Move

Although both reacting and responding are reflexive moves with their pedagogical functions determined by relationships to preceding moves, there are significant differences between these two types of move. Responding moves bear a reciprocal relationship to solicitations and occur only in relation to them; their pedagogical function in the discourse is to fulfill the expectation of soliciting moves. In contrast, reacting moves may be occasioned by any of the four types of moves; their pedagogical function is to *rate* (positively or negatively) and/or to *modify* (by clarifying, synthesizing, or expanding) what was said in the moves that occasioned them. The following excerpts illustrate these distinguishing functions of reacting moves:

Example 1

T/SOL:	What do we import from Denmark?
P/RES:	Modern furniture.
T/REA:	Right, and it's some of the best designed furniture available anyplace in the world.

In this instance, the teacher reacts by positively rating the student's response and by adding relevant information and opinion.

Example 2

P/SOL:	Why don't we raise our tariffs too?
T/REA:	That's a good question.

Here the teacher rates positively the solicitation by the pupil. Note that the reaction is a favorable comment regarding the nature of the question raised by the student and is not an answer to this question.

Example 3

T/STR:	All right, Standard Oil has a little extra money around, and they form a new company and they're going to call it Arabian-American Oil Company.
P/REA:	And the Shah of Arabia, whoever he is, gives them permission to drill on the land, and he also makes provisions that he is to get a certain amount of the profits, usually fifty per cent.

In this excerpt, the student reacts by elaborating the teacher's opening structuring move.

Example 4

P/SOL:	How is it possible for a new nation to increase barriers?
T/RES:	Use any of these devices.
P/REA:	But it has to have trade to survive. I don't see that.
T/REA:	All right, Ghana needs certain things. It wants to develop. All right, Ghana was mentioned before. It wants to industrialize. Now if Ghana doesn't use certain trade barriers, then she might import things, say from the United States—things we export from this country.

In this interchange, the pupil reacts by raising an objection to what the teacher said in response to his question. In turn, the teacher reacts by expanding and clarifying the point brought up by the student.

Reactions may be occasioned by a single move, as in the illustrations cited above, or they may be occasioned by more than one move, as shown in the following example:

T/SOL: What are some of the Malaya's natural resources?
P-1/RES: Tin.
P-2/RES: Rubber.
T/*REA*: The two main things that Malaya has are tin and rubber. Remember rubber and tin in Singapore . . . we said Malaya. And both these countries need these things for many many reasons. So that there is a reason for trade.

In this instance, the teacher reacts to the two pupils by repeating their answers, thus in effect rating their responses positively; in addition, he relates the students' comments to a previous class discussion. (The coding symbol is italicized to designate a reaction to more than one move.)

Another significant characteristic of reacting moves is that they may be occasioned by the "silent language" as well as by the verbal language of the classroom. Pauses occurring in the discourse and physical actions by participants may occasion reactions, as illustrated by the following excerpts from the transcripts:

Example 1

T/SOL: As a country, from day to day what are some of the things we do that are very definitely an indication of the fact that we do have a great deal of international trade?
T/REA-*: Now, you're looking at me but you don't seem to realize that I only want you to answer a question that is right in the chapter.

Here the teacher is reacting to the absence of an expected responding move. Possibly prompted by puzzled expressions of the students, he reacts by giving them a clue where the information may be found. (The asterisk is added to the coding symbol to indicate a reaction occasioned by a pause in the discussion.)

Example 2

T/SOL: . . . But are they? What are the farmer's products? Come on, some other hands!
T/REA-P: Oh, there're too many here who are not saying a word.

In this excerpt, the teacher reacts to the failure of all but a few students to volunteer to answer his question. (The postscript -P indicates that this reaction is occasioned by a physical action.)

These seven examples illustrate the flexibility and versatility that characterize the role of the reacting move in classroom discourse. Its flexibility is demonstrated by the fact that any verbal move, physical action, or pause in the discussion may serve as the occasion for a reaction. Its versatility is apparent in the variety of ways in which it may clarify, expand, synthesize, or rate what has been said in a preceding move. The possibility of reacting to a verbal action or a physical action at any point during the course of play means that participants may attempt to influence events in the classroom at the time and in the manner of their own choosing. The conditions under which it is considered appropriate for participants to react are determined, of course, by the rules of the game that specify the roles of the teacher and the pupil.

Types of Reacting Move

According to the overall system for analysis, pedagogical moves are coded in terms of the substantive and instructional meanings expressed by teachers and pupils. In the excerpts cited above, speakers reacted by communicating both types of meanings. For example, when the teacher reacted positively to the student's question regarding tariffs (page 166), he was expressing instructional meanings; when the student reacted to the teacher's comments about the Arabian-American Oil Company by adding supplementary information (page 166), he was conveying substantive meanings. Since meanings communicated in reactions are substantive and/or instructional in nature, it is appropriate to classify reacting moves into three basic categories: substantive, instructional, and substantive-instructional. Each of these three types serves a different function in the discourse.

Substantive reactions. Reactions of this type express substantive and substantive-logical meanings related to the subject matter under discussion.* Examination of the protocols reveals that in conveying these types of meaning, substantive reactions serve the function of *modifying* in some way substantive content discussed in occasioning moves. The following excerpts illustrate this distinctive function of substantive reactions:

Example 1

P-1/REA:	The U.S. consumer is looking for a lower-priced article, and the Japanese at this point are making lower-priced articles that compete with the exact standards of GE or RCA or anyone in the special electronics fields.
P-2/REA:	They make radios which are better up to a point.

* See pp. 21–26 for definitions of substantive meanings and substantive-logical meanings.

Example 2

T/STR: Now what I started to say I think is that some of us actually prefer foreign goods.
SOL: Well, now give us a few things that have this glamorous appeal to American customers.
P/RES: Watches.
T/REA: Now I thought we made plenty of watches in America.

Example 3

T/REA: All of the instances of foreign investment that Ira and Mary have discussed can be classified in either direct or portfolio types of investment. Both types of investment are important when we talk about the ways in which the United States invests in other countries.

These examples illustrate the variety of ways in which teachers and students may use substantive reactions to clarify, expand, or synthesize statements of preceding speakers. In deciding when to react substantively, participants are limited by their knowledge of the subject matter under discussion and by the rules of the game that specify the circumstances under which teachers or pupils may suggest modifications of what preceding speakers have said.

Instructional reactions. Reactions in this category express instructional and instructional-logical meanings concerned with the social-managerial aspects of the classroom.* In conveying meanings of these types, instructional reactions serve the pedagogical functions of (1) rating positively or negatively what was claimed in an occasioning move or (2) modifying in some way what was said about procedural matters in an occasioning move.

(1) *Rating reactions.* The function of reactions of this type is to rate positively or negatively what is said in preceding moves. One may view rating reactions as metacommunications, since they are communications about previous communications, as illustrated in the following excerpts:

Example 1

T/SOL: Where do we get chicle?
P/RES: South America.
T/REA: South America, yes; it's our great source of that.

* See pp. 26–31 for definitions of instructional meanings and instructional-logical meanings.

Example 2

T/SOL:	In what town in New Jersey, do you think you can remember?
P/RES:	Flemington.
T/REA:	Flemington, New Jersey; all right.

Meanings expressed in rating reactions seem to be closely related both to "critical" meaning and to "evaluative" meaning, as defined by Wellman (21). Critical meaning refers to the use of language to qualify, accept, or reject the claim of a given statement to be rationally justified. "The claim to rationality," writes Wellman, "is the claim that one can support his assertion or actions with reasons, that he has not done violence to the opposing reasons, and that he recognizes the liability to be called before the court of reason" (21:258). Critical sentences are positive or negative, depending upon whether they uphold or reverse the claim they criticize. From this viewpoint, teachers and pupils express critical meanings when they rate what is said and done in the classroom. When a teacher says "That's correct" in reacting to a pupil's comment, he is in effect reaffirming the claim to rationality implicit in the student's statement.

Rating reactions may also be viewed as expressing evaluative meanings. According to Wellman, the central feature of evaluation is partiality. "To be partial, is to be pro or con . . . . To evaluate anything is to place it on a scale ranging from good through indifferent to bad" (21:208, 209). One may therefore interpret evaluative sentences as "putting attitudes into words." From this viewpoint, speakers of reacting moves express favorable or unfavorable attitudes when they rate what is said or done in the classroom. When a teacher says "That's a good answer" in reacting to a student's responding move, he is in effect communicating his attitude of approval of the student's answer.

Inspection of the protocols reveals that speakers of reacting moves, particularly teachers, frequently use such common-sense words as "right," "wrong," "correct," "incorrect," "fine," and "good" in rating what is said and done in the classroom. These words may, in a given reaction, express critical meanings and/or evaluative meanings. For example, when a teacher says "Right" in reacting to a student's response, it may be his intention either to communicate his approval of what the pupil said (evaluative meaning), or to reaffirm the claim to rationality implicit in the pupil's statement (critical meaning), or possibly to convey both types of meaning. In this phase of the research we interpret rating reactions as expressing critical and/or evaluative meanings, and we leave for future study experimental investigation of the distinctions between critical and evaluative meanings in classroom discourse.

(2) *Procedural reactions.* Reactions of this type serve the functions of clarifying, expanding, or synthesizing what preceding speakers have said about procedural matters (assignments, examinations, materials, and classroom routines), as illustrated in the following three examples:

T/REA:	Now this matter that I'm discussing at this moment will become increasingly important to you on Thursday this week when members of the class will make reports to you on the new trade policy that the U.S. is thinking of engaging in.
T/REA:	We studied that just last week when we were talking about the New Deal.
T/REA:	Well there seems to be about a two-to-one vote that you think it would be a good idea.

Substantive-instructional reactions. In the course of class discussion, speakers frequently express both substantive meanings and instructional meanings in a reacting move. For example, a teacher may in a reaction to a student's responding move not only rate positively or negatively what the pupil said, but also expand or clarify the substantive or instructional material discussed by the pupil. The following excerpt illustrates this type of reaction:

T/SOL:	What countries belong to the Common Market?
P/RES:	France.
T/REA:	France. Right. And also Germany and Belgium.

On occasion, a speaker may include reference to both substantive and procedural matters in the same reacting move, as shown in the following example:

T/REA:	We'll have a report later this period, John, that will help to explain the problem you have just mentioned. In connection with this, it's important to keep in mind that the countries in the Common Market are not in agreement on what should be done about it.

In this instance, the teacher not only attempts to clarify the substantive problem raised by the pupil, but also calls attention to a report that will further clarify the matter under discussion.

System for Analysis of Reacting Move

This section presents the system for analyzing reacting moves based on the conceptual framework developed in the preceding section.

Reacting Moves

1. *Reacting move* (REA). Reacting is a reflexive pedagogical move that is occasioned by a structuring, soliciting, responding, or another reacting move. Reactions are classified into three major categories: substantive, instructional, and substantive-instructional. Pedagogically, these moves serve to rate and/or to modify in some fashion what was stated in occasioning moves.

Reacting moves differ from responding moves in that while a responding move is always directly elicited by a solicitation, preceding moves serve only as the occasion for reactions. For example, rating by a teacher of a pupil's response is designated a reacting move; that is, the student's response is the occasion for the teacher's rating reaction, but it does not actively elicit the reaction.

1.1. *Reacting* (REA). A reaction to a single occasioning move is coded REA.

1.2. *Reacting—Italicized (REA).* When the coding symbol is italicized (*REA*), it designates a reaction occasioned by more than one move.

1.3. *Reacting—Pause* (REA-*). The asterisk designates a reaction occasioned by a pause or by the absence of an expected move.

1.4. *Reacting—Physical* (REA-P). The postcript "-P" designates a reaction occasioned by a physical action rather than by a verbal action.

Types of Reacting Move

1. *Substantive reactions* are defined as (a) reactions that convey substantive meanings and associated substantive-logical meanings, and (b) reactions in the instructional and instructional-logical categories that are interpretations of preceding statements (code: statement/interpret STA/INT) and are therefore essentially substantive in nature. Substantive reactions serve to *modify* (by clarifying, synthesizing, or expanding) what was said substantively in the occasioning move.

Example

T/SOL: Now what kinds of capital are there? Paul?
T/RES: Machinery.
T/REA: Now he's using capital in terms of concrete things. You have a tractor; you have a machine. Some of you boys own auto-

> mobiles. Actually you have capital. And other places might have capital simply in terms of money.

2. *Instructional reactions* are defined as reactions that express instructional and associated instructional-logical meanings, with the exception of those coded STA/INT.

2.1. *Rating reactions* are defined as instructional reactions that involve rating processes. Rating reactions serve the pedagogical function of *rating* the truth or falsity or the appropriateness or inappropriateness of what was said in the occasioning move.*

2.11 *Positive.* Distinctly affirmative rating (e.g., yes, right, correct, exactly, precisely).

2.12 *Admitting.* Mildly accepting or equivocally positive rating (e.g., all right, o.k., uh-huh).

2.13 *Repeating.* Implicitly positive rating in which there is only a repetition, rephrasing, or restatement of the occasioning move, with no explicit rating.

2.14 *Qualifying.* Any indication of reservation, however mild or oblique (e.g., yes, but . . . ; however).

2.15 *Not Admitting.* Rating that rejects by stating the contrary, rather than by making an explicitly negative comment.

2.16 *Negative.* Distinctly negative rating (e.g., no, wrong, nope).

2.2. *Procedural reactions* are defined as instructional reactions that convey instructional meanings and associated instructional-logical meanings, with the exception of those that involve rating processes. Procedural reactions serve the pedagogical function of *modifying* by clarifying and/or expanding what has been said about procedural matters (e.g., assignments, examinations, class schedule, materials, and classroom routines) in the occasioning move.

Examples

T/REA: The reason that I didn't cut you off, Ione, was that I was conscious of what Don said and I cut him off too soon.

T/REA: Well now, that is not the question of course I asked.

3. *Substantive-instructional reactions* are defined as reactions that express both substantive meanings and instructional meanings.

3.1. *Substantive-rating reactions* are defined as reactions that include both substantive and rating components.

Example

T/REA: Good point. I'm glad you brought that up. I wasn't thinking of that at the moment, but it's an important problem that

* For complete definitions of the six types of rating reaction see pp. 29–31.

faces us in trade because of its political ramifications as well as just economic.

3.2. *Substantive-procedural reactions* are defined as reactions that include both substantive and procedural components.

Example

T/REA: We'll have a report later this period, John, that will help to explain the problem you have just mentioned. In connection with this, it's important to keep in mind that the countries in the Common Market are not in agreement on what should be done about it.

Types and Characteristics of Occasioning Moves

The categories listed below describe types and characteristics of occasioning moves.

1. *Structuring occasioning move*
1.1. Identification number
1.2. Speaker (teacher, pupil, or audio-visual device)
1.3. Single or multiple components
1.4. Function and method
2. *Soliciting occasioning move*
2.1. Identification number
2.2. Speaker (teacher or pupil)
2.3. Number of components
2.4. Logical meaning
2.5. Information activity
3. *Responding occasioning move*
3.1. Identification number
3.2. Speaker (teacher or pupil)
3.3. Number of components
3.4. Soliciting/responding logical congruence
3.5. Soliciting/responding information activity congruence
4. *Reacting occasioning move*
4.1. Identification number
4.2. Speaker (teacher or pupil)
4.3. Type of reaction
4.4. Logical meaning

Results of Analysis of Reacting Move

For the most part the data are summarized for all 15 classes combined over the four sessions to provide a comprehensive view of reacting moves in the discourse. In some instances, data are presented for each of the 15 classes, for purposes of comparison among the classes. The description is organized around three major questions:

1. What is the function of reacting moves in the discourse of the teacher and the pupil?

2. What types of reacting move occur in the discourse of the teacher and the pupil?

3. What are the relationships of reacting moves by the teacher and the pupil to their occasioning moves?

Function of Reacting Moves in the Discourse

Data presented in Chapter Three revealed that reacting moves represent a little less than one-third of all moves spoken in the 15 classes, with responding and soliciting moves accounting for similar percentages of the discourse. In contrast, only one-twentieth (5.5 per cent) of all moves are structuring moves. In terms of lines, reacting accounts for slightly more than one-third of the discourse, with the remaining two-thirds about equally distributed among the three other moves.

The mean length of reacting moves is 3.5 lines of typescript. This contrasts with the mean length of 9.1 lines for structuring, 2.0 for responding and 1.9 for soliciting. Teacher reactions tend to be longer than pupil reactions: the mean length of teacher reactions is 3.7 lines and of pupil reactions, 2.5 lines.

Roles of the teacher and the pupil in the classroom are defined in part by frequency of behavior in each category of pedagogical moves. Differences in roles are therefore apparent when the percentages of the teacher's discourse and the pupil's discourse devoted to reacting are considered. The data summarized in Table 40 clearly demonstrate that reacting moves play a more significant part in the teacher's discourse than they do in the pupil's discourse. Reactions account for 39.2 per cent of all teacher moves but only 15.1 per cent of all pupil moves. The picture is approximately the same when these data are considered in terms of percentage of lines. Whereas 44.7 per cent of all lines spoken by the teacher are devoted to reacting, only 19.1 per cent of the lines by the pupil are given over to reacting.

Teacher's role. Approximately two-fifths of all teacher moves are reacting moves. The median percentage for the 15 teachers is 38.4, with a high of 43.8 in Class 1 and a low of 30.7 in Class 3. Thirteen teachers are clustered between 37.1 per cent and 43.8 per cent, a range of only seven percentage points. Teachers 11 and 3 are outside this narrow range at the lower end of the distribution, with 34.5 and 30.7 per cent respectively.

If these data are considered in terms of lines spoken, reacting

TABLE 40

Percentage of the Teachers' and Pupils' Moves and Lines Devoted to Reacting for Each of the Fifteen Classes and for All Classes Combined

	Teacher		*Pupil*	
Class	*Moves*	*Lines*	*Moves*	*Lines*
All Combined	39.2	44.7	15.1	19.1
1	43.8	53.5	8.8	10.0
2	37.8	46.5	16.4	26.1
3	30.7	37.8	12.0	9.5
4	40.0	49.9	21.2	16.2
5	37.5	33.7	22.6	29.5
6	37.4	49.4	7.0	8.8
7	37.1	34.0	14.0	15.0
8	40.8	47.7	21.4	29.6
9	38.4	34.6	10.1	11.9
10	40.7	54.0	15.2	31.9
11	34.5	34.5	3.9	4.3
12	38.1	41.4	26.8	29.9
13	43.4	48.5	10.0	10.6
14	42.9	50.9	4.7	3.4
15	41.7	46.4	22.3	30.4

moves account for an even greater percentage of the teacher's discourse. The median percentage of lines devoted to reacting is 46.5 per cent, with a range from 54.0 per cent in Class 10 to 33.7 per cent in Class 5. Nine of the teachers are clustered between 46.4 and 54.0 per cent, a range of only eight percentage points. These findings underscore the significant role that reacting plays in the teacher's discourse.

Pupil's role. Reacting accounts for a smaller amount of pupil activity than it does of teacher activity. The median percentage of moves by students devoted to reacting is 14.0 per cent, with a range from 26.8 per cent in Class 12 to 3.9 per cent in Class 11. Eight classes are clustered within 10.6 percentage points (12.0 to 22.6), but the classes are fairly well distributed over the entire range.

If these data are considered in terms of percentage of lines, the picture is approximately the same. The median percentage of lines devoted by students to reacting is 15.0 per cent, with a high of 31.9 per cent in Class 10 and a low of 3.4 per cent in Class 14. Seven of the classes cluster in the rather narrow range of seven percentage points (8.8 to 16.2). There are six classes at the upper end of the distribution ranging from 26.1 to 31.9 per cent, and two classes at the lower end with 4.3 and 3.4 per cent.

Types of Reacting Move

Table 41 summarizes the distribution of the various types of reacting move. These data reveal that rating reactions account for 40.5 per cent of all reacting moves. Substantive reactions and substantive-rating reactions account for 23.9 per cent and 24 per cent, respectively. Procedural reactions (8.5 per cent) and substantive-procedural reactions (3.1 per cent) occur much less frequently in the discourse.

TABLE 41

Distribution of Reacting Moves by Type of Move for Teacher and Pupil and for Teacher and Pupil Combined

Type of Reacting Moves	*Total*		*Teacher*		*Pupil*	
	%	*f*	%	*f*	%	*f*
All Combined	100.0	4649	100.0	3759	100.0	890
Substantive	23.9	1110	16.8	633	53.6	477
Rating	40.5	1886	46.2	1738	16.6	148
Procedural	8.5	395	6.9	258	15.4	137
Substantive-Rating	24.0	1115	27.2	1021	10.6	94
Substantive-Procedural	3.1	143	2.9	109	3.8	34

Data included in Table 41 help to delineate further the distinctive roles of the teacher and the pupil in the classroom. Rating reactions are obviously a significant part of the teacher's role, but they play only a minor part in the pupil's discourse. In contrast, the largest proportion of pupil reactions are substantive reactions, but a relatively small proportion of teacher reactions are of this type. Reactions that include both substantive and rating components represent a substantial portion of teacher reactions, but only a small portion of student reactions. Procedural reactions and substantive-procedural reactions occur infrequently in the discourse both of the teacher and of the pupil.

Teacher's role. Rating reactions account for the largest percentage of teacher reactions: 46.2 per cent of all reacting moves by the teacher are in this category. This clearly reflects one of the teacher's major functions in the classroom, which is to rate statements made by students. This responsibility of the teacher is further highlighted by the fact that the next highest percentage is substantive-rating reactions, representing 27.2 per cent of all teacher reacting moves. These two types of reaction therefore account for almost three-fourths of all teacher reactions. This is in marked contrast to the pupil, who infrequently speaks reactions that include rating components.

When one considers all teacher reactions concerned with rating (that is, rating reactions and substantive-rating reactions) that are occasioned by pupil verbal moves and by physical actions, he finds that the ratio of positively toned reactions to negatively toned reactions is 4 to 1. Basically positive reactions (positive, admitting, and repeating) account for 80.0 per cent of the teacher's rating reactions, while basically negative reactions (qualifying, not admitting, and negative) represent only 20.0 per cent. It is also interesting to note that each of the three categories—positive, admitting, and repeating—accounts for approximately one-third of the teacher's positively toned reactions. In contrast, qualifying accounts for two-thirds, while negative and not admitting together account for the remaining one-third, of all negatively toned reactions.

These data indicate that when teachers rate what pupils say and do in the classroom they are four times more positive than negative in their reactions; and further, when the teacher does speak a negatively toned reaction, he is much more inclined to qualify rather than not to admit or to express a distinctly negative reaction.

The teacher infrequently reacts substantively: substantive reactions represent only 16.8 per cent of all reacting moves by the teacher. Procedural reactions accounting for only 6.9 per cent and substantive-procedural reactions representing 2.9 per cent occur even less frequently in the teacher's discourse.

Pupil's role. When the pupil reacts, he does so most frequently by expressing substantive meanings: substantive reactions represent 53.6 per cent of all pupil reactions. In contrast, the pupil rarely reacts by rating other participants. Although rating reactions account for 16.6 per cent of the pupil's reactions, the pupil is responsible for only 148 (seven per cent) of the 1,886 rating reactions that occur in the discourse. Fifteen per cent of all pupil reactions are procedural reactions, but these represent over one-third of all procedural reactions that occur in the discourse.

The pupil infrequently speaks reactions that include both substantive and instructional components. Double-component reactions are clearly a part of the teacher's role and not of the pupil's role. The pupil speaks only 94 (nine per cent) of the 1,115 substantive-rating reactions and 34 (23 per cent) of the 143 substantive-procedural reactions that occur in the discourse.

Relationships to Occasioning Moves

In view of the reflexive nature of reacting moves, the relationships of reactions to their occasioning moves are of central importance in the analysis. Virtually all 4,649 reactions are occasioned by vocal actions (i.e., pedagogical moves) rather than by physical actions or by pauses in the discussion. Only 55 reactions occasioned by pauses occur in the 15 classes, and all but one of these are spoken by the teacher. Similarly, a total of 36 reactions occasioned by physical actions occur in the discourse, and all but two of these are by the teacher. The nature of the subject matter under study probably accounts for these results. In a subject such as science, which includes laboratory work involving the manipulation of apparatus, one would expect to find a greater number of reactions occasioned by physical actions.

Two-thirds of all reacting moves are occasioned by responding moves, and one-fourth by reactions; together, responding and reacting account for 92 per cent of all occasioning moves. Only 2.3 per cent of all reactions are occasioned by structuring moves, and 1.4 per cent by solicitations.

The overwhelming number of teacher reactions and pupil reactions are occasioned by single moves. However, a small number of reacting moves occasioned by more than one move occur in the discourse. Reactions of this kind account for 7.1 per cent of all teacher reactions; in only two classes does one find pupil reactions occasioned by more than one move, and these constitute less than 1 per cent of all pupil reactions.

Study of the relationships of reactions to their occasioning moves is helpful in delineating further the distinctive pedagogical roles of the teacher and the pupil. The data reveal that teacher reactions are almost always occasioned by pupil moves, and most of these are pupil responses. The pupil reacts twice as frequently to the teacher as he does to other pupils. When the pupil reacts to the teacher, he typically reacts to a teacher reaction; when he reacts to a fellow pupil, he usually reacts to a pupil reaction or pupil response.

Teacher's role. In classroom discussion, the teacher infrequently reacts to his own verbal moves. As indicated in Table 42, 96.7 per

TABLE 42

Distribution of Types of Teacher Reacting Move by Occasioning Move and Speaker

Speaker and Type of Occasioning Move	*Types of Teacher Reacting Move*											
	Total		*Substantive*		*Rating*		*Procedural*		*Substantive/ Rating*		*Substantive/ Procedural*	
	%	*f*	%	*f*	%	*f*	%	*f*	%	*f*	%	*f*
All Combined	100.0	3759	17.0	633	46.0	1738	7.0	257	27.1	1021	2.9	109
Total T-REA Occasioned by T-Moves	3.1	110	2.0	68	0.1	5	0.3	12	0.1	3	0.6	22
T-SOL	0.1	4	—	1	—	—	0.1	3	—	—	—	—
T-RES	0.6	19	0.3	11	—	1	—	1	—	1	0.1	5
T-STR	—	1	—	—	—	—	—	1	—	—	—	—
T-REA	2.5	86	1.7	56	0.1	4	0.2	7	0.1	2	0.5	17
T-Physical T-Pause T-NOC	—	—	—	—	—	—	—	—	—	—	—	—

Speaker and Type of Occasioning Move	Types of Teacher Reacting Move											
	Total		Substantive		Rating		Procedural		Substantive/ Rating		Substantive/ Procedural	
	%	f	%	f	%	f	%	f	%	f	%	f
Total T-REA Occasioned by P-Moves	96.7	3639	14.9	560	45.9	1733	6.6	241	27.0	1018	2.3	87
P-SOL	0.8	29	0.1	5	0.3	11	0.2	10	—	1	0.1	2
P-RES	74.1	2800	9.3	355	38.6	1458	2.5	92	22.4	843	1.3	52
P-STR	1.5	55	0.2	6	0.8	29	0.3	12	0.2	7	—	1
P-REA	14.9	543	3.5	130	5.2	194	2.0	61	3.7	141	0.5	17
P-Physical P-Pause P-NOC	5.5	212	1.8	64	1.0	41	1.6	66	0.7	26	0.4	15
Total T-REA Occasioned by A-STR	0.2	10	0.1	5	—	—	0.1	5	—	—	—	—

TABLE 43

Distribution of Positive and Negative Rating Reactions by Teachers Following a Sequence of Solicitation-Pupil Response According to Information Activity Congruence of Solicitation and Response

Pupil Response To Which Teacher Reacts	*Teacher Reaction*													
	Total		*Total Positive*		*Positive*		*Substantive/ Positive*		*Total Negative*		*Negative*		*Substantive/ Negative*	
	%	*f*	%	*f*	%	*f*	%	*f*	%	*f*	%	*f*	%	*f*
All Combined	100.0	2301	80.0	1843	51.2	1180	28.8	663	20.0	458	12.1	278	7.9	180
Information Activity Congruence	100.0	2197	80.2	1761	51.1	1124	28.9	637	19.8	436	12.0	264	7.8	172
Information Activity Incongruence	100.0	104	78.8	82	53.8	56	25.0	26	21.2	22	13.5	14	7.7	8

cent of all teacher reactions are occasioned by moves spoken by pupils. Pupil responding moves occasion 74.1 per cent of all teacher reactions. This finding is consistent with data already reported: since virtually all teacher reactions are occasioned by pupil moves and since responding accounts for the major portion of pupil activity, it follows that pupil responses would most frequently be the occasion for teacher reactions. A relatively small percentage (14.9 per cent) of all teacher reactions is occasioned by pupil reactions. The teacher infrequently reacts to pupil structuring or soliciting, each of which occasions less than 2 per cent of teacher reactions.

Since three-fourths of all teacher reactions are occasioned by pupil responding moves, the relationships between these two types of move deserve further analysis. As indicated in Table 42, teachers react to 2,800 or 72.4 per cent of the 3,863 pupil responses that occur in the discourse. (In contrast, pupils react to only 114, or 3 per cent, of all responding moves by fellow pupils.)

Slightly more than one-half (51.8 per cent) of teacher reactions to pupil responses are rating reactions. This again underscores one of the teacher's principal jobs in the classroom. The rating function of the teacher is further highlighted by the fact that 30.2 per cent, the next highest percentage, are substantive-rating reactions. Less frequently, 12.7 per cent of the time, does the teacher react with substantive reactions, and only 5.3 per cent of his reactions are procedural and substantive-procedural reactions.

The importance of the rating function in the teacher's role is emphasized by the fact that 2,301, or 82 per cent, of all teacher reactions to pupil responses include rating components. Of these 2,301 reactions, approximately two-thirds (62.8 per cent) are rating reactions and about one-third (27.2 per cent) are substantive-rating reactions; when the teacher rates pupil responses, he rates pupils more than twice as frequently as he rates *and* suggests some substantive modification of what the pupil said.

It is also interesting to note that the teacher is four times more positive than negative when he rates pupil responses: 80 per cent of teacher ratings are basically positive (i.e., positive, admitting, and repeating) and only 20 per cent are basically negative (i.e., negative, not admitting, qualifying). Even when the teacher expresses negatively toned ratings, he is much more inclined to rate by qualifying rather than by not admitting or by a distinctly negative reaction: qualifying occurs twice as frequently as the not admitting and the negative categories combined.

Table 43 presents the distribution of positive and negative rating

TABLE 44

Distribution of Positive and Negative Teacher Reactions Following a Sequence of Solicitation-Pupil Response According to Logical Congruence of Solicitation and Response

Pupil Response To Which Teacher Reacts	*Teacher Reaction*													
	Total		*Total Positive*		*Positive*		*Substantive/ Positive*		*Total Negative*		*Negative*		*Substantive/ Negative*	
	%	*f*	%	*f*	%	*f*	%	*f*	%	*f*	%	*f*	%	*f*
All Combined	100.0	2301	80.0	1843	51.2	1180	28.8	663	20.0	458	12.1	278	7.9	180
Logically Congruent Response	100.0	2213	80.0	1770	51.0	1130	29.0	640	20.0	443	12.0	267	8.0	176
Logically Incongruent Response	100.0	88	82.9	73	56.8	50	26.1	23	17.1	15	12.5	11	4.6	4

reactions by teachers to pupil responses, according to the information activity congruence of the solicitation and response.* These data reveal that of the 2,301 pupil responding moves that the teacher rates, 95.5 per cent (2,197) are operationally congruent. Of these congruent responses, 80.2 per cent are the occasion for positive ratings by the teacher, and 19.8 per cent for negative ratings. Similarly, of the operationally incongruent responses, 78.8 per cent are the occasion for positive teacher ratings, and 21.2 per cent for negative ratings. Thus, surprisingly enough, the ratio of positive to negative ratings by the teacher both to congruent and to incongruent responses is the same: 4 to 1.

One might reasonably expect the teacher when reacting to an operationally incongruent pupil response to make frequent use of substantive-rating reactions which make it possible for him not only to rate the pupil, but also to suggest some modification or clarification of what the pupil said. However, the data in Table 43 indicate that this is not the case; the teacher uses rating reactions twice as frequently as he uses substantive-rating reactions in reacting to operationally incongruent pupil responses.

The picture is very much the same when one considers the teacher's rating reactions to pupil responses that are logically congruent and logically incongruent with the solicitations that elicted them.** As the data included in Table 44 indicate, 96 per cent (2,213) of the 2,301 pupil responses that the teacher rates are logically congruent, and only 4 per cent are logically incongruent. Of the logically congruent responses, 80 per cent are the occasion for positive ratings by the teacher, and 20 per cent for negative ratings. Of the logically incongruent responses, 82.9 per cent are the occasion for positive ratings, and 17.1 per cent for negative ratings. Thus, the ratio of positive to negative ratings by the teacher both to logically congruent and to logically incongruent responding moves is 4 to 1.

Again, one might reasonably expect that teachers in reacting to logically incongruent responses by pupils would use substantive-rating reactions more frequently than rating reactions. But the data indicate that this is not the case; when the teacher reacts to logically incongruent pupil responses, he uses rating reactions twice as frequently as he uses substantive-rating reactions.

These data thus reveal the surprising fact that the teacher rates

* See Chapter Four, pp. 127–129, for discussion of information process congruence of responding and soliciting moves.

** See Chapter Four, pp. 125–127, for discussion of logical process congruence of responding and soliciting moves.

TABLE 45

Distribution of Types of Pupil Reacting Move by Occasioning Move and Speaker

Speaker and Type of Occasioning Move	*Type of Pupil Reacting Move*											
	Total		*Substantive*		*Rating*		*Procedural*		*Substantive/ Rating*		*Substantive/ Procedural*	
	%	*f*	%	*f*	%	*f*	%	*f*	%	*f*	%	*f*
All Combined	100.0	890	53.6	477	16.7	148	15.3	137	10.6	94	3.9	34
Total P-REA Occasioned by T-Moves	69.9	622	37.8	337	11.5	102	11.1	99	7.2	64	2.3	20
T-SOL	2.9	25	0.3	3	1.0	8	1.6	14	—	—	—	—
T-RES	12.9	115	7.0	62	2.3	21	1.7	15	1.6	14	0.3	3
T-STR	4.5	40	2.8	25	0.1	1	1.2	10	0.3	3	0.1	1
T-REA	49.4	440	27.7	247	8.1	72	6.4	58	5.3	47	1.9	16
T-Physical												
T-Pause	0.2	2	—	—	—	—	0.2	2	—	—	—	—
T-NOC												

Speaker and Type of Occasioning Move	*Type of Pupil Reacting Move*											
	Total		*Substantive*		*Rating*		*Procedural*		*Substantive/ Rating*		*Substantive/ Procedural*	
	%	*f*	%	*f*	%	*f*	%	*f*	%	*f*	%	*f*
Total P-REA Occasioned by P-Moves	29.8	265	15.8	140	5.2	46	4.2	38	3.4	30	1.3	11
P-SOL	0.6	6	0.3	3	—	—	0.3	3	—	—	—	—
P-RES	12.8	114	6.6	59	2.7	24	1.6	14	1.7	15	—	—
P-STR	0.9	9	0.4	4	—	—	0.4	4	—	—	0.2	2
P-REA	13.0	122	7.3	64	2.3	20	1.7	15	1.7	15	0.1	1
P-Physical P-Pause P-NOC	1.9	17	1.1	10	0.2	2	—	—	—	—	1.0	8
Total P-REA Occasioned by A-STR	0.3	3	—	—	—	—	—	—	—	—	0.3	3

TABLE 46

Frequency Distribution of Types of Pupil Reaction According to Types of Occasioning Teacher Reaction

Type of Occasioning Teacher Reaction	*Total*	*Type of Pupil Reaction*				
		Substantive	*Rating*	*Procedural*	*Substantive/ Rating*	*Substantive/ Procedural*
All Combined	440	247	72	58	47	16
Substantive	132	70	24	10	22	6
Rating	100	60	20	10	8	2
Procedural	43	13	6	22	1	1
Substantive/Rating	150	95	20	14	15	6
Substantive/Procedural	15	9	2	2	1	1

congruent and incongruent responding moves by the pupil in the same fashion: the ratio of positive to negative reactions is identical, and the proportion of rating reactions and substantive-rating reactions is almost the same.

Pupil's role. The pupil reacts twice as frequently to the teacher as he does to fellow pupils. As shown in Table 45, slightly more than two-thirds of all pupil reactions are occasioned by teacher moves and slightly less than one-third of all pupil reactions by moves of other pupils. This reflects the typical pattern of interaction in the classes studied: the principal channel of communication is between teacher and pupil, rather than between pupil and pupil.

While responding moves occasion the greatest proportion of teacher reactions, reacting moves by the teacher and fellow pupils occasion the greatest number of pupil reactions. Almost one-half (49.4 per cent) of all pupil reactions are occasioned by teacher reactions. Much less frequently, 12.9 per cent of the time, does the pupil react to teacher responses. Only rarely does the pupil react to teacher structuring and teacher soliciting moves. These two types of move occasion only 7.4 per cent of all pupil reactions.

When the pupil reacts to a fellow pupil, he tends to react to a pupil reaction or to a pupil response: 13.9 per cent of pupil reactions are occasioned by the former and 12.8 per cent by the latter. Although pupil responding accounts for over four times as many moves as does pupil reacting, the pupil reacts to a fellow pupil's reaction just about as frequently as he does to a fellow pupil's response. The pupil infrequently reacts to a fellow pupil's soliciting move or structuring move, which together occasion only 1.5 per cent of all pupil reactions.

The fact that two-thirds of all pupil reactions are to teacher reactions and to reactions of fellow pupils highlights a significant feature of the communication network in the classes studied. The pupil participates in classroom discussion most frequently when directed to respond by a teacher's solicitation, and he usually does not feel free to enter the discussion again with a reacting move until after the teacher has reacted; occasionally the pupil reacts to responding moves, but much more frequently his reactions are to reactions of other participants, usually of the teacher.

Since one-half of all pupil reactions are occasioned by teacher reactions, the relationships between these two speaker-move combinations call for further analysis. Pupils react to 440, or 11.7 per cent, of the 3,759 teacher reactions that occur in the discourse. When one considers the types of teacher reaction that occasion various types of pupil reaction, he finds (Table 46) that the most frequent combination is pupil substantive reaction occasioned by teacher substantive-rating reaction, accounting for 21.6 per cent of all pupil reactions occasioned by teacher reactions. The second highest frequency is represented by pupil substantive reaction occasioned by teacher substantive reaction, which accounts for 70, or 15.9 per cent. The third most frequent combination is pupil substantive reaction occasioned by teacher rating reaction, which represents 60, or 13.6 per cent. Together these three combinations account for 51 per cent of all pupil reactions occasioned by teacher reactions; none of the other 22 possible combinations accounts for more than 5.4 per cent. It is clear that when the pupil reacts to teacher reactions, he does so most frequently by reacting substantively to teacher substantive, teacher substantive-rating, and teacher rating reactions, in that order.

Further examination of the data reveals that the pupil reacts to a higher percentage of teacher substantive reactions and teacher substantive-rating reactions that occur in the discourse than he does to teacher rating reactions: while the pupil reacts to 20.8 per cent of all teacher substantive reactions and 14.6 per cent of all teacher substantive-rating reactions, he reacts to only 5.7 per cent of all teacher rating reactions. Obviously, the pupil is more inclined to view teacher substantive reactions and teacher substantive-rating reactions rather than teacher rating reactions as the appropriate occasion for reacting to the teacher.

Summary

Summarized below are the principal results of the analysis:

1. Reacting moves account for a substantial proportion of the discourse in the classes studied; reactions constitute a little less than one-third of all moves made and slightly more than one-third of all lines spoken.

2. Reacting moves play a more significant part in the teacher's discourse than they do in the pupil's discourse. Reactions account for 38.9 per cent of the teacher's moves, but only 15.1 per cent of the pupil's moves. Similarly, whereas 44.7 per cent of all lines spoken by teachers are devoted to reacting, only 19.1 per cent of the lines spoken by pupils are accounted for by reactions.

3. The roles of the teacher and the pupil are in part defined by frequency of behavior in the various types of reaction. Rating reactions are an important part of the teacher's role, but they play only a minor part in the pupil's role. In contrast, the largest proportion of student reactions are substantive reactions, but only a relatively small

proportion of teacher reactions are of this type. Procedural reactions and substantive-procedural reactions occur infrequently in the discourse both of teachers and of pupils.

4. Virtually all reactions are occasioned by verbal actions (i.e., pedagogical moves) rather than by physical actions or by pauses in the discussion, and most teacher reactions and pupil reactions are occasioned by single moves.

5. Teacher reactions are almost always occasioned by pupil moves, and three-fourths of these are pupil responses. Pupils react twice as frequently to the teacher as they do to fellow pupils. When the pupil reacts to the teacher, it typically is to a teacher reaction; when he reacts to a fellow pupil, it is likely to be to a pupil reacting or pupil responding move. The pupil is much more inclined to view teacher substantive reactions or teacher substantive-rating reactions rather than teacher rating reactions as the appropriate occasions for reacting to the teacher.

6. When teachers rate what pupils say and do in the classroom, they are four times more positive than negative. When the teacher does react negatively to the pupil, he is much more inclined to qualify rather than to not admit or to express a distinctly negative reaction. This is true of the teacher's reactions to incongruent pupil responses as well as to congruent pupil responses.

CHAPTER SEVEN

TEACHING CYCLES: PATTERNS OF PEDAGOGICAL MOVES

FROM THE POINT OF VIEW of research design, the most significant outcome of the early stages of the research was the development of the notion of the pedagogical move. Structuring, soliciting, responding, and reacting served as reliable units of verbal behavior for describing the pedagogical functions that teachers and pupils perform in the classroom. Subsequent research took two forms: (1) intensive study of dimensions of pedagogical moves reported in Chapters Four, Five, and Six and (2) development of the concept of teaching cycles, a larger unit of verbal behavior designed to describe patterns of pedagogical moves and the relationship of moves to each other. Two types of teaching cycle are used in this analysis. *Formally ordered teaching cycles* are designed to provide a basic accounting of all of the possible patterns of pedagogical moves and how they are distributed in the data. *Temporally ordered teaching cycles* are designed to study the sequential ordering of teaching cycles using Markov chains.

Formally Ordered Teaching Cycles

In our overall analysis of classroom discourse, a pedagogical move is seen as comparable to a move in a chess match or a single play in a game of football. Teaching cycles, on the other hand, are seen as an interrelated series of moves or plays. The teaching cycle represents an attempt to conceptualize that larger unit of classroom discourse that seems to be inaugurated by structuring and soliciting moves. It is an effort to see the several pedagogical moves in combination with the expectation that these patterns of moves will provide a fruitful and reliable way of describing the ebb and flow of classroom discourse.

A formally ordered teaching cycle is defined as a series of pedagogical moves that begins either with a structuring move or with a solicitation that is not preceded by a structuring move and ends with the move that precedes a new structuring or a new unstructured solicitation. Since, by definition, both responding and reacting moves are either actively elicited or occasioned by a previous pedagogical move, neither one can be said to begin a cycle, thus substantially limiting the number of combinations of moves.

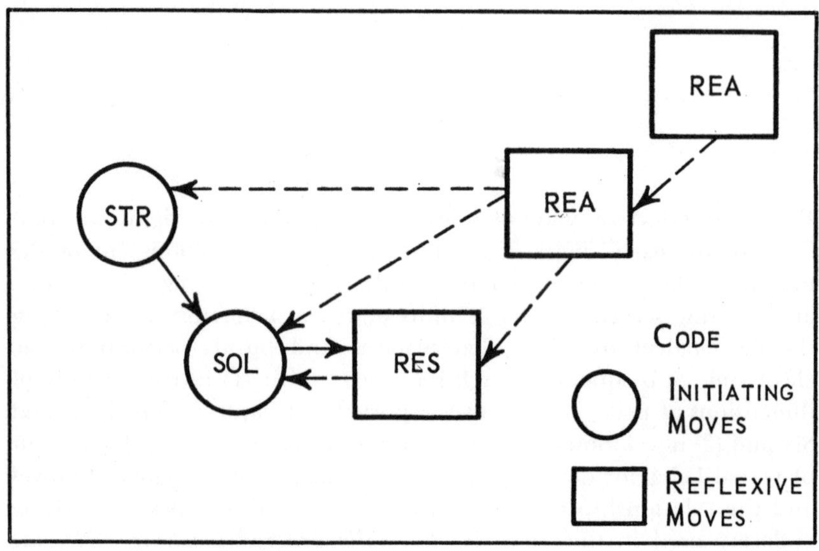

Framework for Analysis

Figure 1 illustrates the interplay among pedagogical moves by indicating the possible paths by which discussion may flow within the framework of a single teaching cycle. The unbroken lines indicate that only a single move in the given direction is possible since a second structuring or soliciting move would initiate a new cycle. The broken line indicates that many such moves are possible within a single cycle; that is, there may be more than one response to a single solicitation and several reactions to any of the other pedagogical moves.

Given a structuring move, there are two subsequent moves that will sustain the cycle: either (1) the structuring leads into a solicitation, or (2) the structuring is the occasion for feedback in the form of reactions. If neither of these moves occurs, a new teaching cycle must begin with the next move.

If the structuring move is indeed followed by a solicitation or if the cycle begins with an unstructured soliciting move, there are two further movements that will sustain the cycle. The more probable one is that the solicitation will elicit a direct response or several direct responses, but there is also the possibility that there will be one or more reactions to the solicitation (e.g., "That's a stupid question") rather than responses to it. Once a speaker makes a responding move, only further responding moves or reactions may follow if the cycle is to continue. Finally, reacting moves may themselves be the occasion for further reacting moves.

Given this model, there are twenty-one possible types of formally ordered teaching cycles, each representing a somewhat different pattern of classroom discourse. The following list presents the twenty-one possible patterns:

Teaching Cycles

1.	STR					
2.	STR	SOL				
3.	STR	REA				
4.	STR	REA	REA . . .			
5.	STR	SOL	RES			
6.	STR	SOL	RES	RES . . .		
7.	STR	SOL	REA			
8.	STR	SOL	REA	REA . . .		
9.	STR	SOL	RES	REA		
10.	STR	SOL	RES	REA	REA . . .	
11.	STR	SOL	RES	REA	RES . . .	
12.	STR	SOL	RES	REA	RES . . .	REA . . .
13.		SOL				
14.		SOL	RES			
15.		SOL	RES	RES . . .		
16.		SOL	REA			
17.		SOL	REA	REA . . .		
18.		SOL	RES	REA		
19.		SOL	RES	REA	REA . . .	
20.		SOL	RES	REA	RES . . .	
21.		SOL	RES	REA	RES . . .	REA . . .

Code

STR—Structuring RES—Responding
SOL—Soliciting REA—Reacting
. . . —one or more additional moves of the kind designated; e.g., "RES . . ." means one or more additional responding moves to the same soliciting move.

For coding purposes, the combining of the pedagogical moves into the several patterns of discourse is determined by the definition

TABLE 47

Distribution of Formally Ordered Teaching Cycles According to Initiatory and Reflexive Patterns for All Fifteen Classes Combined

Initiatory Patterns		*Total*	*No Reflexive Pattern*	*Reflexive Patterns*							
				RES	RES RES . . .	REA	REA REA . . .	RES REA	RES RES . . . REA	RES REA REA . . .	RES REA RES . . . REA . . .
Total	%	97.5*	13.4	25.4	0.9	3.2	1.4	31.7	2.9	9.8	8.8
	f	4478	614	1169	44	141	66	1459	131	450	404
STR	%	4.1	1.9	—**	—	1.4	0.8	—	—	—	—
	f	186	85	—	—	62	39	—	—	—	—
SOL	%	97.3	9.7	22.3	0.8	1.5	0.5	26.0	2.5	9.0	7.0
	f	3642	445	1025	38	67	24	1196	114	413	320
STR-	%	14.1	1.8	3.1	0.1	0.3	0.1	5.7	0.4	0.8	1.8
SOL	f	650	84	144	6	12	3	263	17	37	650

* 114 or 2.5 per cent of the teaching cycles were not codable because tape recordings were partly inaudible.
** Combinations of patterns indicated by dashes are impossible.

of formally ordered teaching cycles with only minor modifications. One involved the so-called "nodding SOL." This is the classroom convention whereby the teacher usually "gives the nod" to the student before he may speak. Normally, this is accomplished simply by calling the student's name. This convention is recorded in the original analysis as T/SOL/–/–/ACV/PRF/1/; that is, the teacher solicits with the expectation that someone will perform a vocal action. Technically, then, "John?" is a solicitation and by definition would inaugurate a new teaching cycle. However, since it merely gives someone the right to speak and is not intended in itself to elicit a specific response, "nodding SOL's" were disregarded for purposes of the teaching-cycle analysis.

The second modification involved those relatively few instances where a complete cycle was interlarded between two moves of another cycle. The following is an example of this situation:

P/SOL:	Now these radios, they would have a quota on them, wouldn't they?
T/SOL:	They'd have a what?
P/RES:	A quota.
T/RES-M3:	They might. I don't really know whether radios do or not—transistor radios.

The "M3" that appears in the coding of the last move indicates that this response is to a solicitation that appeared three moves earlier. It is an answer to the first question. In terms of formally ordered teaching cycles, this is coded as two cycles of type 14 (SOL RES), but with the second response labeled as belonging to the first cycle. Otherwise, if strict temporal order were maintained, the impression would be created that the second solicitation elicited two responses and the first none.

In the analysis using formally ordered teaching cycles, temporal sequence is modified to preserve the integrity of *form* within the teaching cycle. Formally ordered teaching cycles, then, represent a logical reconstruction of the discourse rather than a recapitulation of the precise order in which the pedagogical moves were made. Thus a response is always considered a part of the cycle in which the solicitation that elicited it appeared, and a reaction is considered part of the cycle in which the move that occasioned it appeared, despite the fact that another teaching cycle may intervene between the two moves.

Analysis

Table 47 provides a picture of the patterning of pedagogical moves for all 15 classes combined. The rows indicate the three possible initiatory patterns. The column headings represent the nine reflexive patterns. The most frequent combination is a simple solicitation (row 3) as the initiatory move and a single response followed by a single reaction (column 7) as the reflexive pattern. For the classes as a whole, SOL RES REA accounts for 26 per cent of the total number of cycles. SOL RES (row 3, column 3) is the next most common teaching cycle, accounting for 22.3 per cent of the total. The total percentage of structure-initiated cycles may be obtained by combining the totals for rows 2 and 4 (18.2 per cent). Similarly, one may obtain the total number of teaching cycles that include at least one reaction by combining columns 5 through 10 or the number of cycles which have multiple responses by combining columns 4, 8, and 10. Since a response cannot occur in a cycle in which there is no soliciting move, the six cells in row 2 which include responding moves are invalid.

The analysis of the language of the classroom in terms of percentage distribution of pedagogical moves reveals striking similarities among the 15 classes studied. To some extent, the lack of variability in classroom discourse is borne out in the analysis of teaching cycles. At the same time, however, considerable diversity is observed within the basic pattern. Both the similarities and the differences are reflected in three dimensions of teaching cycle analysis: cycle rate, source, and cycle patterns.

Rate. Rate is described in terms of the cycle activity index, the number of cycles per minute of actual class time. This measure is not substantially related to rate of speech, but to the rate at which verbal interchanges take place in the classroom. These data are summarized in Table 48. A high index, as in the case of Teachers 1 and 13, indicates a rapid flow of discourse; a low index, as in the case of Teachers 9 and 14, indicates low cycle activity. Considerable variability is apparent among these 15 teachers in this aspect of verbal activity. The range of cycle activity indexes is from 0.9 (less than one cycle per minute of class time) to 3.0 (an average of three cycles per minute). The mean and median for the group is 1.8. Over the first three sessions, the mean cycle activity index remains remarkably constant at 1.9, indicating that cycle rate is probably a rather stable characteristic. The drop to 1.4 in the fourth session is probably related to the fact that several of the teachers scheduled reports or debates for that session. Since these activities usually involve long pedagogical moves, the rate of verbal interchange tends to decline.

Source. The second factor in teaching cycle analysis is source; that is, who, teacher or pupil, initiates a given cycle of verbal activity.

TABLE 48

Cycle Activity Indexes for Each of the Fifteen Classes and for All Classes Combined

Class	Session I	II	III	IV	*Unit*
All Combined	1.9	1.9	1.9	1.4	1.8
1	2.4	3.8	2.9	2.2	2.9
2	1.8	1.8	2.3	1.5	1.9
3	1.9	2.1	1.3	1.2	1.6
4	2.5	1.8	1.8	1.4	1.9
5	1.7	2.0	1.8	1.8	1.8
6	1.0	1.2	1.2	1.2	1.2
7	2.1	1.4	2.2	1.7	1.8
8	2.3	2.3	1.5	1.5	1.9
9	0.9	0.9	1.0	0.9	0.9
10	1.2	1.5	1.4	0.9	1.2
11	1.7	1.7	2.4	0.9	1.6
12	1.5	1.5	1.6	1.6	1.6
13	2.7	3.4	2.8	3.0	3.0
14	1.5	1.3	1.1	0.6	1.1
15	2.7	2.9	3.4	1.3	2.6

Source is described in terms of the percentage of teacher-initiated teaching cycles. These data are summarized in Table 49. Of the 4,592 teaching cycles in the 60 class sessions, 84.5 per cent are teacher-initiated. By and large, it is the teacher who delivers the structuring or soliciting move that initiates the teaching cycle. In only one of the sessions (Teacher 5's fourth session) does the percentage of pupil-initiated cycles exceed teacher-initiated cycles. In three of the sessions (Teacher 6's first and Teacher 9's first and third), there are no pupil-initiated teaching cycles.

Over the unit of four sessions, there is again considerable variability among the 15 teachers. The range is from Teacher 9's 96.6 per cent to Teacher 5's 61.2 per cent. The median is 88 per cent and the mean 84.5 per cent. The mean percentages of teacher-initiated teaching cycles remain constant over the first two sessions at 87.2 per cent but drop to 83.4 per cent in the third session and 74.2 per cent in the fourth. This indicates a tendency for pupils to structure and solicit more as the unit progressed. The lower incidence of teacher-initiated teaching cycles in the fourth session is probably due in part

TABLE 49

Percentage of Teacher-Initiated Cycles for Each of the Fifteen Classes and for All Classes Combined

Class	*Session* I	II	III	IV	*Unit of Four Sessions*
All Combined	87.3	87.2	83.4	74.2	84.5
1	97.1	93.4	90.6	90.9	93.1
2	87.1	91.7	91.1	89.8	90.0
3	94.6	93.5	86.6	74.5	89.3
4	93.8	80.3	94.5	79.6	88.0
5	80.0	56.9	71.6	36.9	61.2
6	100.0	90.2	87.0	92.7	92.1
7	84.6	60.9	73.7	85.4	77.4
8	82.1	84.6	72.1	86.7	82.4
9	100.0	92.5	100.0	93.9	96.6
10	95.1	92.0	79.3	85.4	88.5
11	98.7	96.1	93.9	67.6	92.4
12	78.0	73.7	63.1	76.6	72.1
13	89.6	92.6	75.5	91.6	87.4
14	86.6	92.9	87.9	49.9	83.8
15	59.6	84.0	87.6	60.3	75.1

to the pupil reports and debates which took place in several of the classes.

Pattern. The third factor in the analysis is pattern, which refers to distinctive sequences of pedagogical moves. Pattern is described in terms of the percentage distribution of the 21 cycle types in each of the 15 classes (Table 50). Of the 21 types, 6 account for approximately 80 per cent of the total number of teaching cycles for all 15 classes combined. These are cycle 18 (SOL RES REA), which accounts for 26 per cent of all cycles; cycle 14 (SOL RES), which accounts for 22.3 per cent; cycle 13 (SOL), which accounts for 9.7 per cent; cycle 19 (SOL RES REA REA . . .), which accounts for 9 per cent; cycle 21 (SOL REA RES . . . REA . . .), which accounts for 7 per cent; and cycle 9 (STR SOL RES REA), which accounts for 5.7 per cent. None of the other 15 cycles accounts for as much as five per cent of the total.

Cycle 14 (SOL RES) may be seen as a basic pattern in almost all of the verbal interchange in these classrooms. This interchange, however, is modifiable in three ways. First, a reacting move may, and very frequently does, follow the response. Comparison of cycle 18 (SOL RES REA) and cycle 14 (SOL RES) in Table 50 indicates that the extent to which this occurs in the experimental group differs considerably from class to class. Second, a structuring move may precede the solicitation. Some teachers, such as Teacher 9, follow this pattern consistently; others, such as Teacher 13, structure very infrequently. The third major kind of modification involves solicitations that elicit multiple responses or which involve multiple reactions. The distribution of cycle 19 (SOL RES REA REA . . .) and cycle 21 (SOL RES REA RES . . . REA . . .) in Table 50 again indicates considerable variability among these teachers. All three modifications may, of course, occur in combination. A teacher, for example, may structure and react to the same solicitation-response sequence.

Teaching styles. One may infer from these data that while all 15 classes (with the possible exception of Class 9) engaged primarily in soliciting and responding, the teachers did vary in the extent to which they modified the basic solicitation-response interchange. As a matter of fact, considerable variability is evident in all three of the dimensions of teaching-cycle analysis. This suggests that *styles* of pedagogical discourse can be described in terms of cycle activity, percentage of teacher-initiated cycles, and distribution of cycle types. The factors of rate, source, and pattern provide the basis for a kind of typology of classroom discourse which is useful in identifying distinctive modes of linguistic behavior and comparing individual teaching styles. Teachers 2 and 4, for example, are probably most alike in teaching style. Both have the same cycle activity index, a moderate 1.9 (Table 48). They also have comparable percentages of teacher-initiated cycles in the moderate to high range (Table 49). With respect to pattern, these teachers differ only slightly in their relative use of cycle 14 (SOL RES) and cycle 18 (SOL RES REA). Reactions are somewhat more likely to follow responses in Teacher 4's class than in Teacher 2's class. Table 50 indicates that the percentages for cycles 18 (SOL RES REA) and 14 (SOL RES) in Teacher 2's sessions are 19.6 and 24.0, while in Teacher 4's they are 22.5 and 20.2. The higher incidence of cycle 19 (SOL RES REA REA . . .) in Teacher 4's sessions also indicates a greater tendency for reactions to follow reactions in his sessions than in Teacher 2's. Nevertheless, the styles of discourse in Teacher 2's and Teacher 4's sessions may be described as basically similar.

Teaching cycle analysis may be used to describe differences, as well as similarities, among teaching styles. Teachers 1 and 13, for example, have extremely high cycle activity indexes (Table 48). In this respect, therefore, they are alike. Teacher 1's percentage of

TABLE 50

Percentage Distribution of Formally Ordered Teaching Cycles According to Cycle Type for Each of the Fifteen Classes

Cycle Type	*Class*														
	1	2	3	4	5	6	7	8	9	10	11	12	13	14	15
All Types	100.0	100.0	100.0	100.0	100.0	100.0	100.0	100.0	100.0	100.0	100.0	100.0	100.0	100.0	100.0
1	0.4	1.4	1.3	1.5	1.8	2.5	5.3	0.3	11.5	2.1	2.1	1.6	0.3	2.3	1.5
2	0.6	1.1	3.3	1.5	2.5	0.5	1.1	1.3	2.0	0.4	4.2	3.2	0.6	2.0	3.9
3	0.6	0.4	3.0	0.4	4.3	0.5	3.4	0.6	—	0.4	0.3	0.8	0.3	2.0	3.2
4	0.4	1.4	1.3	0.4	0.7	—	1.5	1.3	2.0	0.9	—	1.6	0.2	—	2.0
5	1.7	3.6	3.7	1.5	5.0	2.0	9.1	3.8	3.4	4.3	4.5	4.0	0.8	2.3	2.0
6	—	0.4	0.3	0.4	0.4	—	—	—	—	—	0.3	—	—	—	0.2
7	—	—	0.3	0.4	0.4	—	0.4	—	2.0	0.4	0.3	0.4	—	0.4	0.2
8	—	—	—	—	—	—	—	—	—	1.3	—	—	—	—	—
9	3.6	3.9	6.3	5.6	6.8	3.9	9.1	3.8	17.6	8.1	13.9	9.7	1.0	5.8	2.0
10	0.2	2.1	0.7	1.1	—	0.5	2.3	1.9	1.4	0.4	0.7	2.0	—	0.4	0.2
11	0.6	—	0.7	0.7	0.7	—	—	0.3	—	—	1.4	—	0.3	—	0.2
12	1.3	3.9	1.0	3.7	2.4	1.5	1.9	1.3	—	0.4	0.7	4.9	1.1	2.7	1.5
13	6.1	11.1	20.3	12.4	11.5	6.9	2.8	7.3	4.7	4.7	9.7	9.7	13.7	9.3	8.6
14	20.8	24.0	23.0	20.2	19.7	35.5	18.9	22.4	7.4	25.5	17.7	22.7	28.2	15.2	23.4
15	0.8	1.1	0.7	0.4	0.4	0.5	—	0.6	—	—	0.7	1.6	1.9	—	1.5
16	0.8	1.1	2.7	1.9	2.2	0.5	0.7	—	6.1	0.9	0.7	1.2	1.0	2.3	2.5
17	0.6	—	0.3	0.4	2.5	1.0	—	—	—	—	0.3	—	0.5	0.8	1.0
18	39.7	19.6	18.7	22.5	13.6	28.0	25.6	30.7	30.4	26.4	33.0	14.2	26.0	31.5	23.2

Cycle Type	Class														
	1	2	3	4	5	6	7	8	9	10	11	12	13	14	15
19	7.6	7.5	6.7	10.9	10.0	8.4	9.4	14.4	6.1	10.6	5.2	11.7	8.8	6.2	10.6
20	3.4	4.3	1.7	3.7	2.2	1.5	1.9	1.9	—	2.1	0.3	1.6	4.3	1.6	2.5
21	7.4	9.6	2.0	8.6	8.6	3.4	4.5	5.4	4.7	8.5	2.1	4.9	10.2	12.1	7.1
NC	3.4	3.6	2.0	1.9	4.3	2.0	2.3	2.6	0.7	2.6	1.7	4.0	1.0	3.1	2.7

Legend

1. STR 2. STR SOL 3. STR REA 4. STR REA REA . . .
5. STR SOL RES 6. STR SOL RES RES . . . 7. STR SOL REA
8. STR SOL REA REA . . . 9. STR SOL RES REA
10. STR SOL RES REA REA . . . 11. STR SOL RES REA RES . . .
12. STR SOL RES REA RES . . . REA . . . 13. SOL 14. SOL RES
15. SOL RES RES . . . 16. SOL REA 17. SOL REA REA . . .
18. SOL RES REA 19. SOL RES REA REA . . . 20. SOL RES REA RES . . .
21. SOL RES REA RES . . . REA . . . NC. NOT CODABLE

teacher-initiated teaching cycles (Table 49) is 93.1, compared with Teacher 13's 87.4 per cent. This indicates only a moderate difference. Table 50, however, shows a striking contrast in the ratio of cycle 18 (SOL RES REA) to cycle 14 (SOL RES), a measure of the extent to which a solicitation-response interchange is likely to be followed by a reaction. For Teacher 1 the ratio is 2 to 1, whereas for Teacher 13 it is 1 to 1. These data indicate, therefore, that reactions to responses are about twice as likely to occur in Class 1 as in Class 13.

Two complementary conclusions may be drawn from the data on formally ordered teaching cycles. The first is that the 15 teachers do not deviate radically from a general teaching pattern that consists basically of asking questions and receiving answers. Cycle 14 (SOL RES) and its simplest modification, cycle 18 (SOL RES REA), alone accounted for over 48 per cent of all cycles. In addition, the question-answer interchange forms the core of most of the other major teaching cycles. The second conclusion is that within the basic design there is still considerable variability. This variability may be described in terms of the rate at which verbal interchanges take place, the extent of teacher initiation of teaching cycles, and the manner in which the basic solicitation-response unit is modified.

Temporally Ordered Teaching Cycles

The basic accounting of the patterning of pedagogical moves developed in terms of formally ordered teaching cycles led to speculation about the possibility of identifying even larger patterns of pedagogical moves. One line of investigation sought to determine whether certain cyclical patterns and dimensions of cycles tend to influence the subsequent patterning of pedagogical moves. Statistically this is described through a *Markov chain,* which makes it possible to determine the transition probabilities of moving from one state to another (14). Taking types of teaching cycles as states, the probabilities of moving from one type of cycle to another were investigated as a way of determining whether one pattern of pedagogical moves tends to influence immediately subsequent patterning.

Framework for Analysis

In order to accomplish this type of analysis, emphasis was placed not on the formal ordering of the discourse, as with formally ordered teaching cycles, but on the strictly *temporal ordering* of the cyclical patterns. This procedure necessitated a minor respecification of the concept of teaching cycles. For purposes of this analysis, teaching cycles were defined as beginning either with a structuring move or with a soliciting move that was not preceded by a structuring move and continuing until the last reflexive move (responding or reacting) occurs.

Formally ordered teaching cycles and temporally ordered teaching cycles attempt to account for the patterning of pedagogical moves in slightly different ways. The former regards each new structuring move or unstructured solicitation as the beginning of a new cycle, while the latter occasionally subsumes certain initiatory moves when they occur within a larger patterning. Formally ordered cycles preserve integrity of *form* by treating every initiating move as beginning a new cycle and by reconstructing the discourse in order to achieve it. Temporally ordered teaching cycles preserve integrity of *time* by adhering strictly to the temporal sequence of the cyclical patterns even if this involves the occasional subsumption of minor initiatory moves. Those relatively few cycles that incorporate minor cycles are described as *augmented cycles,* of which there are three types.

Type 1: Repeating. Occasionally the teacher or the pupil finds it necessary to request repetition of certain moves. When a speaker solicits "repeating" within a previously established cycle pattern, the cycle is described as an augmented cycle of Type 1.

Example

P/SOL:	Now these radios, they would have a quota on them, wouldn't they?
* T/SOL:	They'd have a what?
P/RES:	A quota.
T/RES-M3:	They might, I don't really know whether radios do or not—transistor radios.

In contrast to formally ordered teaching cycles which would reconstruct this exchange as two SOL-RES cycles, temporally ordered teaching cycles regard these four moves as one SOL-RES cycle which has been augmented by repeating moves.

Type 2: Directing Performance. A second type of augmentation occurs when a teacher or pupil, within the context of a larger cycle, directs someone to do something that does not involve audible language. Although a solicitation, such a directing move is not regarded as initiating a new cycle but is subsumed within the larger cycle that is coded as an augmented cycle, Type 2.

Example

T/SOL:	Now, what is, what are the things of the home that are mass-produced in America that form a great per cent of our foreign export, Carol?
P/RES:	Electrical appliances.

T/REA:	Right.
* T/SOL:	Now put that down on your list.
T/*REA*-M:	This covers a great many things that are only produced or specialized by American industry. We specialize in it. We don't . . . I don't say we only produce all of these things, but we do specialize in them, and they form a big per cent of our foreign trade.

This interchange is also coded as a single cycle (SOL RES REA REA . . .) despite the fact that a solicitation directing the pupils to do something intervened. (The first reaction is an evaluation of the previous response; the second, an italicized REA, indicates a reaction occasioned by one or more moves in addition to that response.)

Type 3: Clarifying-Expanding. The third type of augmentation occurs when terms, statements, or ideas are clarified or extended within the context of an ongoing teaching cycle. Again, no new cycle is indicated in these instances, but a subscript is added to the coding of the ongoing cycle to show augmentation of this type.

Example

T/SOL:	What Americans would you think who would still be against it [Kennedy trade bill] despite the arguments that we have brought out this period for it? What Americans would still be against it regardless of the arguments we have brought out, Frank?
* P/SOL:	You mean which party or which class of people?
T/RES:	Either way.
P/RES-M3:	Well, I feel the Republicans are still . . . . As you look back in history, the Republicans have always been concerned with high tariffs. You know, they have always wanted high tariffs and never wanted them lower whereas, the Democrats always seem to favor a low tariff. And the last time we had a low tariff was during the term of Roosevelt. Ever since then, there was a high tariff until Kennedy took, you know, until he took the power of his administration, and there is a low tariff now—so . . . .
T/REA:	So that, therefore, you feel that more Republicans than Democrats would be opposed to the proposal on the grounds that Republicans have traditionally, as we look back into history, the Republican Party more than the Democratic Party, has pushed a high tariff.

Despite the fact that a SOL RES exchange takes place during the cycle, only one cycle (SOL RES REA) is coded, with the subscript 3 indicating that the cycle is augmented by expanding-clarifying moves.

Of the 4,081 temporally ordered teaching cycles, 364 are augmented cycles: 130 are Type 1 (Repeating), 66 are Type 2 (Directing Performance), and 168 are Type 3 (Clarifying-Expanding).

Results of Analysis

The analysis of temporally ordered teaching cycles proceeded in terms of three dimensions: the initiator of the cycle, the logic of the cycle, and the type of cycle. In each one, a Markov matrix was used to determine whether and in what ways prior states influenced following states.

Initiator of the cycle. The initiator of the cycle was determined, as in the case of formally ordered teaching cycles, on the basis of who (teacher, pupil, or audio-visual device) delivers the initiatory move. For the fifteen classes, the teacher initiates 85.0 per cent of the cycles, the pupil initiates 14.7 per cent, and audio-visual devices are used to initiate 0.3 per cent. These figures are almost exactly the same as for formally ordered teaching cycles, where the mean percentage for teacher-initiated cycles is 84.5 per cent (Table 49). Examination of Table 51 indicates, however, that once the prior states in terms of cycle initiation are known, the percentages change. For the 15 classes as a whole, the chance that one teacher-initiated cycle will follow another teacher-initiated cycle is approximately 90 per cent, while the chance that a pupil-initiated cycle will follow a teacher-initiated cycle is about 10 per cent.

These percentages change significantly when a pupil-initiated cycle is the prior state. In this case, the chance of the following state being a teacher-initiated cycle is only about 60 per cent and the chance of a pupil-initiated cycle occurring rises to 40 per cent. In the present sample pupil-initiated teaching cycles are, then, four times more likely to occur when they are preceded by other pupil-initiated cycles than when they are preceded by a teacher-initiated cycle. One may hypothesize that if a teacher wishes to encourage pupil participation, he should find some means of having a student initiate a cycle. In this manner, he would strongly increase the probability of subsequent student-initiation, because a prior pupil-initiated cycle seems to invite subsequent pupil-initated cycles to a far greater extent than does a teacher-initiated cycle.

Another significant feature indicated in Table 51 is the relatively wide range among the fifteen teachers in the present sample. The highest percentage of teacher initiation following another teacher initiation is 96.3 per cent for Class 9, while the lowest is 75.5 per cent for Class 5. Class 5 also has the highest percentage of pupil-initiated cycles following pupil-initiated cycles (59.3 per cent), while Class 2

TABLE 51

Percentage Distribution of Temporally Ordered Teaching Cycles by Initiator of Preceding and Following Cycles for Each of the Fifteen Classes and for All Classes Combined

		Following Cycle Per Cent				*Following Cycle Frequency*		
Class	*Preceding Cycle*	T	P	A	*Preceding Cycle*	T	P	A
Total	T	89.5	10.4	0.1	T	3104	360	3
	P	59.4	40.6	—	P	357	244	—
	A	15.4	—	84.6	A	2	—	11
1	T	94.7	5.3	—	T	378	21	—
	P	84.0	16.0	—	P	21	4	—
	A	—	—	—	A	—	—	—
2	T	92.0	7.6	0.4	T	207	17	1
	P	85.0	15.0	—	P	17	3	—
	A	100.0	—	—	A	1	—	—
3	T	89.5	10.5	—	T	214	25	—
	P	73.5	26.5	—	P	25	9	—
	A	—	—	—	A	—	—	—
4	T	90.2	9.8	—	T	185	20	—
	P	83.3	16.7	—	P	20	4	—
	A	—	—	—	A	—	—	—
5	T	75.5	24.5	—	T	117	38	—
	P	39.8	59.2	—	P	37	56	—
	A	—	—	—	A	—	—	—
6	T	94.8	5.2	—	T	165	9	—
	P	66.7	33.3	—	P	9	6	—
	A	—	—	—	A	—	—	—
7	T	86.1	13.9	—	T	167	27	—
	P	48.2	51.8	—	P	27	29	—
	A	—	—	—	A	—	—	—
8	T	85.7	14.3	—	T	204	34	—
	P	69.4	30.6	—	P	33	15	—
	A	—	—	—	A	—	—	—
9	T	96.3	3.7	—	T	130	5	—
	P	83.3	16.7	—	P	5	1	—
	A	—	—	—	A	—	—	—
10	T	93.9	6.1	—	T	185	12	—
	P	63.2	36.8	—	P	12	7	—
	A	—	—	—	A	—	—	—
11	T	95.2	4.8	—	T	236	12	—
	P	57.1	42.9	—	P	12	9	—
	A	—	—	—	A	—	—	—

TABLE 51 (continued)

Class	*Preceding Cycle*	*Following Cycle Per Cent* T	P	A	*Preceding Cycle*	*Following Cycle Frequency* T	P	A
12	T	76.3	23.7	—	T	119	37	—
	P	63.8	36.2	—	P	37	21	—
	A	—	—	—	A	—	—	—
13	T	91.3	8.7	—	T	408	39	—
	P	58.8	41.2	—	P	40	28	—
	A	—	—	—	A	—	—	—
14	T	88.5	11.1	0.4	T	184	23	1
	P	77.8	22.2	—	P	21	6	—
	A	—	—	—	A	—	—	—
15	T	83.0	16.6	92.3	T	205	41	12
	P	47.1	52.9	—	P	41	46	—
	A	7.7	—	—	A	1	—	—

is lowest in this respect (15 per cent). Generally speaking, then, the teacher in Class 9 rarely admits a pupil-initiated teaching cycle into the discourse once he himself has initiated one. This probably is a function of the ground rules that govern verbal behavior in that particular classroom. Apparently students consider it improper or inadvisable to interject questions or otherwise to inaugurate verbal interchanges once the teacher has done so. By contrast, in Class 5 there is the relatively high probability of one chance in four that a teacher-initiated cycle will be followed by a pupil-initiated cycle. Apparently pupils feel much freer here to inaugurate new cycles by asking questions and occasionally by making structuring moves.

Supporting this observation is the fact that once a pupil has initiated such a verbal exchange—broken the ice—either the same pupil or one of the other pupils is actually more likely to initiate the subsequent cycle than is the teacher. This is remarkable in terms of the overall ratio of teacher-to-pupil-initiated cycles, which is roughly 6:1. In contrast to Class 5 is Class 2, where pupils are apparently reluctant to follow the pupil initiation of a cycle with a subsequent pupil-initiated cycle. Another way of interpreting these data is to say that low percentages in pupil-initiated cycles following pupil-initiated cycles, as in the case of Classes 2, 1, 9, and 4, indicate a stronger than usual tendency for the teachers to continue to initiate cycles even when pupil-initiated cycles occur from time to time.

TABLE 52

Percentage Distribution of Temporally Ordered Teaching Cycles by Logical Process According to Logical Process of Preceding Cycles for All Classes Combined

Logical Process of Preceding Cycle	*Logical Process of Following Cycle*												
	1 DEF	2 INT	3 FAC	4 XPL	5 OPN	6 JUS	7 NCL	8 INS	9 NOE	10 NOC	%	*Total f*	*% of Total Cycles*
Total	—	—	—	—	—	—	—	—	—	—	—	4081	100.0
1. DEF	40.2	0.5	19.1	24.8	1.7	0.2	—	11.3	2.0	0.2	100.0	408	10.0
2. INT	7.4	18.5	22.2	33.3	5.6	1.8	—	9.3	—	1.9	100.0	54	1.3
3. FAC	7.4	1.0	49.3	25.7	1.4	0.5	0.1	10.7	3.6	0.3	100.0	1137	27.9
4. XPL	6.4	1.0	21.5	56.2	2.1	0.7	0.1	9.1	2.6	0.3	100.0	1356	33.2
5. OPN	2.6	—	20.0	23.5	28.7	8.7	—	12.2	4.3	—	100.0	115	2.8
6. JUS	—	—	14.9	19.1	12.8	27.7	—	23.4	2.1	—	100.0	47	1.2
7. NCL	—	—	—	66.7	—	—	—	33.3	—	—	100.0	3	0.1
8. INS	6.1	1.8	16.6	15.2	2.3	0.9	0.1	49.8	6.0	1.2	100.0	755	18.5
9. NOE	7.6	1.1	18.4	12.4	3.2	1.1	—	23.8	31.4	1.1	100.0	185	4.5
10. NOC	4.8	—	28.6	28.6	—	—	—	33.3	4.8	—	100.0	21	0.5

Logic of the cycle. The second dimension of the analysis of temporally ordered teaching cycles is the logic of the cycle. For purposes of this analysis, the logic of the cycle was taken to be the type of logical meaning of the soliciting move within the cycle. As indicated previously, the soliciting move is a pivotal one in the cycle because it elicits the response that in turn usually occasions the reaction, and the structuring move is often used to introduce the solicitation. In a typical teaching cycle, for example, a teacher asks for an explanation, the pupil responds by giving an explanation, and the teacher reacts by rating the response. This is regarded as an explaining cycle because its logical character is, in a sense, determined by the solicitation. Those teaching cycles in which a solicitation does not appear (for example, STR REA) are coded as having no overt expectation (NOE).

Table 52 presents the percentage distribution for the logical dimension of temporally ordered teaching cycles indicating the preceding and following states. The pattern is not unlike the one for initiation of cycles. Teaching cycles of a given logical character tend to be followed by teaching cycles of the same logical character to a greater extent than would be indicated by the overall percentage distribution. For example, of the 4,081 temporally ordered teaching cycles, 408, or 10 per cent, include soliciting moves that call for a definition (DEF) and are therefore regarded as defining cycles. When the prior state is a defining cycle, however, the probability of another defining cycle occurring increases to slightly over 40 per cent. A defining cycle, therefore, is much more likely to occur when the preceding cycle is a defining cycle than when the preceding cycle is of some other logical type.

Essentially the same is true for the other logical types. For example, of all the logical dimensions of teaching cycles, explaining (XPL) is the most common, accounting for 33.2 per cent of all cycles. When the preceding state is an explaining cycle, the probability that another explaining cycle will occur increases to 56.2 per cent. The same tendency is present even in the instructional category (INS), which includes all those cycles that are devoted to matters of classroom management, such as assignments, rather than substantive matters relating to international trade. In every one of the logical dimensions in which there are significant frequencies, there is a greater probability of cycles of the same logical character following one another than one would expect on the basis of the overall percentage distribution.

The analysis of the logic of the cycles provides still another basis for describing classroom discourse. All consecutive temporally ordered teaching cycles of the same logical dimension may be seen as consti-

TABLE 53

Percentage Distribution of Temporally Ordered Teaching Cycles by Cycle Type of the Preceding and Following Cycles for All Classes Combined

Type of Preceding Cycle	Type of Following Cycle											Total	Total	% of Total
	1	2	3	4	5	6	7	8	9	10	11	%	f	Cycles
Total	—	—	—	—	—	—	—	—	—	—	—	—	4081	100.0
1	17.9	3.0	25.6	2.7	14.1	9.8	5.4	0.7	3.4	2.4	15.2	100.0	297	7.3
2	2.9	17.7	1.5	13.2	2.9	17.6	—	1.5	1.5	4.4	36.8	100.0	68	1.7
3	7.4	1.0	28.0	1.5	28.1	2.9	11.3	0.3	7.1	0.7	11.7	100.0	789	19.3
4	6.1	1.4	22.5	2.7	32.0	6.8	8.8	3.4	4.1	2.0	10.2	100.0	147	3.6
5	5.0	1.1	17.2	2.1	35.0	6.1	10.6	1.2	9.6	1.8	10.3	100.0	1127	27.6
6	4.2	2.3	13.7	4.9	36.5	10.7	6.1	0.4	7.6	1.1	12.5	100.0	263	6.5
7	8.8	2.2	12.9	6.7	25.8	5.0	14.1	0.7	7.2	3.4	13.2	100.0	418	10.2
8	5.0	7.5	12.5	5.0	17.5	12.5	10.0	5.0	7.5	2.5	15.0	100.0	40	1.0
9	2.6	2.3	14.8	2.9	26.8	8.0	11.6	1.3	12.6	2.9	14.2	100.0	310	7.6
10	6.4	1.3	16.7	5.1	19.2	9.0	15.4	1.3	9.0	—	16.6	100.0	78	1.9
11	10.8	1.8	21.2	4.8	21.0	4.6	10.1	0.7	6.1	1.8	17.1	100.0	544	13.3

Legend

1. SOL 2. STR 3. SOL RES 4. STR SOL RES 5. SOL RES REA
6. STR SOL RES REA 7. SOL RES REA REA . . . 8. STR SOL RES REA REA . . .
9. SOL RES REA RES . . . REA . . . 10. STR SOL RES REA RES . . . REA . . . 11. All Others

tuting one unit of linguistic behavior, possibly a *tactic,* that continues until a new logical dimension is introduced. Thus a teaching tactic may consist of a series of teaching cycles designed to explain why countries trade. When the discourse shifts, for example, from explaining why trade takes place to defining certain terms, the shift may be regarded as the beginning of a new tactic.

An alternate way to conceive of *logically ordered tactics* in teaching would be to collapse the logical categories of fact-stating and explaining, defining and interpreting, and opining and justifying into three logical modes: the empirical, the analytic, and the evaluative. These logical modes in conjunction with a refined system for analyzing the substantive meanings expressed in the classroom might constitute a fruitful way of analyzing the tactics that teachers employ to induce learning. One kind of tactic, for example, may be characterized as dealing analytically with terms such as imports and exports. This may be followed by a tactic in which the discussion centers on expressing opinions and justifying them with respect to whether the United States should export to Communist countries.

Cycle types. The same tendency of prior states to influence following states is found in the third dimension of teaching cycles, cycle type. For ease of presentation, Table 53 indicates the ten most frequently observed cycle types along with an eleventh category comprising the eleven infrequently observed cycle types and those few that were not codable as to cycle type because of a partially inaudible transcription.

As in formally ordered teaching cycles, the cycle SOL RES REA occurs most frequently, accounting for 27.6 per cent of the total of 4,081 temporally ordered cycles. (The comparable figure for formally ordered teaching cycles is 26.0 per cent.) The next most common cycle is again the simple SOL RES, which accounts for 19.3 per cent of the total.

When the preceding states are taken into account, however, these figures again change significantly. When the preceding state is a SOL RES, the probability of a SOL RES REA following is only 17.2 per cent as compared to 26.7 per cent in the overall distribution. But when SOL RES REA is the preceding state, it is followed by another SOL RES REA 35.0 per cent of the time. Whereas the chances of a SOL RES REA occurring are approximately one in four in the overall distribution, the probability of a SOL RES REA occurring when another SOL RES REA is the preceding state is one in three. Furthermore, in the present sample, there is twice the likelihood of a SOL RES REA cycle following another SOL RES REA cycle as there is of a

SOL RES REA following a SOL RES cycle. Similarly, when the preceding state is a SOL RES cycle, the probability of another SOL RES occurring increases from the 19.3 per cent that one would expect from the overall percentage distribution to 28.0 per cent.

Table 54 combines two of the dimensions already discussed. It

TABLE 54

Percentage Distribution of Temporally Ordered Teaching Cycles by Initiator and Cycle Type for Preceding and Following Cycles for All Classes Combined

Type of Preceding Cycle		*Total*		*Type of Following Cycle*							
				1		2		3		4	
		%	*f*	T	P	T	P	T	P	T	P
1	T	6.2	254	34	11	8	1	20	45	7	1
	P	1.1	43	5	3	—	—	9	2	—	—
2	T	1.4	57	1	—	7	4	—	—	7	1
	P	0.2	10	—	1	—	—	1	—	—	1
3	T	13.4	548	23	5	1	—	138	9	2	—
	P	5.9	240	27	3	7	—	23	50	7	3
4	T	3.2	130	9	—	1	1	20	6	2	—
	P	0.4	17	—	—	—	—	4	3	—	2
5	T	26.7	1090	48	3	12	—	154	32	21	—
	P	0.9	37	6	—	—	—	3	5	3	—
6	T	6.2	255	10	1	6	—	30	4	13	—
	P	0.2	8	—	—	—	—	—	2	—	—
7	T	8.2	333	17	5	6	1	24	16	22	1
	P	2.1	85	11	4	2	—	3	11	4	1
8	T	0.9	35	2	—	3	—	3	1	1	1
	P	0.1	5	—	—	—	—	1	—	—	—
9	T	7.3	297	7	1	5	1	34	9	9	—
	P	0.3	13	—	—	1	—	2	—	—	—
10	T	1.8	74	5	—	1	—	10	3	3	1
	P	0.1	4	—	—	—	—	—	—	—	—
11	T	9.7	394	42	4	4	1	53	27	18	—
	P	3.4	139	12	1	3	1	16	19	3	5
		100.0	4081								

Legend

1. SOL 2. STR 3. SOL RES 4. STR SOL RES
5. SOL RES REA 6. STR SOL RES REA
7. SOL RES REA REA . . . 8. STR SOL RES REA REA . . .
9. SOL RES REA RES . . . REA . . .
10. STR SOL RES REA RES . . . REA . . . 11. All Others

presents the distribution of cycles type by initiator of the cycle. For ease of presentation, the cycles initiated by audio-visual devices, which accounted for only 0.3 per cent of the cycles, are not included in the table. Of the thirteen instances of audio-visual-initiated cycles, one occurred in Class 14 and the other twelve in Class 15. Generally

TABLE 54 (continued)

Percentage Distribution of Temporally Ordered Teaching Cycles by Initiator and Cycle Type for Preceding and Following Cycles for All Classes Combined

Type of Following Cycle													
5		6		7		8		9		10		11	
T	P	T	P	T	P	T	P	T	P	T	P	T	P
30	4	25	3	7	6	1	1	4	1	6	1	24	14
8	—	1	—	—	3	—	—	5	—	—	—	6	1
—	—	12	—	—	—	1	—	—	—	3	—	8	12
2	—	—	—	—	—	—	—	1	—	—	—	—	4
187	1	8	—	61	5	1	—	49	—	5	—	45	8
27	7	13	2	8	15	1	—	5	2	1	—	17	22
44	1	10	—	8	2	4	—	6	—	3	—	11	2
1	1	—	—	—	3	—	1	—	—	—	—	—	2
382	6	65	—	103	13	12	1	103	2	20	—	101	12
4	2	4	—	—	3	1	—	2	1	—	—	2	1
92	1	28	—	16	—	1	—	19	1	3	—	28	2
3	—	—	—	—	—	—	—	—	—	—	—	1	2
90	1	19	—	34	9	2	1	24	3	11	1	34	12
12	5	2	—	8	8	—	—	3	—	2	—	5	4
5	1	5	—	1	3	2	—	2	1	1	—	2	1
1	—	—	—	—	—	—	—	—	—	—	—	2	1
78	1	24	1	29	5	4	—	38	—	8	—	35	7
3	1	—	—	1	1	—	—	1	—	1	—	2	—
15	—	6	—	10	1	1	—	6	—	—	—	11	1
—	—	1	—	1	—	—	—	1	—	—	—	1	—
97	3	16	—	37	1	3	1	25	1	6	—	44	10
12	2	7	2	9	8	—	—	6	1	2	2	8	20

Legend

1. SOL 2. STR 3. SOL RES 4. STR SOL RES
5. SOL RES REA 6. STR SOL RES REA
7. SOL RES REA REA . . . 8. STR SOL RES REA REA . . .
9. SOL RES REA RES . . . REA . . .
10. STR SOL RES REA RES . . . REA . . . 11. All Others

speaking, Table 54 reinforces the pattern indicated by Tables 52 and 53. Of the 4,081 cycles, 1,090 or 26.7 per cent were teacher-initiated SOL RES REA cycles. Teacher-initiated SOL RES cycles account for the second highest percentage, 13.4 per cent. Typically, then, the teacher solicits and the pupil responds. In addition, however, for the 15 classes as a whole, the teachers are twice as likely to react in some form of these responding moves than they are to initiate a new teaching cycle following the response. This is suggested by the 2 to 1 ratio of teacher-initiated SOL RES REA cycles to teacher-initiated SOL RES cycles.

The pattern is quite different in pupil-initiated cycles. The highest percentage of pupil-initiated cycles is 5.9 per cent for the SOL RES cycle, while the pupil-initiated SOL RES REA cycle accounts for only 0.9 per cent of the total. Generally, then, when the pupil initiates cycles in the classes under study, the verbal pattern tends to be of the simple soliciting-responding variety and rarely includes the reacting move that is characteristic of teacher-initiated cycles. This reinforces the notion that one of the general rules for pupil behavior in the classroom is that the pupil rarely comments upon or rates the responding moves he elicits.

The second highest percentage of pupil-initiated cycles is in the "all others" category (3.4 per cent), indicating that pupil-initiated cycles have a tendency to follow unusual patterns such as SOL REA and STR REA REA . . . to a greater extent, proportionately, than do teacher-initiated cycles. Only two of the eleven cycles in the "all others" category, for example, include responding moves. For the present sample, therefore, pupil-initiated cycles not only account for a for smaller percentage of the total than do teacher-initiated cycles, but also tend to be distributed differently. In terms of the temporal analysis, however, one might still note the tendency for like patterns to cluster together, although the low frequencies make it difficult to generalize.

Patterns in Pedagogical Discourse

The data point to the fact that pedagogical discourse, rather than occurring haphazardly, seems to follow regular patterns. Certain regularities, such as following a basic soliciting-responding pattern in teaching, seem to be common to all of the 15 classes in the sample. Other regularities, such as the rate at which verbal exchanges take place, are basically consistent from one session to another within a given class, but vary from one class to the next. This latter kind of patterning, which sets some classes apart from others, may be seen as constituting classroom style. Once these regularities are identified, both in terms of teaching in general and in terms of individual classrooms, the relationships among the events that compose the pattern become the basis for prediction.

In all of the dimensions of teaching cycles analyzed by means of the Markov chain, a kind of inertia seems to exist by which each of the states tends to be followed by another state with the same characteristics. A pupil-initiated cycle tends to give rise to a subsequent pupil-initiated cycle; a teaching cycle of a given logical character tends to give rise to another cycle of the same logical character; and each of the cycle types, as well as cycle type in combination with initiator, tends to be followed by cycles with the same characteristics to a greater extent than would be indicated by the overall percentage distribution of these cycle dimensions. It is as if each of the states possessed some kind of internal dynamic that tends to influence the characteristics of subsequent cycles.

This tendency for cycle states to perpetuate themselves has the effect of increasing one's ability accurately to predict certain linguistic events in the classroom. If, for example, ten observers were to enter ten different classrooms in the present sample while classes were in session, one could predict with reasonable accuracy that one of the ten ongoing verbal exchanges between the teacher and the pupils would involve definition of terms. If, however, one knew that in each case the preceding teaching cycle had been a defining cycle, one could then place the odds at four in ten that the subsequent cycle would also involve defining. The temporal analysis, then, by establishing statistical relationships between prior and following states defined here as teaching cycles, permits a more refined description of classroom verbal behavior by greatly improving the ability to see relationships among classroom variables.

This refined ability to predict is probably best illustrated in terms of initiation of teaching cycles. By using data such as frequency and percentage distributions in combination with Markov matrices, one can describe not only the relative proportion of teacher-to-pupil-initiated cycles, but the probabilities of certain linguistic events following certain other linguistic events. In terms of simple frequency for the group of 15 teachers, teacher-initiated cycles far outnumber pupil-initiated cycles; but when the preceding state is a pupil-initiated cycle, another pupil-initiated cycle is almost as likely to occur as a teacher-initiated cycle. For one class of the 15, the probability of a pupil-initiated cycle occurring under these circumstances is even somewhat greater than for a teacher-initiated cycle. While it is not possible to generalize the present data to all kinds of teaching on all levels, the regularities in the patterning of classroom discourse in the present sample suggest the hypothesis that similar kinds of regularities may be found in other samples of classroom verbal behavior.

In another sense, the analysis of teaching cycles using the Markov chain permits one to broaden the study of the *sequence* of verbal exchanges in the classroom instead of limiting the analysis to the individual teaching cycles themselves. Just as the notion of teaching cycles permits analysis of patterns of pedagogical moves, the Markov chain makes possible the analysis of the patterning of teaching cycles. Using this technique, it is possible, for example, to study typical sequences of teaching cycles and to compare and contrast the patterns in individual classes. For any of the dimensions of classroom verbal behavior investigated here, entire class sessions may be plotted showing movement from one kind of patterning to another.

Summary

In the analysis of patterns of classroom discourse, two types of teaching cycles are used. The first type, formally ordered teaching cycles, is used to account for all of the patterns of pedagogical moves and to establish the distribution. Analysis of the second type, temporally ordered teaching cycles, uses Markov chains to determine whether prior cycles tend to influence succeeding ones.

Formally Ordered Teaching Cycles

A formally ordered teaching cycle is defined essentially as a series of pedagogical moves beginning with a structuring move or a solicitation that is not preceded by a structuring move and ending with the move that precedes a new structuring or a new unstructured solicitation. Given this definition, 21 types of teaching cycle are possible. In attempting to account for all the patterns within the discourse, strict temporal sequence is occasionally sacrificed.

Of the 21 cycle types, SOL RES REA, which accounts for 26 per cent of the total, and SOL RES, which accounts for 22.3 per cent, occur most frequently. Six teaching cycles account for 80 per cent of the total of 4,592. Considerable variability is present when the data are analyzed in terms of the three dimensions of formally ordered teaching cycles: rate, source, and pattern. The number of cycles per minute of class time ranges from 0.9 for Teacher 9 to 3.0 for Teacher 13. Both the mean and the median are 1.8. Cycle activity tends to remain constant over the four sessions. The analysis of source, defined as percentage of teacher-initiated cycles, indicates that 85 per cent of the cycles are teacher-initiated. In 3 of the 60 class sessions, there are no pupil-initiated teaching cycles. The median percentage of teacher-initiated cycles is 88 and the mean is 84.5. The range for the unit as a whole is from 96.6 per cent for Teacher 9 to 61.2 per cent for Teacher 5. In terms of individual class sessions, the range is from 100 per cent to 36.9 per cent. In the pattern analysis, all the 15 teachers, with the possible exception of Teacher 9, are seen as following a basic SOL RES pattern. Teachers seem to differ, however, in the way they shape and frame this basic interchange.

Temporally Ordered Teaching Cycles

A temporally ordered teaching cycle is defined in essentially the same way as a formally ordered teaching cycle except that three types of minor initiatory maneuvers—repeating, directing performance, and clarifying-expanding—are subsumed when they occur within larger cycles. The cycles in which this occurs are called augmented teaching cycles. Of the 4,081 temporally ordered teaching cycles, 364 are augmented. Repeating accounts for 130 of these, 66 involve directing performance, and 168 include a clarifying-expanding exchange. In the analysis of temporally ordered teaching cycles using Markov chains, each cycle is regarded as a state, and matrices are designed to indicate whether prior states influence following states.

Three lines of analysis were used: initiator of the cycle, logic of the cycle, and cycle type. When a teacher-initiated cycle is the prior state, it is followed by a pupil-initiated cycle only about 10 per cent of the time. However, when a pupil-initiated cycle is the prior state, about 40 per cent of the following cycles are pupil-initiated. This indicates that pupils are four times more likely to initiate a cycle when the preceding cycle is also pupil-initiated than when the preceding state is a teacher-initiated cycle. The logic of the cycle is also influenced by the preceding state. Defining cycles, for example, are four times more likely to occur following another defining cycle than would be expected in terms of the overall distribution. This tendency is present in all of the logical categories. Cycle type is also influenced by the prior state. A SOL RES cycle, for example, is much more likely to occur following another SOL RES cycle than following a SOL RES REA cycle.

CHAPTER EIGHT

CLASSROOM VARIABLES AND TEST RESULTS

IN TEACHING, as in all practical activities serving human purposes, some criterion of success is needed if teachers are to know whether they are accomplishing what they set out to do. The criterion of success for both teachers and students playing the game of teaching is evidence that the student participants have learned the desired skills and knowledge; learning on the part of students is the successful outcome or "upshot" of teaching. It is therefore important to distinguish learning as the outcome of teaching from the activity of teaching itself. Discussions about teaching and learning have been plagued by confusion between the two. The teacher's job is to teach students; he does not, indeed cannot, "learn" them.

Experience in carrying out this research has led us to recognize the importance of distinguishing between the perspective from which the teacher in the classroom evaluates learning outcomes and the perspective from which the researcher interested in the consequences of classroom discourse might describe outcome variables. Undoubtedly, it is appropriate for the teacher to identify certain skills and knowledge that he feels his students *should* learn and then to judge the success or failure of his teaching on the basis of whether his students in fact do learn the desired skills and knowledge. But for research aimed at discovering relationships between linguistic variables in the classroom and subsequent learning outcomes, it is more appropriate to approach the problem of identifying the learning outcomes on the basis of observable consequences apart from any notion of what *should* be learned. It is, therefore, more useful for the researcher to raise the question, "What kinds of classroom events are related to what kinds of learning outcomes?" rather than the question, "What are the relationships between discourse variables and measures of learning based on some notion of what *should* be learned?" In other words, descriptive investigation of outcome variables is as significant as descriptive investigation of classroom discourse itself.

Study of the relationships between classroom variables and measures of learning thus becomes appropriate once the complex events of the classroom *and* the outcome variables have been systematically and reliably described. This research focused primarily on description of classroom variables; full-scale study of the outcomes of instruction was beyond the scope of the present project. However, preliminary investigations of the relationships between classroom variables and outcome variables represented by scores on the test of economic knowledge and the attitude scale (Appendix C) were undertaken and may serve as a useful guide in developing subsequent research.

The outcome measures developed in this research—the test of economic knowledge and the attitude scale—are limited measures of the outcomes of four days of teaching. The consequences of teaching, however, are no less diverse and complex than is the process of teaching, and to attempt to incorporate the results of teaching in a single test score is to oversimplify the problems involved in describing the outcomes of instruction. Cronbach has expressed this idea cogently:

> Outcomes of instruction are multidimensional, and a satisfactory investigation will map out the effects of the course along these dimensions separately. To agglomerate many types of post-course performance into a single score is a mistake, since failure to achieve one objective is masked by success in another direction. Moreover, since a composite score embodies (and usually conceals) judgments about the importance of the various outcomes, only a report that treats the outcomes separately can be useful to educators who have different value hierarchies. (8:235)

Recognizing, then, that the test on international trade and the attitude scale used in this research represent very limited measures of learning outcomes, the following discussion of classroom variables and outcome variables is presented principally as an empirical basis for guiding further research, suggesting hypotheses for investigation. In this discussion no effort is made to present the results of these preliminary investigations in complex statistical terms, which are likely to misrepresent the purpose of this study. The results are discussed rather in terms of inspection of the data, with the aim of posing problems for subsequent investigation.

Analysis of Attitude Change

The scores on the attitude pre-test are fairly homogeneous for the total group of students. The mean for the total group is 3.8, with a standard deviation of 0.59. Test item number 4, which is closest to this mean rating of the total group, reads "Studying economics is interesting. It is a useful subject that serves the needs of many students" (See Appendix C). This item can probably be characterized as reflecting a mildly positive attitude toward studying economics. The mean scores on the attitude post-test for the total group shows almost no change: 3.7, with a standard deviation of 0.86. Thus, as a total group the students show almost no change in attitude as a result of the experimental teaching unit.

Considered separately, however, there was a modest range of differences in amount of change among the 15 classes, ranging from the greatest positive change of +.7 for Class 9 to the greatest negative change of —1.5 for Class 12. On the post-test, the most positive average class rating was 2.6 (Class 10), which is about halfway between a strong and a moderately positive attitude toward studying economics. This class, however, showed almost no change, having started with a pre-test rating of 2.7. The most negative rating was 5.5, obtained for Class 12, which represents a very mildly positive attitude and also reflects a considerable shift in the negative direction for this class. No relationship between attitude change and classroom variables could be established.

Analysis of Test of Economic Knowledge

The scores on the test of economic knowledge were analyzed, taking into account verbal intelligence and class size. The pairs of vocabulary scores and scores on the post-test, which measured knowledge of international trade of the 345 students for whom all relevant scores were available, were used to determine the regression of test scores on verbal intelligence. Each test score was then adjusted by subtracting from the student's score the score predicted for the student on the basis of his verbal intelligence. The mean adjusted score for each class was then determined as shown in Table 55. The table also gives the estimated standard error for each mean. The standard error was determined by taking the square root of a pooled estimate of the variance of the adjusted scores within each class divided by the number in each class.

When the ratio of each class mean to its estimated standard error is examined (Table 55), it is observed that the ratios for eight of the 15 classes, namely Classes 2, 4, 5, 7, 9, 13, 14, and 15, are larger than 1.643, the normal deviate value that is exceeded by chance in either direction only 10 per cent of the time. It seems reasonable, therefore, that the means for Classes 2, 4, and 5 indicate an average performance that exceeds the expected, while the means for Classes 7, 9, 13, 14, and

TABLE 55

Mean Adjusted Scores on the Test of Economic Knowledge, Standard Error of the Mean, and Class Size for Each of the Fifteen Classes

Class	*Mean Adjusted Score*	*Standard Error of the Mean*	*Class Size*
2	+5.44	1.46	28
4	+2.99	1.49	27
5	+2.73	1.46	28
3	+2.62	1.69	21
12	+2.09	1.99	15
8	+2.09	1.69	21
6	+1.81	1.77	19
1	+0.01	1.55	25
10	−1.28	1.87	17
11	—2.38	1.52	26
9	−2.40	1.46	28
7	−2.70	1.61	23
14	−3.00	1.69	21
13	−3.10	1.69	21
15	−6.78	1.77	19

15 indicate an average performance that falls short of the expected; and it also seems reasonable that these results are not due to chance. For purposes of describing relationships between dimensions of pedagogical moves, teaching cycles, and learning, Classes 2, 4, and 5 are regarded as having significantly higher-than-predicted mean scores on the post-test on international trade; Classes 7, 9, 13, 14, and 15, on the other hand, are regarded as having significantly lower-than-predicted mean scores on that test.

Pedagogical Moves and Test Results

Tables 56–61 presents data relevant to the investigation of the relationships between pedagogical moves and test results and teaching cycles and test results. Table 56 presents data on teacher activity in terms of percentages of total moves and lines and percentages for each of the pedagogical moves. No one factor sharply differentiates the three classes judged significantly high from the five classes judged significantly low. As a group, however, the teachers in the "high" group are relatively less active in terms of percentage of lines spoken than are the teachers in the "low" group. In the "high" group, no more than 61.5 per cent of the lines are spoken by any of the three teachers. In contrast, three of the teachers included in the "low" group (in Classes 7, 13, and 14) speak slightly more than 70 per cent of the lines and the teacher of Class 9 speaks 92.8 per cent of the lines; the exception is Teacher 15, who speaks 60.8 per cent of the lines.

With respect to the percentages of pedagogical moves, there seems to be little to differentiate the two groups—with the exception, perhaps, of the percentages of structuring moves. The range for the three classes judged significantly high is very restricted (4.1 per cent to 5.2 per cent), but the group judged significantly low includes both extremes of the range for all 15 classes (1.2 per cent and 13.2 per cent). This suggests that there may be an optimum frequency for the use of the structuring move by the teacher as a way of launching interaction between teacher and pupils and as a means of introducing subject matter.

Table 57 presents data on certain dimensions of the soliciting move for the two groups and for all classes combined. The data are presented in terms of teacher activity, with the base in each case being all substantive solicitations by the teacher. One factor in which there seems to be some difference between the two groups is the teacher's use of solicitations calling for a pupil to assign a truth function. The mean of means for the "high" group (12.9 per cent) is roughly the same as the mean of means for the group of 15 classes combined (12.5 per cent) but the mean of means for the "low" group is considerably below it (8.0 per cent).

In terms of the logical dimension of soliciting, the teachers in the "low" group make greater use of the empirical mode than do the teachers in the "high" group. The mean of means for the five classes judged significantly low is 35.3 per cent for fact-stating and 46.0 per cent for explaining; for the three classes judged significantly high, the figures are 25.2 per cent for fact-stating and 42.2 per cent for explaining. When constructing is the information process activity of the teacher solicitation and fact-stating or explaining is the logical dimension, further differences between the two groups are observed. Teachers in the "low" group require pupils to construct a factual or explanatory response to a greater percentage of their substantive soliciting moves than do teachers in the "high" group. For the five classes judged significantly low, the percentage of teacher solicitations calling for the construction of factual responses is 26.9, and the percentage for teacher solicitations calling for the construction of ex-

TABLE 56

Data on Pedagogical Moves for Three Classes Judged Significantly High and Five Classes Judged Significantly Low

Class	T *Moves*: *All Moves*	T *Lines*: *All Lines*	T/SOL: *All Moves*	T/RES: *All Moves*	T/STR: *All Moves*	T/REA: *All Moves*
All Classes						
Mean of Means	62.6	72.2	28.9	3.4	5.5	24.2
Range	57.8–72.1	60.3–92.8	21.4–36.8	1.1–5.9	1.1–13.2	20.0–28.5
Three Classes Judged Significantly High						
Mean of Means	59.6	61.0	28.0	3.3	4.7	23.1
Mean of Class 2	59.0	61.5	29.9	1.2	4.8	22.4
Mean of Class 4	61.4	60.3	29.6	2.8	4.1	24.8
Mean of Class 5	58.3	61.3	24.5	5.8	5.2	22.0
Five Classes Judged Significantly Low						
Mean of Means	64.1	73.8	27.8	3.8	6.1	25.7
Mean of Class 7	63.9	72.0	25.7	5.8	7.8	23.6
Mean of Class 9	72.1	92.8	29.0	1.7	13.2	28.0
Mean of Class 14	66.6	72.6	29.8	2.7	4.5	28.4
Mean of Class 13	60.0	70.9	30.1	3.7	1.2	24.2
Mean of Class 15	57.8	60.8	24.6	5.3	3.6	24.2

TABLE 57

Data on Soliciting Moves For Three Classes Judged Significantly High and Five Classes Judged Significantly Low

Class	T/SOL-A: T/SUB SOL	T/SOL-C: T/SUB SOL	T/SOL-FAC: T/SUB SOL	T/SOL/XPL: T/SUB SOL	T/SOL-C/FAC: T/SUB SOL	T/SOL-C/XPL: T/SUB SOL
All Classes						
Mean of Means	12.5	78.9	33.9	44.8	24.5	38.3
Range	1.6–21.0	62.4–94.4	19.0–49.4	31.0–60.4	10.0–41.0	24.5–53.9
Three Classes Judged Significantly High						
Mean of Means	12.9	76.0	25.2	42.2	17.2	36.6
Mean of Class 2	11.8	75.3	25.3	53.2	17.2	43.0
Mean of Class 4	10.9	81.7	31.4	42.3	24.5	38.9
Mean of Class 5	16.0	71.0	19.0	31.0	10.0	28.0
Five Classes Judged Significantly Low						
Mean of Means	8.0	84.6	35.3	46.0	26.9	41.0
Mean of Class 7	7.2	88.2	40.5	37.9	35.3	34.0
Mean of Class 9	1.6	94.4	25.8	54.8	24.1	51.6
Mean of Class 14	8.4	81.7	20.9	55.5	15.2	47.6
Mean of Class 13	7.4	87.5	49.4	37.6	41.0	34.6
Mean of Class 15	15.2	71.2	39.9	44.4	19.0	37.4

TABLE 58

Data on Congruence of Soliciting and Responding Components For Three Classes Judged Significantly High and Five Classes Judged Significantly Low

	Congruence of Pupil Responding Component with Teacher Soliciting Component					
	Logical Process			*Information Process*		
Class	*Congruent*	*Incongruent*	*Ignored*	*Congruent*	*Incongruent*	*Ignored*
All Classes						
Mean of Means	92.2	3.8	4.0	89.6	6.9	4.1
Range	86.7–96.6	0.–7.8	0.–11.0	85.0–95.5	0.8–10.6	0.–10.2
Three Classes Judged Significantly High						
Mean of Means	88.4	4.7	6.9	86.5	6.7	6.8
Mean of Class 2	90.6	3.4	6.0	88.0	6.0	6.0
Mean of Class 4	87.9	7.8	4.3	86.4	9.2	4.4
Mean of Class 5	86.7	2.8	10.5	85.1	4.8	10.1
Five Classes Judged Significantly Low						
Mean of Means	92.4	3.8	3.8	89.8	6.1	4.1
Mean of Class 7	89.0	—	11.0	89.0	0.8	10.2
Mean of Class 9	91.6	2.9	5.5	85.9	8.3	5.8
Mean of Class 14	91.2	7.0	1.8	89.1	9.1	1.8
Mean of Class 13	94.9	4.7	0.4	90.9	8.7	0.4
Mean of Class 15	95.2	4.3	0.5	94.2	3.7	2.1

planatory responses is 41.0. The comparable percentages for the group of three classes judged significantly high are 17.2 and 36.6. Teachers in the "high" group thus place less reliance on eliciting constructed empirical responses than those in the "low" group. Fact-stating and explaining soliciting moves that call for a constructed response by the pupil comprise more than two-thirds of the teacher moves in the "low" group and only slightly more than half in the "high" group.

Table 58 presents data on the congruence between teacher-soliciting components and pupil-responding components. (See Chapter Four, pp. 124–129, for discussion of soliciting-responding congruence.) The only notable differences between the two groups seem to be these: a higher percentage of soliciting components is ignored by pupils in the "high" group than by those in the "low" group, while a higher percentage of pupil responding components is congruent with teacher soliciting components in the "low" group than in the "high" group.

The data on dimensions of teacher structuring moves are presented in Table 59. One notable tendency is for some of the classes judged significantly low to deviate rather sharply from the means, while the range for the three classes judged significantly high is relatively restricted. In each of the first four items listed in Table 59, extremes for the group of all 15 classes are found in the five classes judged significantly low. This includes the highest percentage (100 per cent) for teacher launching components, the lowest (0 per cent) and the highest percentage (11.0 per cent) for teacher halting/excluding components, the highest percentage (73.1 per cent) for teacher launching and announcing components, and the lowest percentage (1.9 per cent) for teacher launching and stating propositions components. Although these variables are not independent, it may be that in these dimensions of the structuring move there is an optimum frequency for the use of the structuring move. There is a somewhat higher percentage of structuring components involving reason-giving in the "high" group (mean of means: 29.4 per cent) as compared with the "low" group (mean of means: 19.7 per cent).

The percentage distributions for the "high" and "low" classes for the five types of reacting moves identified in Chapter Six are presented in Table 60. As a group, the five teachers in the classes judged significantly low devote a relatively high percentage of their reacting moves to substantive reactions and a relatively low percentage of their reactions to rating reactions. The mean of the means of substantive reactions in the "low" group is 15.6; in the "high" group it is 11.1. For rating reactions, it is 44.5 per cent for the "low" group and 55.1

TABLE 59

Data on Structuring Moves for Three Classes Judged Significantly High and Five Classes Judged Significantly Low

Class	T/STR-*Launch:* T/STR	*T/STR-Halt-Exclude:* T/STR	T/STR-*Launch-Announce:* T/STR	T/STR-*Launch-State Propositions:* T/STR	T/STR-*Launch-Announce & State Propositions:* T/STR	T/STR *with Reason-Giving:* T/STR
All Classes						
Mean of Means	95.4	4.6	48.9	13.9	32.6	24.2
Range	89.0–100.	0–11.0	8.5–73.1	1.9–36.7	3.3–56.3	9.9–50.0
Three Classes Judged Significantly High						
Mean of Means	94.5	5.5	58.0	5.0	31.5	29.4
Mean of Class 2	95.2	4.8	50.8	4.8	39.6	30.2
Mean of Class 4	93.3	6.7	62.2	6.7	24.4	31.1
Mean of Class 5	95.1	4.9	61.0	3.6	30.5	26.8
Five Classes Judged Significantly Low						
Mean of Means	94.3	5.7	52.3	10.5	31.5	19.7
Mean of Class 7	92.4	7.6	43.5	16.3	32.6	12.0
Mean of Class 9	89.0	11.0	33.0	16.5	39.5	24.2
Mean of Class 14	100.	—	73.1	1.9	25.0	21.2
Mean of Class 13	96.2	3.8	53.8	11.6	30.8	17.2
Mean of Class 15	94.0	6.0	58.2	6.0	29.8	23.9

TABLE 60

Data on Reacting Moves for Three Classes Judged Significantly High and Five Classes Judged Significantly Low

Class	T/REA-SUB: T/REA	T/REA-RATE: T/REA	T/REA-PRC: T/REA	T/REA-SUB/PRC: T/REA	T/REA-SUB/RATE: T/REA	T/REA-RATE/POS: T/REA-RATE
All Classes						
Mean of Means	16.9	43.9	7.1	3.2	28.3	80.0
Range	9.9–29.4	21.9–60.2	1.5–13.5	1.3–8.1	13.7–54.7	60.7–90.2
Three Classes Judged Significantly High						
Mean of Means	11.1	55.1	9.5	1.5	19.4	82.8
Mean of Class 2	10.6	53.0	11.0	1.7	13.7	81.5
Mean of Class 4	12.7	52.2	10.2	1.6	23.3	85.4
Mean of Class 5	9.9	60.2	7.4	1.3	21.2	81.4
Five Classes Judged Significantly Low						
Mean of Means	15.6	44.5	5.5	2.0	32.4	80.2
Mean of Class 7	14.5	44.8	5.4	0.9	34.4	81.1
Mean of Class 9	20.3	21.9	1.5	1.6	54.7	86.7
Mean of Class 14	13.0	42.3	6.7	2.8	35.2	73.3
Mean of Class 13	17.9	59.9	3.7	2.3	16.2	80.0
Mean of Class 15	12.5	53.5	10.2	2.3	21.5	80.1

per cent for the "high" classes. Not only are the teachers in the "low" classes more likely to make substantive reactions to pupil moves, but two of them also show a tendency to combine substantive with rating components. This type of reaction comprises more than half of the teacher reactions in Class 9 (54.7 per cent) and more than a third in Class 14 (35.2 per cent) and in Class 7 (34.4 per cent). In contrast, the mean of means for the "high" group is 19.4 per cent, with no teacher devoting as much as one-fourth of his reactions to this type. Differences between the two groups are also observed for procedural reactions and for reactions with both substantive and procedural components, which, however, involve rather low frequencies. The groups are about equally positive in their rating reactions.

Teaching Cycles and Test Results

Certain tentative hypotheses may be formulated on the basis of comparing the "high" and "low" learning groups in terms of dimensions of teaching cycles. Perhaps the most clear-cut involves cycle rate (Table 61), which was one of the factors in the analysis of teaching cycles.

Table 48 presented the Cycle Activity Indexes (number of teaching cycles per minute of class time) for each of the 15 classes and for the group as a whole. Both the mean and the median for the group is 1.8. The mean of means for the group as indicated in Table 61 is 1.7. The three classes that scored significantly higher than expected on the post-test (Classes 2, 4, and 5) are all remarkably close to the mean and the mean of means for the group. The indexes for Classes 2 and 4 are 1.9; for Class 5, 1.8. These indexes indicate a moderate pace of slightly less than two cycles per minute. Four of the classes that scored significantly lower than expected, however, deviated sharply from that figure. This group includes the fastest-paced class, Class 13, with an index of 3.0 (an average of three cycles per minute), and another unusually fast-paced class, Class 15 (2.6), as well as the two slowest-paced classes, Classes 9 (0.9) and 14 (1.1). The exception is Class 7, with an index of 1.8. Even taking into account the limited size of the sample, one may hypothesize on the basis of these data that there may be an optimum pace of classroom verbal activity for achieving certain kinds of verbal learning.

A second dimension of teaching cycles which was investigated was the proportion of teacher-initiated in contrast to pupil-initiated teaching cycles (Table 61). Of the 4,592 formally ordered teaching cycles, 84.5 per cent are initiated by teachers. It was also noted that

TABLE 61

Data on Formally Ordered Teaching Cycles for Three Classes Judged Significantly High and Five Classes Judged Significantly Low

Class	*Number of Cycles* / *Minutes of Class Time*	T/STR-*Initiated Cycles:* / *All Cycles*	*Cycles That Do Not Include* REA *Following* RES: / *All Cycles*
All Classes			
Mean of Means	1.7	18.4	26.7
Range	0.9–3.0	3.7–41.2	12.8–37.9
Three Classes Judged Significantly High			
Mean of Means	1.9	17.4	26.1
Mean of Class 2	1.9	17.1	30.0
Mean of Class 4	1.9	15.4	22.5
Mean of Class 5	1.8	19.7	25.8
Five Classes Judged Significantly Low			
Mean of Means	1.9	20.0	24.1
Mean of Class 7	1.8	27.2	29.4
Mean of Class 9	0.9	41.2	12.8
Mean of Class 14	1.1	15.6	18.2
Mean of Class 13	3.0	3.7	31.1
Mean of Class 15	2.6	12.3	28.8

teachers differed in the extent to which they used structuring moves to initiate the cycles. Combining these two factors, the frequencies for each type of formally ordered teaching cycle were used to compute the percentage of all cycles which were both teacher-initiated and structure-initiated. For the 15 classes as a group, 16 per cent of all cycles are initiated by teachers using structuring moves, rather than the more common soliciting moves. The mean of means for the 15 classes is 18.4 per cent. As has already been noted, structuring moves may be used for different purposes and in different ways (see Chapter Five), but in terms of teaching cycles they are regarded simply as an alternate means of inaugurating a verbal exchange in the classroom. The three teachers of the classes that scored significantly higher on the post-test do not differ markedly from the mean of means for the whole group (18.4 per cent). In Class 2, 17.1 per cent of the cycles are initiated by teacher structuring moves. For the teachers in Classes 4 and 5 the figures are 15.4 per cent and 19.7 per cent. Of the five classes in the low-learning group, two do not deviate sharply from the mean of means, but one of the others, Class 9, has the highest percentage of teacher-structure-initiated cycles (41.2), and the other class, Class 14, has the lowest percentage (3.7). While the differences between the high and low learning groups with respect to teacher structuring may not be so well defined as in the case of cycle rate, it may be that more intensive study of teaching cycles initiated by teacher structuring moves will reveal differences in kind and function as well as the differences in degree already noted.

A third area that offers promise for future investigation is one involving those teaching cycles that do not have reacting moves following responding moves. While structuring moves serve the function of getting a cycle under way, reacting moves often serve to seal them off, sometimes by rating the previous moves, sometimes by modifying or expanding them. Of the two reflexive moves, responding and reacting, the reaction is the optional one; the response is elicited by the solicitation, but the reacting move may or may not be made depending on the circumstances and the inclination of the player.

Of the twenty-one formally ordered teaching cycles, four (cycles 5, 6, 14, and 15) do not include reacting moves following responses. For the 15 classes as a group, these four cycles account for 27.1 per cent of the total number of cycles, with a mean of means of 26.7 per cent. The range is from 12.8 per cent (Class 9) to 37.9 per cent (Class 6). Again, the three high-learning classes are reasonably close to the mean of means (26.7 per cent): Class 2 is 30.0 per cent, Class 4 is 22.5 per cent, and Class 5 is 25.8 per cent. Of the five low-learning classes, three (Classes 7, 13, and 15) are also close to the mean of means (29.4 per cent, 31.1 per cent, and 28.8 per cent), but Classes 9 and 14 are the two lowest-ranking classes with percentages of 12.8 and 18.2, indicating that reacting moves are more likely to follow responses in these classes than in the other 13.

Summary

While many kinds of relationship are possible between various dimensions of pedagogical moves, teaching cycles, and test results, only a few have been presented as illustrative of the direction future research may take. Whether the factors cited are actually related to any of the identifiable criteria of success in teaching remains to be determined. Future research using a different sample and specifically designed to determine the presence or absence of such relationships may prove fruitful. It is unlikely, however, that any single dimension of classroom discourse described here will be found to have a consistent relationship to any single dimension of learning. Rather, it seems likely that further studies might seek to identify clusters of variables—types of teaching profiles—that might possibly be related to certain outcome variables.

In general, the results of the investigation of classroom variables and outcome variables suggest that the next step in the study of teaching should be to expand the descriptive focus, using the techniques developed in the present project to describe not only classroom discourse but also the variety of outcomes that might be associated with classroom activity.

CHAPTER NINE

RULES OF THE LANGUAGE GAME OF TEACHING

WITHIN THE theoretical framework of this research, the results reported in the preceding chapters may be summarized in terms of the rules of the classroom game of teaching. Even though teachers rarely state the rules explicitly, and although classes differ somewhat in details, the results indicate that common elements underlie much of the teaching game: pupils and teachers follow a set of implicit rules with few deviations. These rules define the teaching game. It may be useful to summarize these rules explicitly, *not as a prescriptive guide to teacher behavior, but rather as a descriptive model of what actually occurs in classrooms in the present study.*

General Rules

The classroom game involves one person called a teacher and one or more persons called pupils. The object of the game in the classrooms observed is to carry on a discourse about subject matter, and the ostensible payoff of the game is measured in terms of the amount of learning displayed by the pupils after a given period of play. In playing the game, the players follow a set of complementary rules. The person playing the role of teacher follows one set of rules; a person playing the role of pupil follows a somewhat different set of rules. Some deviations from these rules are permitted, and the subsequent pattern characterizes the player's individual style of play. These deviations, however, are relatively minor in comparison with the general system of expectations. In fact, the basic rule is that if one is to play the game at all, he will consistently follow the rules specified for his role.

Within the general set of rules that define the game, there are individual differences among classes in style of play. For example, a teacher may play most of the game structuring, while the pupil attends to the structuring and responds whenever called upon to do so. A teacher may, on the other hand, choose to play the game principally as a soliciting-responding exercise; if he so chooses, he is also responsible for reacting to pupil responses. The teacher may even choose a style of play characterized by a larger proportion of reactions than is usually seen in this game. If a pupil is playing the game with such a teacher, his responsibility to react may be almost as compelling as his responsibility to respond.

Within the general rules of the game, the style of play may, therefore, be modified in one way or another. Once the ground rules for a particular game have been set, however, it is not wise for either the teacher or the pupil to assume the other player's role. Part of the responsibility of the person playing the role of teacher is to set the ground rules and to see that these rules are obeyed. In this sense, the teacher is expected to serve not only as coach and as one of the players but also as referee of the game. The pupil's role demands that he learn the ground rules of the game, even if these rules are not explicitly stated by the teacher.

There are five general rules that guide the play of the teacher and the pupil in the classrooms observed:

1. The basic verbal maneuvers that the teacher and the pupil make in playing the game are pedagogical moves: structuring and soliciting, which are initiatory moves; and responding and reacting, which are reflexive moves. Each of the four types of move plays a distinctive role in the discourse, and the specific rules covering these moves for the teacher and for the pupil will be presented later. Soliciting, responding, and reacting each accounts for slightly less than one-third of the moves in a given classroom, and structuring accounts for the remaining small fraction of moves. In terms of amount of speech (i.e., lines of transcript), reacting accounts for three-eighths of the lines spoken, and the remaining five-eighths is about equally distributed among the remaining three moves.

2. The teacher is the most active player in the game. He makes the most moves; he speaks most frequently; and his speeches usually are the longest. He is permitted some flexibility in the exact amount by which his activity exceeds the total activity of all pupil players, but in general the ratio of his speech to the speech of all other players is approximately 3 to 1 in terms of lines spoken and 3 to 2 in terms of the number of moves made. Moreover, these ratios remain constant over several class sessions, unless the teacher directs another player to assume his role temporarily.

3. If the game is played within the field of economics, the major part of the game is played with substantive meanings specified by the teacher's structuring of the game. From time to time, however, players are permitted to depart from this central focus, sometimes to topics tangential to the substantive material of the game and occasionally to a topic that is irrelevant to the subject matter under study. The teacher usually initiates these off-target discussions, sometimes as a means of introducing a substantive point. Occasionally, a pupil player introduces an irrelevancy, but he does not do so often in a single class session; the exact frequency depends upon the reactions of the teacher. In general, however, the discussion takes place within the substantive framework of the teacher's structuring.

4. Players generally use the empirical mode of thought (fact-stating and explaining) in dealing with the substantive material under discussion. The analytic mode (defining terms and interpreting statements) is used much less frequently. The frequency of evaluative statements (opining and justifying) is also relatively low in comparison with empirical statements; that is, expressions of personal opinion about economic policies or attempts to justify opinions appear rather infrequently. However, players are free to report opinions of others, such as public officials, or to report the arguments used by others to justify their opinions. This does not mean that players are completely prohibited from expressing their own opinions and justifications, but that the general rules under which the game is played encourage the use of the empirical mode of thought.

5. In gauging wins and losses, players should keep in mind that this is not a game in which one player, such as the teacher, wins, while another player, such as one of the pupils, loses. Rather, there are relative degrees of winning and losing, and the teacher's winnings are a function of the pupil's performances. This is a peculiar, but important, characteristic of this game. While the teacher undeniably has the greater power and freedom in the course of play, he is ultimately dependent on his pupils for the degree of success he achieves in playing the game.

This feature of the game is a consequence of the criterion of success: the eventual aim of the game, the ostensible reason for playing, is the pupil's learning of substantive and substantive-logical meanings. Learning is usually measured by test performance; the teacher's success depends therefore upon the pupil's test performance. If a pupil fails the test, implying that he has not learned, then the teacher, by implication, has not taught successfully. Thus, insofar as that pupil is concerned, the teacher has lost the game. An individual teacher, of course, typically plays the game with more than one student; his wins and losses are scored over the total group of pupils, much as the team point system is used to score track meets. In calculating the results, several test failures may be offset by a number of brilliant test scores, although the precise formula depends upon the educational setting in which the game occurs. For some schools, success requires at least minimal performance by all pupils; in such schools, the teacher's overall score is considerably reduced for even one or two test failures, with proportionately less credit for high test scores. For other schools, a few exceedingly high scores overbalance a substantial number of low test results. In this latter setting, a few special pupil prizes awarded by outside sources, such as Regents Scholarships and Merit Scholarships, may very well counterbalance many failures.

The general formula for computing a teacher's final score cannot be written because the weights assigned to various kinds of test scores depend upon decisions made by people outside the classroom. Principals, superintendents, school board members and the general public help establish the criteria for determining success.

Rules for Soliciting and Responding

The soliciting-responding pattern comprises the core of the classroom game and accounts for slightly more than three-fifths of all moves made.

Rules for the Teacher

The person playing the role of teacher in the classrooms observed follows these rules:

1. The teacher's primary role is that of solicitor: about one-half of his moves are solicitations. Furthermore, the teacher makes a majority of all soliciting moves in the game.

2. In a majority of his soliciting moves, the teacher calls for the performance of a substantive task; that is, in about three-fifths of his moves he attempts to elicit information from pupils about the subject matter under study. In approximately two-fifths of his moves he calls for an instructional task, directing pupils to perform activities related to the management of the classroom as a social unit.

3. The teacher generally makes it known that he expects only one pupil to respond at a time, although other interaction patterns are possible. As a major exception to this rule, when the task is an instructional one, he may sometimes expect all pupils to respond in unison; but when the task is a substantive one, he rarely expects pupils to respond in unison unless a vote to indicate opinion is involved.

While the teacher is the only speaker who may expect the agent to perform some activity outside the classroom and/or at some future time, even he does not attempt to elicit such activity very frequently.

4. The teacher seldom calls for the performance of more than one task in a given move. If he chooses to do so, at least one of the tasks is normally a substantive one; only infrequently does he make a move presenting more than one instructional task. In his multi-task moves, the teacher expects the same information process in both components—most often constructing—but expects two different logical process activities, usually fact-stating and explaining.

5. The teacher elicits information with empirical meaning in over one-half of his soliciting moves, and expects explaining more often than fact-stating. He does not frequently expect evaluative meanings; when he does, he expects opining more often than justifying. When the teacher calls for a response with analytical meaning, and he does so in less than one-fifth of the substantive task moves, he calls more often for defining than for interpreting. With instructional tasks, he most frequently expects extra-logical meanings, especially performing-oral and repeating.

6. When the teacher solicits, he generally expects the information process activity to be constructing. When he does not expect constructing, he expects assigning a truth function more often than constructing/assigning or selecting from alternatives. He shifts from constructing to assigning a truth function most notably when the logical activity involves opining or justifying. When the process of the instructional task is logical rather than extra-logical, the teacher also tends to shift from constructing to assigning a truth function.

7. As the chief solicitor, the teacher normally attempts to keep the game in focus by using three types of moves: substantive task/explaining/constructing; substantive task/fact-stating/constructing; and instructional task/perform oral/constructing.

8. The teacher frequently presents clues regarding the terms appropriate to the responding move, especially when the task is a substantive one. The clue most often is a propositional function word and the one he relies upon most heavily is "what," although he also frequently uses "why" and "which." He may offer a clue to parallel terms and may even combine this clue with a propositional function. On occasion, he offers combinations of clues; but when he does, he seldom offers more than three clues in one move. The teacher occasionally offers the leading clue (i.e., "Don't you think that . . .") when the logical process activity involves the evaluative mode.

9. The teacher frequently makes elliptical moves and often makes

incomplete moves. Especially with substantive tasks, he interlards information. The teacher is usually the only player to provide amplification in the soliciting move; that is, he attempts to give further clues regarding the information process activity or logical process activity without changing the topic or the task.

10. As a respondent, the teacher may add tasks the pupil does not call for, perform an unexpected information process, or ignore a task. It is characteristic of the teacher to disregard not only the information process of assigning a truth function when the task is instructional but also the process of selecting from alternatives with substantive tasks. More than the pupil, the teacher is likely to respond with logical meanings of an ascending or descending nature; he does not, however, shift from one logical mode to another.

Rules for the Pupil

The person who plays the role of the pupil in the classrooms observed follows these rules:

1. The pupil's primary role is that of respondent. He normally devotes about two-thirds of his moves to responding, and he speaks most of the responding moves. When he responds, he usually performs the task and the primary activity expected by the solicitor. He may, however, ignore one of the tasks when there are two in the solicitation. When the pupil's responding move does not reflect primary congruence, the incongruence usually involves a shift from one logical mode to another or some substitution for the information processes of selecting from alternatives and assigning a truth function.

2. The pupil speaks about ten per cent of the solicitations. Like the teacher, he expects substantive tasks in about three-fifths of his moves and instructional tasks in about two-fifths. He almost never presents two tasks in one move. He usually expects empirical meanings, with fact-stating almost twice as frequent as explaining. With instructional tasks he seldom expects the extra-logical processes, but he may expect a speaker to repeat a previous move.

3. When the pupil solicits, he most frequently expects the information process of assigning a truth function. The pupil is more likely to expect constructing with an instructional task than with a substantive task. More than the teacher, he expects selecting from alternatives, but the process is not an important one for him.

4. In presenting a substantive task, the pupil is as likely to expect explaining as he is to expect fact stating; but in presenting an instructional task he is almost certain to expect fact-stating rather than explaining. He may occasionally expect analytical meanings, most

notably interpreting with an instructional task. Evaluative meanings account for more of the pupil's moves than they do of the teacher's; the pupil expects evaluative meanings with instructional tasks rather than with substantive tasks.

5. In his most frequent solicitation the pupil expects a substantive task, the logical process of fact-stating, and the information process of assigning a truth function. In his next most frequent solicitation, the pupil expects the performance of a substantive task, the logical process of explaining, and the information process of constructing.

6. The pupil seldom provides amplification; that is, he does not attempt to give further clues regarding the primary activities he expects once he has presented the task. When he does offer amplification, the task is a substantive one and the information process is assigning a truth function.

7. The pupil frequently offers clues to terms appropriate for the responding move. Most often he will offer a propositional function word, but he also offers a leading clue for the truth function he expects (e.g., "Don't you think that . . ."). More than the teacher, he offers clues with instructional tasks.

8. The pupil most often solicits the teacher, rather than a fellow pupil. He never expects the agent to perform outside the classroom or at some future time. He very seldom expects non-linguistic behavior, and never of the teacher. His directive is usually a simple request and he never commands the teacher to act.

Rules for Structuring

Both the teacher and the pupil in the classrooms observed follow these general rules:

1. Players must keep in mind that structuring is a directive move whose function it is to set the context for classroom behavior by launching or halting-excluding interaction between pupils and teachers. The speaker structures by indicating dimensions of the interaction, such as time, agent, activity, topic, and cognitive process; regulations; reasons; and instructional aids. Structuring moves may set the context for the classroom game as a whole and/or for one or more sub-games.

2. Players may structure at any time during the course of play. Participants usually distribute their structuring moves throughout a class session, allowing for a slight clustering at the beginning and at the end of the session.

3. Both the teacher and the pupil usually speak one-component moves; that is, moves that present one set of directives for the entire

game or for a single sub-game. The teacher is given some leeway in this matter, and on occasion he may structure two or more sub-games in a single move; but the "one component per move" rule strictly applies to pupils.

4. Speakers of structuring moves generally set the context for some kind of language activity, most frequently oral activity. Occasionally, a player structures non-oral language activities, such as written assignments; but only rarely does he structure non-language activities, such as the collection of homework and distribution of materials.

Rules for the Teacher

The person playing the role of the teacher in the classrooms observed follows these rules:

1. The teacher structures less than he solicits or reacts but more than he responds. The ratio is approximately one teacher structuring move to 12 other teacher moves. On the average, the teacher speaks longer in a structuring move than in any other move, although the total number of lines spent in structuring is less than in soliciting or in reacting.

2. The teacher most often launches a sub-game that is to begin at once and is to continue for only a segment of the class session. This means that he structures sub-games as the class moves along; only infrequently does he structure a series of sub-games for a particular session or for the several sessions that make up a unit. Rarely does the teacher explicitly halt or exclude a sub-game; rather, he signals the end of one sub-game by launching another.

3. The teacher generally launches a sub-game by announcing a substantive topic and a classroom activity. In addition, he frequently announces who is to be involved in the activity. Occasionally, he specifies the logical process with which participants are to deal with the substantive topic under study.

4. When announcing the activity for a sub-game, the teacher generally states that the class will "talk about" or "take up" a specified topic; rarely is he more specific in indicating the type of oral activity. From experience, the pupil understands that the class will engage in a verbal exchange consisting primarily of soliciting by the teacher and responding by the pupils.

5. Occasionally, the teacher cites regulations, specifies instructional aids, and gives reasons for launching the game or sub-game. The teacher should keep in mind that he, not the pupil, is responsible for specifying regulations and giving reasons.

Rules for the Pupil

The person playing the role of the pupil in the classrooms observed follows these rules for structuring:

1. The pupil structures less than he solicits, responds, or reacts. The ratio is approximately one structuring move to 60 other moves. The pupil speaks self-initiated structuring moves and teacher-assigned structuring moves in the ratio of about 3 to 2.

2. When the pupil structures, he usually launches a sub-game that is to begin immediately and to last for a segment of a session. The pupil rarely launches activities for the entire session or launches more than one sub-game at a time. Under no conditions does he halt or exclude a sub-game; this is the prerogative of the teacher.

3. When the pupil launches on his own initiative, he generally does so by announcing his intention of asking the teacher a question. On the other hand, when he structures in accordance with previous assignment by the teacher, he usually does not announce his topic, but proceeds immediately to speak on the assigned topic. In such assigned structuring moves the pupil speaks for a relatively long period of time.

4. The pupil does not set forth regulations or give reasons for the games or sub-games he structures. He does, however, use or refer to instructional aids such as newspapers, radio, television, or other news media.

Rules for Reacting

Both the teacher and the pupil in the classrooms observed follow these general rules:

1. Approximately one out of every three moves in the game is a reacting move, and slightly more than one-third of all lines spoken is devoted to reacting.

2. Players use reacting moves to rate (positively or negatively) and/or to modify (by clarifying, synthesizing, or expanding) what is said or done during the course of play.

3. Almost all reactions are occasioned by pedagogical moves, although pauses occurring during the discussion and physical actions may also be taken by players as the occasion for reacting. Since any pedagogical move is potentially an occasioning move, speakers of reacting moves may attempt to influence the course of events in the classroom at a time and in a manner of their own choosing. The conditions under which it is considered appropriate for players to react are indi-

cated in the rules specifying the roles of the teacher and the pupil.

4. A player's reaction may be to one or more preceding moves, and a given move may occasion more than one reaction by one or more players.

Rules for the Teacher

The person who plays the role of the teacher in the classrooms observed follows these rules:

1. Approximately two out of every five moves by the teacher will be reactions, and each reaction will be about three and one-half lines in length.

2. The teacher rarely reacts to his own verbal moves. Practically all teacher reactions are occasioned by pupil moves and most of these are pupil responses. Furthermore, most of the teacher's reactions are occasioned by single pupil moves.

3. The teacher reacts most frequently by rating moves of pupils. Three-fourths of all teacher reactions involve rating, which is one of the most important functions of the teacher in the game. In the majority of instances, the teacher's rating reactions are at least somewhat positive. Frequently he will tell a pupil explicitly that he has made a "correct" or "good" response; in any case, he is expected at least to "admit" the pupil's statement, often by a short phrase such as "all right." When the teacher does react negatively to the pupil, he usually does not make this rating completely negative by reacting with such remarks as "no," or "you're wrong." Rather, he offers some sort of qualifying evaluation, such as "yes, but . . . ," or he points out that the pupil's response was not entirely correct or to the point. This applies to incongruent pupil responses as well as congruent pupil responses.

Rules for the Pupil

The person who plays the role of the pupil in the classrooms observed follows these rules:

1. One in every six or seven pupil moves is a reaction. Virtually all pupil reactions are occasioned by single moves.

2. Pupils should keep in mind that they are expected to participate in classroom discussion most frequently when directed to respond to the teacher's solicitation, and that they are usually not expected to enter the discussion again until the teacher has reacted to the response. At that time the pupil may react to the teacher's reactions; occasionally he reacts to responding moves, but much more frequently his reactions are to reacting moves of other participants.

3. The pupil reacts twice as frequently to the teacher as he does to fellow pupils. When he reacts to the teacher, he usually reacts to a teacher reaction; when he reacts to a fellow pupil, he is likely to react to a pupil reaction or response.

4. When the pupil reacts, he does so most frequently by expressing substantive meanings. In contrast, the pupil rarely reacts by rating moves of other participants; rating is definitely a function of the teacher. If the pupil does rate a fellow pupil's response, his rating should not be too strong either in a positive or in a negative direction.

Except under extraordinary circumstances, pupils overtly accept the teacher's statements as the spoken truth. The pupil does not explicitly rate a statement made by the teacher; that is, the pupil does not tell the teacher he is right or wrong, that he is doing well or doing badly. If the pupil has impulses in this direction, he must inhibit them, for they have no place in the classroom game.

On the other hand, if one speaks the role of pupil, he must remember that merely uttering a statement does not guarantee that it will be accepted as true. In fact, an important part of the teacher's responsibility is to challenge, though mildly, pupil statements that he believes to be invalid. In certain classes, pupils may even be challenged occasionally by other pupils.

Rules for Teaching Cycles

The overarching rule of classroom verbal behavior that is indicated by investigation of teaching cycles by means of the Markov chain might be called "the classroom law of inertia." Any given state tends to influence the following state in a temporal sequence. Taking teaching cycles as states, this influence is in the form of increasing the probability that the following state will have the same characteristics as the preceding state. Thus, for all of the dimensions of teaching cycles that were studied—initiator of the cycle, logic of the cycle, and cycle type—teaching cycles once set in motion tend to remain in motion to a greater extent than would be indicated by the overall percentage distribution of cycle characteristics. Many of the rules listed below may be seen as corollaries of this basic "law."

It should be noted that there are variations in the basic rules of the game. These variations are comparable to styles of play in games like basketball or bridge. For example, while all bridge players normally follow certain general rules, individual players or teams are free to follow different bidding conventions and styles of play. Similarly, teachers, as a general rule, initiate teaching cycles; that is, teachers rather than pupils take the initiative in getting verbal exchanges under way. This is true of all classes. When a pupil does initiate a cycle, however, this may signal a different style of play in certain classes where pupils tend to initiate subsequent cycles to a far greater extent than is ordinarily the case. In some classes, then, a pupil-initiated cycle acts as a cue for other pupils to initiate subsequent cycles to a much greater extent than the rules normally specify.

1. The teacher initiates approximately 85 per cent of the teaching cycles. However, when the preceding cycle is a teacher-initiated cycle, the chance that another teacher-initiated cycle will follow is about 90 per cent. The percentage of total teacher initiation of cycles varies from class to class, but teacher initiation of cycles remains relatively constant from one session to the next in the same class unless procedures such as debates and student reports are introduced.

2. Variations in style of play may be observed in the rate at which teaching cycles occur, in the extent to which teachers rather than pupils initiate cycles, and in the way the basic solicitation-response interchange is introduced and modified.

3. The pupil initiates about 15 per cent of the teaching cycles. However, when the preceding cycle is a pupil-initiated cycle, the chance that another pupil-initiated cycle will follow is approximately 40 per cent. Classes differ in the extent to which pupil-initiated cycles follow pupil-initiated cycles, indicating that modified ground rules govern this as well as other aspects of the classroom game.

4. Teaching cycles of a given logical type tend to occur in clusters of two or more. An explaining cycle, for example, tends to follow another explaining cycle to a greater extent than would be indicated by the overall percentage distribution. The same holds for defining cycles, for fact-stating cycles and for the other logical processes.

5. A teaching cycle constituting a particular pattern of pedagogical moves tends to be followed by the same pattern to a greater extent than is indicated by the overall distribution of cycle types. Thus a SOL RES REA cycle tends to increase the probability of a subsequent SOL RES REA, and a SOL RES tends to increase the probability of a subsequent SOL RES. The typical sequences of pedagogical moves that determine teaching cycle types, therefore, are subject to the same principle of inertia that influences other characteristics of teaching cycles.

6. Teachers generally follow a soliciting-responding interchange with a reacting move. The ratio of presence to absence of a reacting move following a teacher-initiated SOL RES cycle is approximately 2:1. However, the typical pupil-initiated teaching cycle is SOL RES

rather than SOL RES REA. Pupils, then, generally refrain from commenting upon or evaluating the responses they elicit.

7. The pupil, more than the teacher, initiates unusual teaching cycles such as those that involve reactions to structuring and soliciting moves.

Further Research

That the rules cited above are the rules of the game as played in the classes studied is obvious from the data. One can only speculate on why teachers and pupils so consistently follow these rules. Perhaps high school teachers like those represented in this study have found the "teacher soliciting–pupil responding–teacher reacting" pattern of instruction to be the most effective method of instruction. One might view this as a kind of pragmatic evolution, a process by which the most effective techniques have survived through years of usage. On the other hand, this pattern of teaching may be based on teachers' assumptions about how high school pupils learn; that is, teachers may assume that if they lectured a great deal, which is more characteristic of classes at the college level, pupils would tend to become bored. Teachers may also assume that if much of the class time is devoted to pupil reacting, such a process might degenerate into a sharing of ignorance.

From another point of view, teachers may assume that students "learn by doing." Their aim would be, therefore, to stimulate and guide the "doing" by repeated solicitations. From this point of view, classroom discourse may be seen as a rehearsal of cognitive processes or, in short, an opportunity to practice thinking as viewed by these teachers. Since thinking begins with a problem, one way for the teacher to encourage pupils to think is to pose a problem in the form of a question. Thus, the aim of teaching is to stimulate and shape the pupil's cognitive responses. The teacher stimulates and directs the response by posing a problem that initiates the pupil's thinking; that is, he asks a question that requires an answer. The teacher further modifies this response by his subsequent reactions.

Another possible explanation concerns the end point or payoff of the teaching game. In most instances, the payoff is the pupil's learning as measured by a test. If a pupil does well on the test, presumably showing that he has learned, both the pupil and the teacher win the game. Similarly, if the pupil fails the test, presumably showing that he has not learned, both the pupil and the teacher lose the game. If this is indeed the case, one might view the classroom discourse as preparation or rehearsal for the payoff test; thus, the teacher conducts the class in essentially the same form in which a test is presented in order to maximize transfer to the test situation. The discourse, therefore, might be viewed as a series of tests in preparation for the final testing situation.

None of these speculations can be proposed with a high degree of confidence, and certainly the data do not warrant choosing one set of speculations over another. Perhaps all of the factors discussed influence the pattern of classroom discourse to some extent. In any event, the more important issue concerns continued investigation of the pedagogical pattern of interaction that has been identified in this research and careful evaluation of its effectiveness in terms of specific consequences.

Problems for Further Research

Several promising lines for further investigation have become apparent during the course of this research:

1. One of the most important lines for continuing study concerns the reformulation of the antecedent-consequence nature of research in teaching to recognize the need for descriptive studies both of classroom variables and of outcome variables. Instead of investigating various dimensions of classroom behavior in relation to some arbitrary measure of "learning," it may be more useful in the long run to formulate investigations in terms of the general question, "If a given set of events occurs in the classroom, then what are the observable outcomes?" For this kind of research, the usual tests devised to measure "learning" will probably not be adequate. At the beginning, at least, one would want to explore as fully as possible a wide range of possible outcomes, perhaps using a variety of interview techniques to collect data from pupils and, on the basis of such information, gradually to develop more formalized instruments that in all likelihood will be considerably different from the kind of measure used in the present study.

2. With appropriate modifications in the categories labeled "substantive meanings," the system of analysis devised in this research provides a potentially useful technique for investigation of classroom teaching in a variety of high school subjects, such as English, social studies, mathematics, and science. The results of such studies together with the findings of the present research would provide a basis for comparing and contrasting the patterns of teaching in the four basic subjects traditionally included in the high school curriculum.

3. The present research was concerned with patterns of pedagogical discourse in the high school classroom; the question therefore arises whether the method of analysis is also useful in studying

teacher-student interaction in elementary schools and colleges. Further research might extend the study of classroom teaching to elementary and college classes to determine whether the general approach developed in this study is applicable to these levels, and what adaptations in the method of analysis are necessary when applied to these levels of instruction.

Implications for Research Design

The design of this research was a compromise between rigorous experimental laboratory procedures and more informal techniques represented by typical case history methods. In retrospect, this seems to have been a fortunate compromise, in that the data clearly reflect the complex interactions of actual, ongoing classes; yet the research procedures permitted sufficient control to yield results that could be treated within practical limits and interpreted with reasonable confidence.

When classroom interaction is viewed from a research perspective, it appears as a complex maze of interrelated phenomena. Twenty or thirty people are continually interacting in a variety of multidetermined ways, each action dynamically influencing subsequent events. The entire process rapidly and constantly changes while the researcher tries to identify meaningful dimensions of observation. In part, it is probably this extraordinary complexity that has mitigated against research in classroom settings and has led scholars to view educational problems either from a more philosophical position relatively independent of controlled empirical investigations, or from the perspective of highly artificial laboratory conditions.

Certainly both points of view have much to offer in the search for knowledge about the teaching process. The present research, which clearly illustrates this premise, began with the concept of language games developed in the philosophical work of Wittgenstein and others and relied heavily on analytic philosophers, such as Feigl, in devising the categories of meaning. Yet throughout the research, the interplay between theoretical concepts and empirical data was of utmost importance. While the initial theoretical concepts guided attempts to observe and describe the complex events of classroom interaction, the daily confrontation of these concepts with the primary data of actual classes led to revisions and refinements of earlier notions that would have been impossible without the constant check of the empirical material.

This study also borrowed from the tradition of laboratory research. Although it was not possible to achieve the kind of rigorous control often established in certain types of experimental investigations, the research procedures of this study offered at least a modicum of both statistical and experimental control of the data using techniques paralleling those of the laboratory. Without such controls, the researcher could hardly deal meaningfully with the complex phenomena of the classroom. The complexity itself, however, suggests that the inevitable simplification of laboratory research precludes a realistically meaningful view of the teaching process. In a typical psychological learning experiment, for example, subjects are selected for the particular study on the basis of certain relevant criteria, but, in most instances, the interaction of the experimenter and subjects begins and ends with the experiment. In contrast, the teacher and pupils in each of the classrooms sampled in this research had a history of interaction, and this research was only a short time sample in that history. Undoubtedly, the events observed in this time sample were inextricably related to events prior to the classes' participation in the research, and in a sense the unique tradition of each class was part of the problem under investigation. If an "experimental" teacher had been introduced in each classroom; if the teaching unit had been completely independent of the course of study; if the research had been conducted in laboratory rooms specially designed to increase sound fidelity of the recordings, certain experimental advantages would have been gained. But the study would *not* have been a study of actual classroom interaction.

The research procedures, without doubt, influenced the behavior of teachers and pupils; probably few people are totally unaffected by the presence of apparatus that is recording every word spoken. But efforts were made in the direction of minimizing such distractions. Observations made during the study suggest that, by and large, this aim was accomplished with a fair degree of success.

To some extent, the procedures chosen by different researchers to investigate the same general problem are a matter of personal taste or professional style. Indeed, at the current stage of knowledge about the teaching process, a variety of widely different approaches to the same problem is probably desirable. Nevertheless, experience in this study would suggest that research within actual classroom settings, with some degree of control, is an especially useful mode of investigation in the study of classroom teaching.

BIBLIOGRAPHY

1. Bellack, Arno, A., Joel R. Davitz, *et al. The Language of the Classroom* U.S. Department of Health, Education and Welfare, Cooperative Research Program, Project No. 1497. New York, Institute of Psychological Research, Teachers College, Columbia University, 1963.
2. Bellack, Arno A., *et al. The Language of the Classroom: Part Two.* U.S. Department of Health, Education and Welfare, Cooperative Research Program, Project No. 2023. New York, Institute of Psychological Research, Teachers College, Columbia University, 1965.
3. Belnap, Nuel D., Jr. *An Analysis of Questions: Preliminary Report.* Santa Monica, California, System Development Corporation Technical Memorandum (TM Series), 1963.
4. Brown, Roger. *Words and Things.* Glencoe, Illinois, The Free Press, 1958.
5. Calderwood, James D. *International Economic Problems.* Minneapolis, Curriculum Resources, Inc., 1961.
6. Cohen, Felix S. "What Is A Question?" *The Monist,* **39** (1929), 350–364.
7. Copi, Irving M. *Introduction to Logic.* 2nd ed. New York, The Macmillan Company, 1961.
8. Cronbach, Lee J. "Evaluation for Course Improvement." Robert W. Heath, ed. *New Curricula.* New York, Harper and Row, 1964.
9. Feigl, Herbert. "Logical Empiricism." Herbert Feigl and Wilfrid Sellars, eds. *Readings in Philosophical Analysis.* New York, Appleton-Century-Crofts, Inc., 1949.
10. Fitch, Joshua G. *The Art of Questioning.* 9th ed. Syracuse, New York, C. W. Bardeen, 1879.
11. Hamburger, Martin. "Realism and Consistency in Early Adolescent Aspirations and Expectations." Ph.D. Dissertation. New York, Teachers College, Columbia University, 1958. Typewritten.
12. Hamilton, Eric R. *The Art of Interrogation: Studies in the Principles of Mental Tests and Examinations.* New York, Harcourt, Brace and Company, 1929.
13. Hyman, Ronald T. "An Analysis of High School Teaching: The Structuring Move in the Language of Selected Classrooms." Doctor of Educa-

tion Project Report. New York, Teachers College, Columbia University, 1965. Typewritten.

14. Kemeny, John G., and J. Laurie Snell. *Mathematical Models in the Social Sciences.* Boston, Ginn and Company, 1962.
15. Kliebard, Herbert M. "Teaching Cycles: A Study of the Pattern and Flow of Classroom Discourse." Doctor of Education Project Report. New York, Teachers College, Columbia University, 1963. Typewritten.
16. Phenix, Philip H. *Realms of Meaning: A Philosophy of the Curriculum for General Education.* New York, McGraw-Hill Book Company, 1964.
17. Smith, B. Othanel, Milton O. Meux, *et al. A Study of the Logic of Teaching.* U.S. Department of Health, Education and Welfare, Cooperative Research Program, Project No. 258 (7257). Urbana, Bureau of Educational Research, College of Education, University of Illinois, n.d.
18. Smith, Frank L., Jr. "Analysis of Classroom Discourse: Soliciting Moves in the Language of Selected Classrooms." Doctor of Education Project Report. New York, Teachers College, Columbia University, 1965. Typewritten.
19. Thorndike, Robert L. "Two Screening Tests of Verbal Intelligence." *Journal of Applied Psychology,* **26** (April, 1942), 128–135.
20. Thorndike, Robert L., and George H. Gallup. "Verbal Intelligence of the American Adult." *The Journal of General Psychology,* **30** (January, 1944), 75–85.
21. Wellman, Carl. *The Language of Ethics.* Cambridge, Massachusetts, Harvard University Press, 1961.
22. Wittgenstein, Ludwig. *Philosophical Investigations.* Oxford, Basil Blackwell, 1958.
23. Yamada, Soshichi. "A Study of Questioning." Reprinted from *Pedagogical Seminar,* **20** (June, 1913), 129–186.

APPENDIX A

CODING INSTRUCTIONS

1. *General Coding Instructions*
   1.1. Coding is from the viewpoint of the observer, with pedagogical meaning inferred from the speaker's verbal behavior.
   1.2. Grammatical form may give a clue, but is not decisive in coding. For example, SOL may be found in declarative, interrogative or imperative form. Likewise, RES may be in the form of a question—frequently indicating tentativeness on the part of the speaker.
   1.3. All missed statements and all noncodable statements (e.g., er, ah, mmm, well . . . , etc.) are coded T/NOC or P/NOC. Partially missed statements are coded only if there is enough information to code the pedagogical move, the substantive-logical meaning and/or the instructional meaning and instructional-logical meaning. Those moves immediately following a move coded T/NOC or P/NOC are coded as usual, if the context is clear and unambiguous. If alternative codes are clearly possible, code T/NOC or P/NOC for these moves also.
   1.4. A line of discourse is a four-and-a-half-inch segment of transcript in elite type.
   1.5. All complete utterances of less than one line are counted as one line.

   Examples

   T: Yes. (1 line)

   T: Rubber. (1 line)

   1.6. In longer utterances, the final line segment is counted as one line if it exceeds half the line. If it does not, it is discounted.

Examples

T: Well, it has more to do, Kenny, with the problem of being self-sufficient in case of war. (2 lines)

T: What does he plan to do with the industries that might be hurt? (2 lines)

1.7. In utterances that comprise more than one pedagogical move, partial line segments (italicized below) are combined in determining the line count.

Examples

T: Correct. / *Can you think of any other* way that we can approach this big *problem of tariffs?* — REA (1 line) SOL (2 lines)

T: That is perfectly correct. / *Briefly, now,* I'd like to turn to a completely dif*ferent subject.* — REA (1 line) STR (2 lines)

1.8. In utterances that contain more than one pedagogical move, each pedagogical move is counted as at least one line.

Example

T: We trade much more with large industrialized countries. / Right? — RES (2 lines) SOL (1 line)

2. *Pedagogical Moves*

2.1. The postscript -M is added to the coding of a pedagogical move when the speaker resumes the same move after it has been interrupted or mediated by one or more intervening pedagogical moves. If the interlarded move is ambiguous (e.g., mmm, er, ah), code it T/NOC or P/NOC.

Examples	*Code*
P: Well, if you get 4 billion dollars each year . . .	P/SOL/TMB/XPL/2/–/–/–
T: Mmmm.	T/NOC/1
P: . . . how are you going to pay it off?	P/*SOL-M*/TMB/XPL/1/–/–/–
P: How can we have a balance, a favorable balance of trade . . .	P/SOL/TMB/XPL/2/–/–/–
T: Yes.	T/REA/TMB/–/–/STA/POS/1
P: if we lose 4 billion dollars of gold each year?	P/*SOL-M*/TMB/XPL/1/–/–/–

2.2. A SOL begins with the first manifestly eductive statement and ends with:

a. The end of the utterance

b. The beginning of a STR, RES, or REA

2.3. Solicitations that give someone permission to speak (acknowledging SOL's) are coded: T/SOL/IMX/–/–/*ACV*/*PRF*/1

Example	*Code*
T: Allan?	T/SOL/IMX/–/–/*ACV*/*PRF*/1
T: Yes?	T/SOL/FOD/–/–/*ACV*/*PRF*/1

Acknowledging SOL's are not coded separately when they occur in connection with another solicitation.

The only type of response (RES) that can follow this kind of SOL is a RES-M, but any other kind of pedagogical move may occur.

2.4. Tentative and optional assignments, as well as prescribed ones, are coded as SOL's.

Example	*Code*
T: Sombody might be interested in examining the *Purdue Poll on Teenagers*. There's a booklet on the American teenager in the library. Any one of you might be interested in examining how teenagers feel about different topics.	T/*SOL*/NTR/–/–/*ASG*/PRF/6

25. When checking statements (e.g., "Fellow Me?" "Get it?") occur within a STR or a REA, SOL is not coded unless there is a pause or verbal cue indicating a RES is expected. Such statements when they occur within a larger move do not appear as part of the code for the larger move.

2.6. Implicit in any SOL is the concept of knowing or not knowing. Therefore, code RES for any one of the range of possible responses (including invalid ones), and also for any reply referring to knowing or not knowing (e.g., "I don't know").

2.7. Occasionally a teacher or student responds to a SOL with a question. Coding in these instances is in terms of context and intent. For example, students frequently respond with a question to indicate the tentativeness of their responses. These are coded RES. If, however, the "responding" question is a genuine solicitation (i.e., expects a RES), it is coded SOL.

2.8. A SOL which calls for a fact is coded FAC, but if the RES gives both a fact *and* an explanation, the substantive-logical meaning of the RES is coded XPL.

Example	*Code*
T: What do we import from Bolivia?	T/SOL/IMX/*FAC*/1/-/-/-
P: We import tin from Bolivia because we don't have any in this country.	P/RES/IMX/*XPL*/2/-/-/-

2.9. A SOL which calls for an opinion is coded OPN, but if the RES gives both an opinion and a justification, the substantive-logical meaning of the RES is coded JUS.

Example	*Code*
T: Should we lower our quotas?	T/SOL/TRA/*OPN*/1/-/-/-
P: No, because it would hurt the American businessman.	P/RES/PFT/*JUS*/1/-/-/-

2.10. Responses are normally coded as having been elicited by the immediately preceding pedagogical move. When the solicitation which elicits the response occurs earlier in the discourse, the postscript -M (i.e., SOL-M), along with a numeral indicating the position of the soliciting move, is added. The number is determined by counting back to the last explicit expression of the solicitation.

Example	*Code*
T: Come on. Mention another economic group that we belong to.	T/SOL/TRA/FAC/2/-/-/-
P: Monetary Fund	P/RES/TRA/FAC/1/-/-/-
T: Monetary Fund	T/REA/TRA/-/-/STA/RPT/1
P: UNICEF	P/*RES-M3*/TRA/FAC/1/-/-/-
T: UNICEF	T/REA/TRA/-/-/STA/RPT/1
P: UNESCO	P/*RES-M5*/TRA/FAC/1/-/-/-
T: UNESCO	T/REA/TRA/-/-/STA/RPT/1
P: WHO	P/*RES-M7*/TRA/FAC/1/-/-/-

2.11. A speaker cannot respond to his own solicitation. (1) If the speaker answers his own question immediately after asking it, the question is taken to be rhetorical and a stylistic device rather than a true SOL. (2) If a speaker answers his own question after an intervening incorrect answer, the correct answer to the solicitation is coded as a reaction to the incorrect answer, since the purpose of the question was not to elicit a response from the questioner. (3) If a speaker answers his own question after a *pause,* the answer is coded as a reaction, indicating that the speaker is primarily reacting to the *absence* of an expected response. An asterisk is indicated as part of the coding of the REA (i.e., REA-*) when this occurs.

Example	*Code*
T: Now what is the escape clause then?	T/SOL/BAT/DEF/1/-/-/-
(pause) The escape clause, then, is the provision in all of our reciprocal acts which provides that if imports come in under the Reciprocal Act in too great a quantity, and large enough to cause severe damage to any particular industry, anyone in industry may petition the Tariff Commission to have the rate put back up where it was before.	T/*REA-**/BAT/DEC/9/-/-/-

2.12. The postscript -P is added to the coding of reactions (i.e., REA-P) when the reaction is occasioned by a physical action rather than a verbal action.

Example	*Code*
T: Who can raise your hand . . . in what respect we have discussed the European Common Market this year . . .	T/SOL/PFT/-/-/PRC/FAC/3
not quite so many hands now.	T/*REA-P*/PFT/-/-/ACP/FAC/1

2.13. A reaction begins at the beginning of an utterance or following a nonverbal response or the absence of an expected move. A REA is still in progress when the speaker:

a. Evaluates or otherwise discusses a previous move
b. Rephrases a previous move or makes reference to it
c. Expands a previous move by stating its implications, interpreting it, or drawing conclusions from the same point or sub-point.

A REA ends when any of the following occurs:

a. The utterance ends
b. A SOL begins
c. The speaker indicates the end of the REA by some verbal convention, such as, "All right, now let's turn to . . ."
d. A distinct (not parenthetic) shift occurs to another substantive area not heretofore mentioned or not under immediate discussion

e. A distinct (not parenthetic) shift occurs from any substantive category to an instructional category not heretofore mentioned or not under immediate discussion.

2.14. When a reaction (REA) to a verbal move is followed by a summary reaction (*REA*), both reactions are coded separately even when they occur within the same utterance.

2.15. A brief or passing reference to what has gone before does not constitute a summary reaction (*REA*). *REA* is coded for a genuine summary or review and/or for a reaction to more than one move.

2.16. *REA* frequently occurs when a teacher concludes a unit of discussion and moves to something new. In these instances, it is necessary for the coder to determine when the summary ends (*REA*) and the focusing on new material begins (STR) and to code appropriately.

2.17. A reaction to a solicitation occurs only when the reaction is *about* the solicitation and not a response to the solicitation.

Example	*Code*
P: Why don't we raise our tariffs too?	P/SOL/BAT/XPL/1/–/–/–
T: That's a good question.	T/REA/BAT/–/–/STA/POS/1

3. *Teaching Cycles*

3.1. All teaching cycles are coded on the first pedagogical move of the cycle (STR or SOL).

Example	*Code*
T: Why do countries trade?	/6/18/5 T/SOL/TRA/XPL/1/–/–/–

The first number (6) indicates that this cycle is the sixth in this session. The second number (18) indicates that the cycle is an example of cycle type 18 (SOL RES REA). The third number (5) indicates that there is a total of five lines of transcript in the cycle.

3.2. All acknowledging SOL's, that is, solicitations that simply give someone permission to speak, are ignored for purposes of coding teaching cycles. No cycles, therefore, can be initiated simply by calling a person's name. Acknowledging SOL's are excluded from the line count in the coding of teaching cycles.

3.3. When a formally ordered teaching cycle is resumed after an intervening cycle, the moves are coded as part of the original cycle.

Example	*Code*
	/36/14/2
P: Do we export to Africa?	P/SOL/IMX/FAC/1/-/-/-
	/37/14/2
T: To where?	T/SOL/IMX/-/-/ACV/RPT/1
P: Africa.	P/RES/IMX/-/-/ACV/RPT/1
	/36/
T: Oh, a little.	T/RES-M3/IMX/FAC/1/-/-/-

Since the latter RES was elicited by the first SOL, it is coded as part of cycle number 36, not cycle 37.

4. *Substantive Meanings*

4.1. Coding of substantive meanings is in terms of the main context of the discussion. If, for example, in a discussion of direct foreign investment (FOD) a speaker mentions avoidance of tariffs as one reason for this kind of investment, the explanation is coded FOD. A shift to tariffs (BAT) is indicated only if the discussion actually centers on the nature of tariffs, the kinds of tariffs, etc.

4.2. In coding, indicate whenever possible the substantive content to which the move refers or the substantive context of the move. The speaker may or may not explicitly refer to the substantive material. The absence of substantive-logical coding in these instances indicates that no substantive meanings were actually expressed.

Example	*Code*
T: In what does this country specialize?	T/SOL/FSP/FAC/1/-/-/-
P: Heavy machinery	P/RES/FSP/FAC/1/-/-/-
T: Right.	T/REA/*FSP*/-/-/STA/POS/1
T: Turn out the lights, please.	T/SOL/*PFT*/-/-/ACP/PRF/1

5. *Substantive-Logical Meanings*

5.1. Only when defining is the main focus is a move coded as defining. When the definition is within the immediate context of other substantive-logical meanings, defining is not coded.

5.2. Responses giving facts within the context of an explanatory move or in a sequence of explanatory moves are coded explaining (XPL), except when the SOL which elicits the fact-stating clearly calls for a fact, not an explanation. In the latter case, both the SOL and the RES are coded fact-stating (FAC).

Example	*Code*
T: What are the reasons most cars are made around the Detroit area?	T/SOL/FSP/*XPL*/2/-/-/-
P: The Great Lakes.	P/RES/FNR/*XPL*/1/-/-/-
T: What do the Great Lakes provide?	T/SOL/FNR/*FAC*/1/-/-/-
P: Transportation.	P/RES/FNR/*FAC*/1/-/-/-
T: They provide transportation for what?	T/SOL/FNR/*FAC*/1/-/-/-
P: Raw materials.	P/RES/FNR/*FAC*/1/-/-/-

5.3. "Reverse" definitions, which give the definition and call for the term, are coded as defining moves.

Example	*Code*
T: What do we call a tax on imports?	T/SOL/BAT/*DEC*/1/-/-/-
P: A tariff.	P/RES/BAT/*DEC*/1/-/-/-

5.4. When more than one substantive-logical process occurs within a single pedagogical move, code according to the following order of priority:
a.) JUS (justifying)
b.) XPL (explaining)
c.) OPN (opining)
d.) FAC (fact-stating)
e.) INT (interpreting statements)
f.) DEF (defining terms)

5.5. An incorrect statement intended as the description of a state of affairs, such as, "Ghana grows most of the cotton produced in Africa," would be coded FAC even though it is empirically incorrect.

6. *Instructional Meanings*

6.1. Occasionally, within longer moves (e.g., a STR or a REA), reference is made to more than one of the instructional categories. In coding, identify the primary instructional function of the move or its principal focus, and code appropriately.

6.2. Use the following order of precedence when more than one of the instructional categories are involved and the main intent of the discourse cannot be readily determined:
a.) STA (statement)
b.) LOG (logical process)
c.) ASG (assignment)
d.) MAT (instructional material)
e.) PRC (procedure)

f.) PER (person)
g.) ACT (action-general)
h.) ACV (action-vocal)
i.) ACC (action-cognitive)
j.) ACP (action-physical)
k.) ACE (action-emotional)
l.) LAM (language mechanics)

6.3. MAT is coded without an instructional-logical category only when substantive material is asked for or given *with reference to materials of instruction* such as textbooks, films, graphs, and maps. MAT is coded only when the reference to materials is explicit.

Examples	*Code*
T: What does the book say we export most?	T/SOL/IMX/FAC/1/*MAT*/-/-/-
P: Agricultural products.	P/RES/IMX/FAC/1/*MAT*/-/-/-
T: What does the book say we products do we have to import?	T/SOL/IMX/FAC/2/*MAT*/-/-/-
P: Rubber.	P/RES/IMX/FAC/1/*MAT*/-/-/-

6.4. ACC/FAC is coded when the cognitive process is the main intent of the move.

Examples	*Code*
T: Remember that?	T/SOL/TMB/-/-/*ACC/FAC*/1
T: You know that?	T/SOL/REL/-/-/*ACC/FAC*/1
P: I don't know.	P/RES/TDI/-/-/*ACC/FAC*/1
P: I can't seem to remember.	P/RES/FOR/-/-/*ACC/FAC*/1

6.5. ACC/FAC is *not* coded when the reference to a cognitive process is incidental.

Examples	*Code*
P: I think we do have a quota on transistor radios.	P/RES/*BAQ/FAC*/1/-/-/-
T: I think it was Hamilton.	T/RES/*BAT/FAC*/1/-/-/-
T: As I recall, it's about 17%.	T/REA/*IMX/FAC*/1/-/-/-

6.6. Both ACC/FAC and the substantive and substantive-logical meanings are coded when the statement gives them approximately equal prominence.

Examples	*Code*
P: I'm not sure, but it's about 17%.	P/RES/*IMX/FAC/1/ACC/FAC/1*
P: I don't know, but I think we do have a quota on transistor radios.	P/RES/*IMX/FAC/1/ACC/FAC/1*
T: I can't remember exactly, but it's somewhere in Asia.	T/RES/*FNR/FAC/1/ACC/FAC/1*

7. *Instructional-Logical Meanings*

7.1. Use the following order of precedence in evaluative reactions when more than one instructional-logical categories are involved:

a.) QAL (qualifying)
b.) POS, NEG, PON (positive, negative, positive or negative)
c.) ADM, NAD, AON (admitting, not admitting, admitting or not admitting)
d.) RPT (repeating)

7.2. RPT is coded in evaluative reactions when there are no additional accepting, rejecting, or qualifying statements.

7.3. In evaluative reactions, only explicit evaluations are coded.

Examples	
T: No.	T/REA/IMX/*-/-/STA/NEG/1*
T: You're not thinking.	T/REA/FOR/*-/-/ACC/FAC/1*
T: No. That's wrong. You're not thinking.	T/REA/TRA/*-/-/STA/NEG/1*
T: This can be in capital equipment which represents dollars.	T/REA/TMB/FAC/2/-/-/-
P: But it's never actually gold bullion.	P/REA/TMB/FAC/1/*STA/QAL/1*
T: Yes, it is.	T/REA/TMB/*-/-/STA/NAD/1*

7.4. Any indication of reservation with POS, NEG, ADM, or NAD is coded as QAL.

Examples	*Code*
T: You're right, but I'm not sure of your wording.	T/REA/IMX/-/-/STA/*QAL/2*
T: Well, I don't know whether or not your word "temporary" is the proper word to use, but you got the idea that the im-	

mediate effect of this, of course, is to put a lot of American workers out of jobs.	T/REA/PFT/–/–/STA/*QAL*/7

7.5. In STA/QAL reactions, code a minimum of one line as the instructional-logical segment of the move when additional substantive matter is included. If the move is only one line in length, code only as STA/QAL with nothing for the substantive-logical part of the move.

Examples	*Code*
T: Yes, but we export wheat.	T/REA/IMX/–/–/STA/QAL/*1*
T: Yes, but we never actually send gold bullion to these foreign countries.	T/REA/TMB/FAC/1/STA/QAL/2
P: But if we do continue to admit these cheap transistor radios, our American manufacturers will have to go out of business.	P/REA/BAR/XPL/2/STA/QAL/2

7.6. Interpreting (INT) is coded as instructional-logical meaning for clarifying solicitations and responses in which the speaker asks for or gives the referent or antecedent in a previous move.

Examples	*Code*
P: It's unconstitutional	P/RES/TDI/FAC/1/–/–/–
T: What's unconstitutional?	T/SOL/TDI/–/STA/*INT*/1
P: He is in favor of joining the Common Market.	P/RES/PFT/FAC/2/–/–/–
T: Who is?	T/SOL/PFT/–/STA/*INT*/1
P: Macmillan.	P/RES/PFT/–/STA/*INT*/1
P: We all went up there to a meeting.	P/REA/NTR/FAC/1/–/–/–
T: Where?	T/SOL/NTR/–/–/STA/*INT*/1
P: Upstate New York.	P/RES/NTR/–/–/STA/*INT*/1

If, however, the speaker supplies the terms in which the response is to be phrased, code FAC as the substantive-logical meaning indicating additional substantive material of a factual nature.

Examples	*Code*
P: We all went up there to a meeting.	P/REA/NTR/FAC/1/–/–/–
T: Do you mean *upstate New York?*	T/SOL/NTR/*FAC*/1/–/–/–
P: Yes.	P/RES/NTR/*FAC*/1/–/–/–

T: What do we mean by the slogan, "Buy American—The job you save might be your own."?	T/SOL/IMX/*INT*/3/–/–/–
P: The workers would be put out of jobs.	P/RES/IMX/*INT*/1/–/–/–
* T: Do you mean *American* workers?	T/SOL/IMX/*FAC*/1/–/–/–
P: Yes, American workers.	P/RES/IMX/*FAC*/1/–/–/–

(* "Did you *say* American workers?" would be coded ACV/FAC)

If the speaker requests or gives a clarifying response involving the definition of *terms* code DEF, DEC, or DED as appropriate.

Examples	*Code*
T: The capital outflow has reached dangerous proportions.	T/REA/TMB/OPN/2/–/–/–
P: What do you mean by capital outflow?	P/SOL/TMB/*DEF*/1/–/–/–

7.7. Code interpreting (INT) as the instructional-logical meaning when interpretations of graphs, maps, charts, or reading matter are involved.

Example	*Code*
T: What does this yellow section stand for?	T/SOL/IMX/–/–/*MAT*/*INT*/1
P: The amount of exports.	P/RES/IMX/–/–/*MAT*/*INT*/1

7.8. When the instructional-logical process performing (PRF) is used with instructional categories such as MAT, ASG, or PER it is always understood that an *action* is the referent and that this action is associated with the appropriate instructional category. Thus, when "Open your books" is coded MAT/PRF, the code is interpreted to mean "Perform an action associated with materials of instruction." The SOL, "Wash your face" would be coded PER/PRF and, interpreted, "Perform an action associated with your person."

APPENDIX B

EXCERPT FROM A PROTOCOL

T: However, to get back to our main point once more, in talking about the U. S. role in, in all this international trade. Our export trade is vital to us. Our import trade is vital to us, and it would upset and shake American economy to a tremendous extent if we were to stop importing or stop exporting. Let's turn to American in- T/REA/IMX/XPL/5/PRC/FAC/1
vestments abroad. You suppose we do invest much T/STR/FOR/-/-/PRC/FAC/1 (20/5/3)
money outside of the U. S. ? T/SOL/FOR/FAC/1/-/-/-

P: Yes. P/RES/FOR/FAC/1/-/-/-

T: In what ways, in what fields? How would it be done? T/SOL/FOR/XPL/1/-/-/- (21/18/7)

P: Well, a lot of the big companies here in the U. S. will set up companies over in other countries, and that way they can give the workers over there a chance to work and to sell their products and the foreign countries can get the tax off that. P/RES/FOD/XPL/5/-/-/-

T: I think you put the most important thing last,

but that's true. The branch office in a foreign T/REA/FOD/-/-/STA/QAL/1

country, which involves the exportation of American capital, is so often done to avoid paying

/22/14/4

what? T/SOL/FOD/XPL/3/-/-/-

P: Taxes. P/RES/FOD/XPL/1/-/-/-

/23/14/2

T: What kind of taxes? T/SOL/FOD/FAC/1/-/-/-

P: Import. P/RES/FOD/FAC/1/-/-/-

/24/14/2

T: Hm? T/SOL/FOD/-/-/ACV/RPT/1

P: Import. P/RES/FOD/-/-/ACV/RPT/1

T: Why would a company open up a branch in England,

/25/21/70

or Germany or France or Italy? T/SOL/FOD/XPL/2/-/-/-

P: Corporation won't have to pay tax? P/RES/FOD/XPL/1/-/-/-

T: No, if it's an American corporation it's still going to have a, have to pay corporation tax over here. It might save a little bit on the income earned by its branch office until it brings that income back to this country it is not taxed, but ultimately it would be. But it's a different kind of tax. T/REA/FOD/XPL/6/STA/NEG/1

P: The tariff. P/RESOM3/FOD/XPL/1/-/-/-

T: The tariff. We're not the only country in the world, you know, that has a tariff. If we want to send our goods inside... Well, take tobacco, for example. Most countries in the world have placed a very, very high tariff on American cigarettes coming in. They don't want their people to buy our cigarettes. And I mean it's expensive in some countries. You go across Europe and try to buy American cigarettes--they're available but you pay an enormous price. You usually pay at least twice what you pay for a pack of cigarettes here. If a pack of cigarettes here is 30¢, it's about 60¢. Why, in, in Canada some American brands go as high as 70 -- I've paid 75¢ in Canada for a pack of American cigarettes. This is some years ago, but this is called the duty, the tariff. Now, if you open a branch and you ship in the raw tobacco and you manufacture the cigarette in, say, Germany, give it a different name but let it be known that it's American tobacco, which people would recognize, anyway. If they liked the taste, you avoid that tax. I've forgotten.... T/REA/FOD/XPL/22/STA/RPT/1

26/14/3

P: Why can't you do it /missed/ say, in English. P/SOL/FOD/XPL/1/-/-/-

T: That has to do with corporation laws and copyrights on names and such, but two years ago when T/RES/FOD/XPL/2/-/-/-
I was in Germany, I was, at the time, smoking Salem, and I noticed this pack of cigarettes one day, and I thought, "Oh, a pack of Salem." And then I looked again, and it was the iden-

APPENDIX C

TEST AND SCALES

Test of Knowledge of International Trade

NAME ______________________

SCHOOL ______________________

DATE ______________________

SECTION 1

Listed below are a number of terms commonly used by economists in discussions of international trade. You are to define each of these terms in two ways: (1) first, write a *general definition* of the term, giving the major ideas or characteristics to which the term refers; (2) second, give a *specific example* of the term. Even if you don't know an actual example of some of the terms, make up an example that is reasonable.

For example, suppose you were asked to define the term, "International trade." First, give a general definition, "Buying and selling of goods and services between two countries." Then, give a specific example, "The U.S. buys coffee from Brazil, and Brazil buys machinery from the U.S."

Remember, for each term, write a general definition and then give a specific example.

1. *specialization*

   general definition:
   specific example:

2. *factors of production*

   general definition:
   specific example:

3. *exports*

   general definition:
   specific example:

4. *imports*
   general definition:
   specific example:

5. *foreign investment*
   general definition:
   specific example:

6. *tariff*
   general definition:
   specific example:

7. *quota*
   general definition:
   specific example:

8. *exchange control*
   general definition:
   specific example:

9. *export controls*
   general definition:
   specific example:

10. *rate of exchange*
    general definition:
    specific example:

SECTION 2

Briefly answer each of the following questions. Simply write the main idea or the major points answering each question, without going into too much detail.

A sample question and the kind of answer required is presented below.

Question: What is the fundamental reason for countries trading with each other?

Answer: Because of the uneven distribution of factors of production, such as human skills, natural resources, and capital equipment.

1. In what important ways does international trade differ from domestic trade?
2. Explain why countries specialize in production of some goods and trade with other countries to obtain certain other goods they need rather than become totally self-sufficient.
3. How do the factors of production influence a country's productivity?
4. Why is the largest amount of international trade between highly industrialized countries?
5. How is the U.S. economy dependent on exports?
6. How is the U.S. economy dependent on imports?

7. What are the major reasons for direct foreign investment?
8. How does the trade between two countries influence the economy of each country?
9. What are the major reasons for a country maintaining barriers to international trade?
10. What are the major reasons for a country reducing barriers to international trade?

SECTION 3

Briefly answer each of the following questions. A sample question and the kind of answer required are presented below.

Question: The U.S. lacks industrial diamonds but produces large quantities of machinery. How does the U.S. obtain industrial diamonds?

Answer: Import diamonds from countries that produce diamonds and export machinery to countries that need machinery.

1. A heavily wooded country, such as Finland, concentrates on industries directly related to wood products and depends on imports from other countries for many other kinds of products she needs. Why doesn't Finland try to become more self-sufficient and produce the products she now has to import?
2. Even if India received huge sums of money and equipment for automobile factories, why would it still be difficult for her to put millions of unemployed people to work immediately producing automobiles?
3. Burmese farmers desperately need American farm equipment and other American goods. Yet, there is relatively little trade between Burma and the U.S. today. Why?
4. Why does our country have to export certain agricultural products such as wheat?
5. Although America is a land of coffee drinkers, why do we buy all our coffee from other countries instead of trying to grow our own coffee?
6. Why does General Motors have an automobile factory in Canada when it already has factories a few miles away in the United States?
7. If we cut down the amount of coffee we buy from Brazil, how does that affect Brazil's import of goods from us?
8. Suppose you were a Congressman arguing for an increase in the tariff imposed on bicycles imported from England. What would be the major reasons you'd use to support your argument? State these reasons in specific terms directly related to the manufacturing and importing of bicycles.
9. Suppose you were a Congressman arguing for a reduction in the tariff imposed on peanuts imported from Nigeria. What would be the major reasons you'd use to support your argument? State these reasons in specific terms directly related to growing and importing of peanuts.
10. Suppose the owner of a large supermarket in New York City was trying to decide on whether he should purchase olives from California or from Spain. Assuming the price of the olives delivered in New York was the same for both California and Spanish olives, and that the quality of the

olives was the same, what kinds of problems would the owner of the supermarket have in purchasing the olives from Spain in contrast to purchasing them from California?

Attitude Scale

NAME ______________________________ DATE ______________

SCHOOL ___________________________ GRADE _____ AGE _____

BOY GIRL (circle one)

What is your father's occupation? (or mother's if father not working)

____

Listed below are seven short paragraphs, each describing how a person might feel about studying ECONOMICS. Please read all the descriptions, and then check the paragraph that best describes how *you feel* about studying economics. Even if you've never studied economics in school and don't know exactly what it would be like, just give us your best guess. There is no right or wrong answer. We're interested only in your opinion, so check the paragraph that best describes how you feel about studying economics.

_____ 1. Studying economics is of tremendous value, and I'd really enjoy it. It is one of the most important subjects I know, and everyone should be required to study it.

_____ 2. Studying economics is very profitable for everyone who takes it. It is a worthwhile subject and most students should have the chance to study it.

_____ 3. Studying economics would benefit a student. It deals with universal problems and teaches you to think accurately and efficiently.

_____ 4. Studying economics is interesting. It is a useful subject that serves the needs of many students.

_____ 5. Studying economics is all right. It has its merits and fulfills its purpose. I'd be willing to spend time studying this subject.

_____ 6. Studying economics is not a bore. It has its merits and its drawbacks, but on the whole I think its merits probably somewhat outweigh its drawbacks.

_____ 7. Studying economics won't do anybody any harm. I haven't any definite like or dislike for this subject. It might be worthwhile if it were taught right.